W9-CWT-730

Direct Store Delivery

Andreas Otto • Franz Josef Schoppengerd
Ramin Shariatmadari
Editors

Direct Store Delivery

Concepts, Applications and Instruments

Editors

Prof. Dr. Andreas Otto
University of Regensburg
Chair of Controlling and Logistics
Faculty of Economics
Universitätsstraße 31
93053 Regensburg
Germany
andreas.otto@wiwi.uni-regensburg.de

Franz Josef Schoppengerd
Vice President Emerging Solutions
& Architecture
Industry Solution Management
Consumer Products & Life Sciences
Product Technology Unit Industries
SAP AG
Dietmar-Hopp-Alle 16
69190 Walldorf
Germany
franz.josef.schoppengerd@sap.com

Dr. Ramin Shariatmadari
Business Transformation Consulting Process
Consumer Industries and Trade
SAP Deutschland AG & Co. KG
Hasso-Plattner-Ring 7
69190 Walldorf
Germany
ramin.shariatmadari@sap.com

ISBN 978-3-540-77212-5 e-ISBN 978-3-540-77213-2

DOI 10.1007/978-3-540-77213-2

Library of Congress Control Number: 2008940142

Cover design: WMXDesign GmbH, Heidelberg, Germany

Printed on acid-free paper

9 8 7 6 5 4 3 2 1

springer.com

Contents

Contributors

Somjit Amrit
General Manager and Global Head – Consumer Goods Practice, Wipro Research Cell for Consumer Packaged Goods Industry, Wipro Technologies, 475-A, Old Mahabalipuram Road, Sozhananganallur, Chennai 600041, India
e-mail: somjit.amrit@wipro.com

Jörg Becker
Westfälische Wilhelms-Universität Münster, European Research Center for Information Systems (ERCIS), Leonardo-Campus 3, D-48149 Münster
e-mail: becker@ercis.de

Serhan Dagtas
UALR, 2801 S. University Avenue, Little Rock, AR 72204, USA
e-mail: sxdagtas@ualr.edu

Philippe Fuchs
Westfälische Wilhelms-Universität Münster, European Research Center for Information Systems (ERCIS), Leonardo-Campus 3, D-48149 Münster
e-mail: philippe.fuchs@ercis.de

Paris Gogos
The Nielsen Company, 200 W. Jackson Boulevard, Suite 2500, Chicago, IL 60606, USA
e-mail: requests.dme@nielsen.com

Peter Klaus
Friedrich-Alexander-Universität Erlangen-Nürnberg, Rechts- und Wirtschaftswissenschaftliche Fakultät, Lehrstuhl für Betriebswirtschaftslehre, insb. Logistik, Schlossplatz 4, D-91054 Erlangen
e-mail: klaus@logistik.uni-erlangen.de

Herbert Kotzab
Department of Operations Management, Copenhagen Business School, Solbjerg Plads 3, DK-2000 Frederiksberg
e-mail: hk.om@cbs.dk

Stefanie Müller
Hochschule Offenburg Campus Gengenbach, Professur für Speditions-, Transport- und Verkehrslogistik, Klosterstraße 14, D-77723 Gengenbach
e-mail: stefanie.mueller@fh-offenburg.de

Yuri Natchetoi
SAP Research, 111 Duke Street, Montreal, 1 Quebeck, H3C2M1, Canada
e-mail: yuri.natchetoi@sap.com

Vinay Natu
Empresas Polar, 2 da Ave. de los Cortijos de Lourdes, Edificio Centro Empresarial Polar, Caracas, 5474, Venezuela
e-mail: vinay.natu@empresas-polar.com

Andreas Otto
Chair of Controlling and Logistics
Faculty of Economics, University of Regensburg, Universitätsstraße 31, D-93053 Regensburg
e-mail: andreas.otto@wiwi.uni-regensburg.de

Leon Pieters
Deloitte, Laan van Kronenburg 2, Postbus 300 (P.O. Box), NL 1180, AH Amstelveen
e-mail: leonpieters@deloitte.com

Neil Preddy
The Nielsen Company, 200 W. Jackson Boulevard, Suite 2500, Chicago, IL 60606, USA
e-mail: requests.dme@nielsen.com

Pavel Pucelik
SD&M Business Systems Manager, Plzeňsky Prazdroj, a.s., U Prazdroje 7, CZ 30497, Plzeň
e-mail: pavel.pucelik@pilsner.sabmiller.com

Jon Rasmussen
Director, Consumer Goods, Industry Marketing, Intermec Technologies Corporation, 550 Second Street S.E., Cedar Rapids, IA 52401, USA
e-mail: jon.rasmussen@intermec.com

Wayne Rigney
The Nielsen Company, 200 W. Jackson Boulevard, Suite 2500, Chicago, IL 60606, USA
e-mail: requests.dme@nielsen.com

Emiel van Schaik
Senior Vice President, Consumer Industries,
SAP AG, Dietmar-Hopp-Allee 16, D-69190 Walldorf
e-mail: emiel.van.schaik@sap.com

Franz Josef Schoppengerd
Vice President Emerging Solutions & Architecture, Industry Solution Management – Consumer Products & Life Sciences, Product Technology Unit Industries, SAP AG, Dietmar-Hopp-Allee 16, D-69190 Walldorf
e-mail: franz.josef.schoppengerd@sap.com

Ramin Shariatmadari
Business Transformation Consulting Process, Consumer Industries and Trade, SAP Deutschland AG & Co. KG, Hasso-Plattner-Ring 7, D-69190 Walldorf
e-mail: ramin.shariatmadari@sap.com

Koen De Staerke
Deloitte, Berkenlaan 8 B, B-1831 Diegem
e-mail: kdestaerke@deloitte.com

Alan Thomas
Deloitte, 200 Clarendon St., Boston, MA 02116, USA
e-mail: alathomas@deloitte.com

Mukai Wesley
SAP Research, 3475 Deer Creek Road, Palo Alto, CA 94304, USA
e-mail: wesley.mukai@sap.com

Axel Winkelmann
Westfälische Wilhelms-Universität Münster, European Research Center for Information Systems (ERCIS), Leonardo-Campus 3, D-48149 Münster
e-mail: axel.winkelmann@ercis.de

Alberto Zamora
Movilitas GmbH, Käfertalerstraße 164, D-68167 Mannheim
e-mail: alberto.zamora@movilitas.com

Chapter 1
Success in the Consumer Products Market – Understanding Direct Store Delivery

Andreas Otto[1], Franz Josef Schoppengerd[2], and Ramin Shariatmadari[3]

[1] Chair of Controlling and Logistics, Faculty of Economics, University of Regensburg, Universitätsstraße 31, D-93053, Regensburg, tel.: +49 941 943 2686, e-mail: andreas.otto@wiwi.uni-regensburg.de

[2] Vice President Emerging Solutions & Architecture, Industry Solution Management – Consumer Products & Life Sciences, Product Technology Unit Industries, SAP AG, Dietmar-Hopp-Allee 16, D-69190 Walldorf, tel.: +49 6227 748820, e-mail: franz.josef.schoppengerd@sap.com

[3] Business Transformation Consulting Process, Consumer Industries and Trade, SAP Deutschland AG & Co. KG, Hasso-Plattner-Ring 7, D-69190 Walldorf, tel.: +49 6227 7 45283, e-mail: ramin.shariatmadari@sap.com

Abstract

Direct Store Delivery (DSD) is a business process that manufacturers use to both sell and distribute goods directly to the point of sales or point of consumption including additional product and market related services such as merchandizing, information gathering, or equipment service. This chapter introduces the Global Direct Store Delivery Analysis and reports the major results. It explains and organizes both the logistics and the sales & marketing related motives for companies to use DSD as a mode of distribution. Further on, it presents empirical insights on how companies run DSD. This chapter is geared to lay the terminological and conceptual basis for the reminder of the book and should be used as a starting point to explore the book.

1.1 Introduction

In 1975 Irving Shapiro of Du Pont Company summed up the first oil crisis: "Everything is history … The future is a whole new game." In the meanwhile the international markets have witnessed many crisis and shocks. In fact, the business communities get more and more used to handle change. Change has become stable. Nevertheless, competing in today's markets, especially in the consumer product (CP) market remains a challenge. The principal actors in this game, consumers, retailers, manufacturers, logistics service providers, and technology providers remain "unstable", demand new services, offer new solutions, strive for

A. Otto et al., *Direct Store Delivery*,
DOI: 10.1007/978-3-540-77213-2_1, © Springer-Verlag Berlin Heidelberg 2009

better positions in the value chains, and finally struggle to produce ever growing rates of return to hungry shareholders. This is by no means typical only for the Consumer Products market, but due to the very nature of this market, it has become to a very competitive arena. An ongoing concentration allows mighty retailers to control access to consumers and to extend their footprint "backwards" into the supply chain, penetrating manufacturers with "pick up logistics". Manufacturers, keen to understand consumer preferences, strive to bridge the gap between their realm and the point of sale. Going vertical seems to be one of the promising temptations the industry considers. The quest for sustainability is likely to witness a final breakthrough in the coming years. Its advents are clear rises in transportation cost and "carbon footprints", allowing consumers to reward "green" production and logistics. Despite all this change, the logistics agenda remains pretty much the same. As a recent study revealed, reducing logistics cost, improving customer responsiveness, and improving working capital efficiency remain the top most goals.

To sum up: The question is not what to achieve but how to achieve. How can manufacturers make their products available to millions of consumers in emerging markets – even when there is hardly any retail structure in place? How can manufacturers distribute products to thousands of micro-stores? How can manufacturers control logistics costs while order sizes go down? How can manufacturers gain more precise and on time feedback on customer satisfaction? How can manufacturers change preferences while the consumer is at the shelf? How can manufacturers reduce out of stocks? How can retailers remain profitable while continuously reducing point of sale prices? How can retailers offer more customized products to consumers? How can retailers respond to unpredictable demand swings? How can retailers manage for smooth product flows while buying from thousands of manufacturers?

It is this particularly demanding environment in which an "old" concept, going direct, becomes more and more prominent in the logistics area. Many companies and a huge portion of daily consumes are shipped directly to the shelves. In line with common business practice we suggest to call this the "DSD" (Direct Store Delivery) model. As our analysis has shown, DSD is a key method of selling and distributing products. This holds for a large variety of industries. Within the consumer products industry, DSD is primarily employed for the distribution of food, beverages, and tobacco products. As of 2006, 80% of the world's top 30 FMCG companies in fact did run DSD. 96% of the FMCG manufacturers as well as 88% of the retailers identified major benefits and reported to gain competitive advantages coming out of the DSD business process. Furthermore, also outside the CP Industry, many other industries adopted the DSD model, such as wholesale distribution, oil & gas, or the service industries.

Consider the following numbers indicating the extensive usage of DSD in the industry today: Food retailers in the US receive well over half a billion deliveries each year via DSD, which is outnumbered only by the US Postal service in the number of items delivered (GMA Forum 2006, p. 60). On a worldwide scale, eight out of ten food manufacturers use DSD. In the beverage industry all of the ten largest worldwide manufacturers use DSD. Within the US, DSD produces up to 30% of total retail sales volume of small- and large-format retail stores in the US and contributes more than 80% of retail dollar growth for the top 20 CPG categories in large-format stores. Furthermore, 5 of top 10 packaged foods at retail today and 6 of top 10 categories of large format stores today are delivered by DSD (GMA 2005, p. 9). In the US, typical small- and large-format stores receive, respectively, some 1,100 and 12,000 DSD deliveries a year. Typical small-format stores receive nearly 80,000 items from its combined DSD suppliers – while a large-format store receives three million items (GMA Forum 2006, p. 60).

The growing acceptance of DSD in the consumer products market can be taken for granted. Indeed, it actually poses a list of interesting questions:

- Why do companies use DSD? Compared to other distribution models, DSD is more expensive for the manufacturer – so which benefits does DSD create to outweigh its cost?
- How should companies execute the daily DSD processes not only to reduce cost but also to reap all potential benefits?
- Understanding that DSD is a more expensive model, how can companies calculate whether their operation is not more expensive, but too expensive?
- How should companies support the DSD process via software and mobile technology?
- Which product groups should be fed into the DSD pipeline? What are the criteria to identify DSD products?
- Which regional markets, which emerging markets can be addressed with DSD? Which particular combinations of countries and products should not be approached with DSD?

We consider these questions as relevant to DSD adopters, i.e. to manufacturers and retailers already using DSD. They will help them improving their DSD business both on an operational and on a strategic-tactical level. But we also consider them as relevant to non-DSD companies while verifying their set of distribution modes.

1.1.1 The Empirical Base of the Book

While approaching DSD from both an academic and a practitioner perspective it became clear to us that the empirical base of knowledge is quite limited. However, some pieces of research have been available:

- Coca-Cola Retailing Research Group Europe (CCRRGE)/Consulenti Associata di Gestione Aziendale (GEA): Cooperation between industry and trade in supply chain management (1994)
- Gjaja and Vogel: The power of DSD (2000)

- Grocery Manufacturers Association (GMA): E-commerce opportunities in direct store delivery (2002a)
- GMA and Berger: Reducing out-of-stocks in the grocery channel – an in-depth look at DSD categories (2002b)
- GMA: Unleash the power of DSD: Driving DSD supply chain efficiencies and profitability (2005)
- GMA: Global data synchronization and DSD (2006).

Looking for a more systematic and comprehensive appreciation of DSD we had to do:

- Research not limited on one region only
- Research not limited on one industry only
- Research not limited to retail or manufacturing only
- Research not limited on appreciating DSD as a "logistical tool" only
- Research not excluding execution aspects.

Consequently and in 2006, the University of Regensburg and Germany based SAP corporation joined to set up a comprehensive empirical study, termed the Global DSD Analysis (GDA), designed to supply a broad and up to date empirical basis for further research on DSD. Some of the companies represented in this book took part; however the coverage was much larger. It included 203 manufacturing companies in the fast moving consumer goods (FMCG) sector and 49 grocery retailing companies (Table 1.1). 24 of the top 30 FMCG manufacturers and 11 of the top 15 retailers joined the GDA. The involved companies represent more than 15 million DSD deliveries to points of sales. The GDA covered the regions of Western Europe, Eastern Europe, Middle East and Africa, North America, Latin America, Asia Pacific, and Australia (Fig. 1.1).

Table 1.1 Characteristics of the Global DSD Analysis (GDA) 2007

Consumer Products: (n=203)*	Retail: (n=49)*
24 out of the Top 30 FMCG companies	11 out of the worldwide Top 15 Retailers
Food:	Americas:
8 out of the worldwide Top 10 companies	10 out of the Top 30 Retailers
Beverage:	Europe:
8 out of the worldwide Top 10 companies	7 out of the Top 10 Retailers
Tobacco:	Germany:
6 out of the worldwide Top 10 companies	> 80 % of the German Retail market

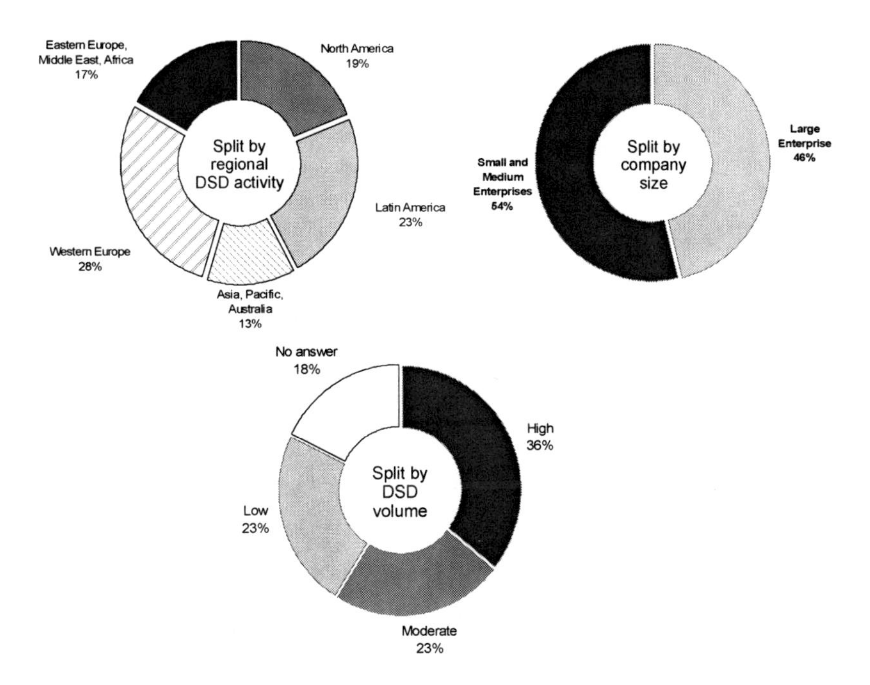

Fig. 1.1 Participants of Global DSD Analysis (Otto and Shariatmadari 2008)

1.2 What is Direct Store Delivery?

According to literature, DSD can be defined as a business process that manufacturers use to both sell and distribute goods directly to point of sales (PoS) or point of consumption (PoC) including additional product and market related services such as merchandizing, information gathering, or equipment service and bypassing any retailer or wholesaler logistics (Otto and Shariatmadari 2008, p. 11). A company that performs DSD does not send goods to any locations using any independent third party actor – neither an independent wholesaler, nor the retailer's own warehouses (Vinod 2004, p. 359). The high-level DSD process is illustrated in the following figure (Fig. 1.2).

Hereby and as illustrated by the above figure, DSD products are delivered directly from the manufacturer's plant or distribution center to the customer's retail location or even directly to consumers (e.g. deliveries to homes and offices,

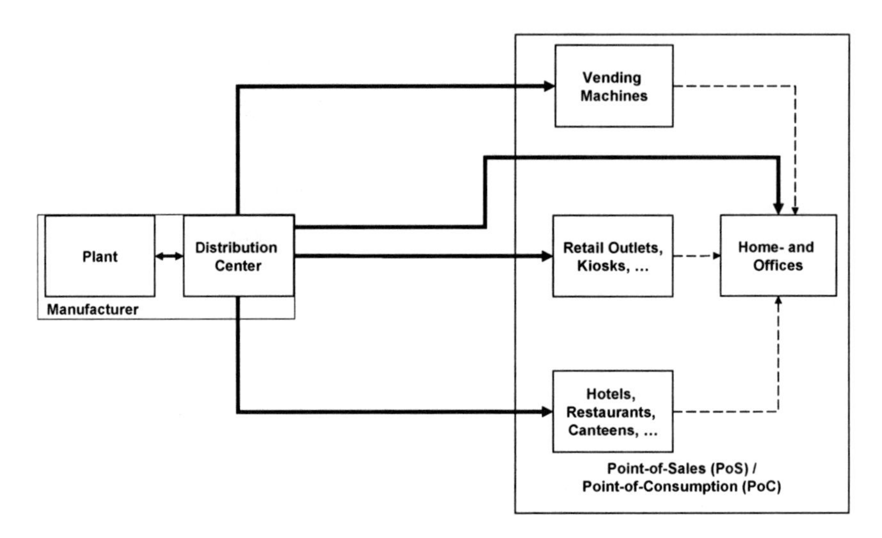

Fig. 1.2 The high-level DSD process (Otto and Shariatmadari 2008)

vending machines). In the CP industry, DSD receives an extensive relevance. Although DSD receives an extensive importance in the industry, the topic seemed to be neglected from academia side.

1.3 Empirical Insight: Why do Companies Perform DSD?

The Global DSD Analysis revealed that companies employ DSD for a multitude of reasons. This section will set the focus in particular to the manufacturers and will try to trace and to systemize why they run DSD. The following figure summarizes arguments in favor of using DSD. It is organized according to the value reference framework (Fig. 1.3).

Ultimately, CP manufacturers' motives to employ the business process of DSD are headed to add value to the firms' financial results. For this, companies have two basic options to generate a net value-add: increase revenue or decrease costs. Accordingly, manufacturers can launch activities to increase revenue (i.e. activities related to the area of sales & marketing) or they can try to reduce cost elements (i.e. actions to total costs of distribution) associated to their business processes. With DSD, both areas can be addressed. Hence, the above illustrated arguments will be discussed under the pillars of sales & marketing-related and logistics-oriented aspects in the following.

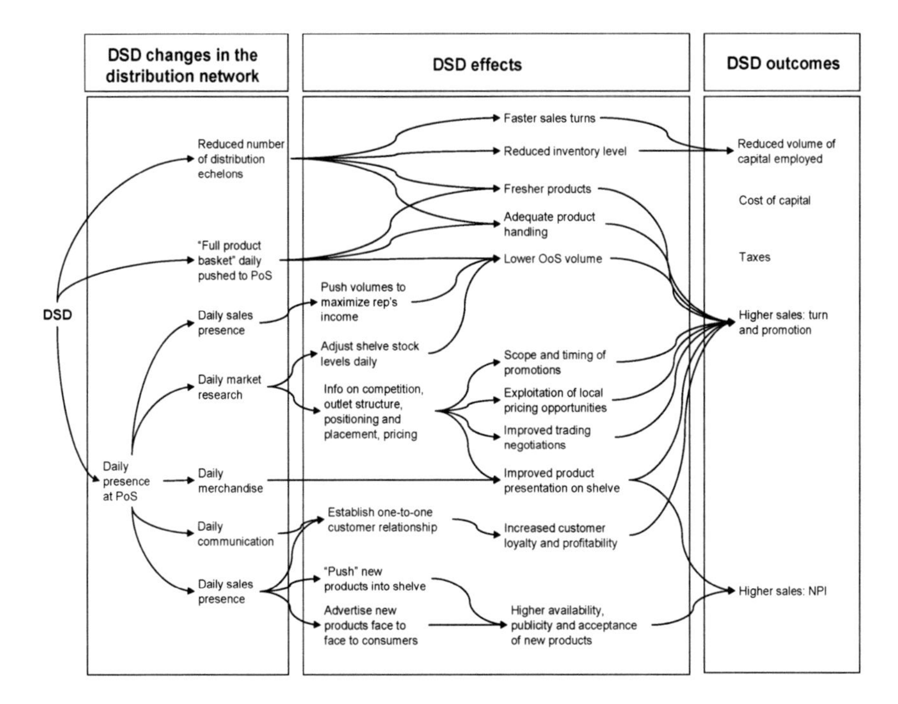

Fig. 1.3 Why do manufacturers run DSD? (Otto and Shariatmadari 2008)

1.3.1 Motives in the Area of Logistics

For the logistics area, numerous benefits and advantages can result from the DSD business process. Mainly, these are the following:

1.3.1.1 DSD Ensures Faster Replenishment Cycles

In DSD, the order fulfillment cycle is fast, since the order to delivery lead-time is typically less than 48 h – sometimes even less than 24 h. As the following figure (Fig. 1.4) illustrates, more than 50% of retail respondents in the GDA confirmed the goods receipt within the next 48 h.

This ensures an adequate product constitution for perishable food in the shelf. Hereby, products in the categories of bakery, meat & poultry, fish and dairy are often delivered directly by the suppliers (Kaipia and Tanskanen 2003, p. 171; US Federal Trade Commission 2003, p. 52).

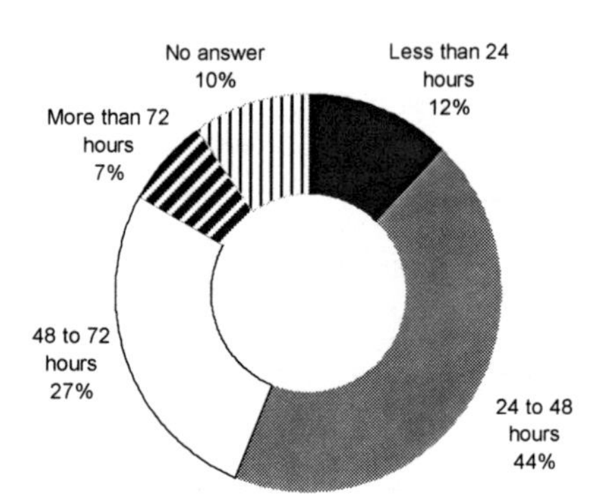

Fig. 1.4 Fast order fulfillment in DSD (Answers of retail respondents in the GDA) (Otto and Shariatmadari 2008)

1.3.1.2 DSD Allows Adequate Product Handling

Also other major DSD categories require a special focus on product handling, such as soft drinks, beer, bread and fresh baked goods or fragile items, such as salted snacks and some gourmet items (Saltzmann et al. 1999, p. 8; Hennessy 1994). For ice cream, product handling and maintaining a consistent temperature to avoid heat shock are the most important factors (Parlin 2002; Pamplin 2001). Hereby, the DSD concept revolves around a business crucial product control. It also brings the manufacturer into the position to ensure appropriate product handling until the product arrives to its final selling destination (such as the cooler) (Merkel 1997, p. 44).

1.3.1.3 DSD Reduces the Inventory Level

In a DSD system, the manufacturer owns the complete distribution up to the point of sale or point of consumption. DSD suppliers tend to deliver directly to the final in-store destination (e.g. shelf, cooler, display). Hereby and similar to a vendor managed inventory (VMI) system, the DSD supplier often takes the responsibility for the inventory of its customer (Hertel et al. 2005, p. 192). In such a process, the main inventory replenishment decisions will be done by the manufacturer on behalf of the customer. He also monitors the buyer's inventory levels and makes supply decisions regarding order quantities, shipping and timing (Waller et al. 1999, p. 183).

Based on the on-site insights through DSD, the supplier is in the position to match demand and replenishment continuously. In fact, the inventory situation of the average product is reviewed more frequently than purchase orders are placed. On average, the more frequent review in DSD eliminates the ordering delay in the information. As of it, replenishment decisions can be scheduled and made better.

Safety stock levels throughout the supply chain – especially on retail level – can be reduced as they are managed by the manufacturer. Hence, the overall inventory level can be lowered by DSD.

1.3.1.4 DSD Lowers the Average Out-of-Stock

If comparing DSD categories to warehouse-delivered products, the average out-of-stock rates for DSD products differ among the previous performed studies related to the topic of on-shelf availability. While the Coca-Cola Retailing Research council reported a stock-out average of 6.5%, GMA and Roland Berger evaluated about 7.4% for DSD (GMA and Berger 2002). Anyhow, DSD products show a better average performance in terms of on-shelf availability if compared to the worldwide average of out-of-stock 8.3% based on the Corsten/Gruen study. Even further, some of the analyzed DSD categories showed significantly lower out-of-stocks than the average (Snacks 5.3%).

Surely, a positively influencing factor of DSD is the route personnel which visit outlets on a regular basis, often several times a week. Frequently these DSD representatives carry sales incentives and maintain shelves and displays – keeping products on-shelf even while they are on promotion (Neff 2001).

1.3.1.5 DSD Secures Product Availability Across the Country

In emerging countries, distribution is one of the most challenging problems for consumer-products businesses. "In Latin America, product distribution is a blood sport that few foreign companies can stomach. In Colombia, 15% of soft drinks pass through rebel-controlled territories where shippers are vulnerable to robbery or extortion. Throughout the region, liquor transporters must disguise themselves to avoid pilferage. In Mexico City, beverage trucks cannot be insured unless the shipper contracts with a high tech security service to protect against hijackers." (Gonzalez 2002, p. 2).

While supermarket and hypermarket retailers are increasingly present in major capital cities, consumers living on the peripheries of these cities and on the countryside continue to purchase the large majority of goods through local shops (CCRRC and Booz Allen 2003, p. 3). The tendency of most multinational companies entrancing these markets is to focus initially on the bigger chains in the major cities to build up volume quickly, without having to invest in costly sales and distribution systems.

However, one major difficulty with this strategy is that most of these consumer products companies then neglect 50–90% of the typical market. As of it, delivering mainstream beverages to the majority of the population is still a huge challenge for manufacturers (USA Today 2005). Such a strategic approach also puts manufacturers into a dangerous position with the major retailers, if it comes to negotiation. Thirdly, failing to build quickly a broad distribution base also allows competitors to combat new entering manufacturers easier.

1.3.2 Motives in the Area of Sales & Marketing

As shown in the previous chapter, DSD is a quick distribution process enabling lowered reaction time to market opportunities, reduced level of overall supply chain inventory, and better out-of-stock rates. But additionally and based on these benefits from the logistics area, several benefits result from the DSD business process in sales & marketing.

1.3.2.1 DSD Enables Unhindered Communication to Customers and Consumers

DSD is a business process that companies use to both sell and distribute goods directly to customer locations. Hereby, the CP manufacturer and the respective customer outlet work together directly. This unhindered access on a regular basis is unique for the DSD business process – and thereby, generates unique opportunities for the supplier. Actually, no other process enables the supplier to directly interact with its trading partners in such frequent manner.

Thereof and by DSD, the CP manufacturer can leverage a unified and consistent communication to the customers and – vice versa – gets a better understanding about the needs of them. The management of the customer relationship between the supplier and its trading partners as well as consumers is a focal point in this context. In fact, CP manufacturers see the direct access to customers and consumers by DSD as an important and effective instrument to understand their true needs better, as the Global DSD Analysis showed.

1.3.2.2 DSD Allows Improved Product Presentation

Enabled by DSD, CP manufacturers gain direct contact to customers, and hence, also the consumer-product interfaces in the respective PoS. Depending on category and product attributes, these interfaces can be manifold (e.g. shelves, displays, coolers). Very often and especially when goods distribution is done via retailer-owned distribution centers, the consumer products presentation in the store does neither match the consumers' expectation nor the manufacturers' ambition. The reason is quite simple as retail personnel often do not manage the products appropriately (e.g. in terms of appearance or freshness). Nor are most retail employees willing to do the merchandizing work to ensure a proper consumer interface. Even worse, suppliers are mostly not aware of the suboptimal presentation of their products in the outlet. Not matching consumers' expectations can result in missed sales opportunities for the consumer products manufacturer.

By DSD, about 80% of the CP respondents perform direct product merchandizing according to their standards, as the Global DSD Analysis revealed. Hereby, the sales representatives directly work on the presentation of products within the store and execute activities to ensure a proper consumer-product interface. Amongst others, building up additional product placements and/or displays are tasks to reach that aim.

1.3.2.3 DSD Enables Access to Prime Market Information

Not limited to short-term effects, companies use the DSD process also to improve their business on long-term perspective. Optimizing products and processes via various functional areas require detailed and up-to-date information about multiple interactions with customers. Relevant information from these interactions serves as the basis for future interactions (Peppers and Rogers 1997).

As the Global DSD Analysis revealed for the first time in this extent, the collection of information is the top activity performed in DSD besides physical distribution. In fact, a broad majority of 84% of CP respondents stated to collect downstream data often or very often. Although differing slightly in the levels, it remains valid for all regions and segments.

The survey also showed that DSD companies collect a wide variety of all kinds of downstream information. But the capturing of data in categories of sales, inventory, out-of-stock, quality of product/assortment/merchandizing, competitive intelligence, and outlet structure have been preeminent. In fact, the kind of information gathered and its extent seem to be company- as well as segment-specific.

1.3.2.4 DSD Enables Better Product Pricing

Based on various competitive situations and circumstances, buyers in different regions show a different willingness to pay. Hence, regionally dispersed markets act different in terms of price elasticity (Kamen 1989, p. 38). Analyzing prices of product categories can help CP manufacturers to identify more profitable pricing decisions by quantifying the sales response to base-, promoted-, and cross-price variation of their products (IRI 2006, p. 19). As most DSD categories experience a high level of consumption elasticity (meaning that consumers purchase many DSD products on impulse and consume them rapidly), such opportunities by setting more adequate prices are extremely valid for the DSD business.

Taking into consideration the current circumstances in the industry's environment (especially the diversifying consumer behavior), the price analyses need to be performed on a regional – or even better – on a local, PoS-specific level. Key for these analyses but difficult to gain, comprehensive information on store-level (e.g. such as consumer preferences, local competitive intensity or respective PoS environment data) have to be integrated.

Enabled through the direct access to their customers, many DSD suppliers have already created such a visibility on store-level (Forrester Research 2006, p. 9). They combine their improved customer and consumer insights with researches on price elasticity in order to determine the optimal target price to consumers at retail. Hereby, the strong relationship to their trading partners (again, enabled by DSD) as well as the in-depth understanding of the local needs help DSD companies to realize the appropriate prices at customer location (Fig. 1.5).

As the GMA evaluated in a recent study, 78% of DSD companies set their prices locally. Furthermore, the analysis found out that "virtually no companies outside direct store delivery (DSD) look at elasticity at a regional level, meaning they do not capitalize on regional and local pricing opportunities" (GMA 2005, p. 3).

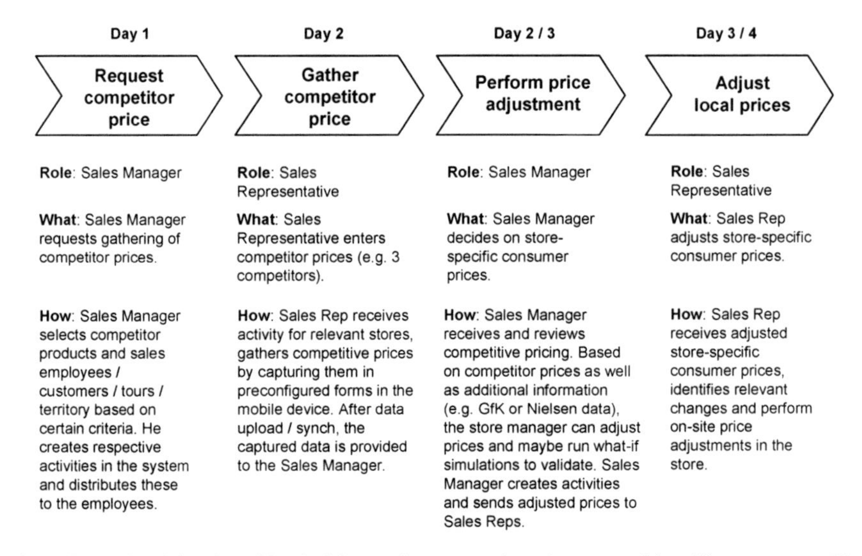

Fig. 1.5 Local pricing in DSD: Quick reaction on market changes and handling store specific consumer prices (Otto and Shariatmadari 2008)

1.3.2.5 DSD Increases Efficiency of New Product Introductions

In order to increase the success rate for new product introductions, sensing demand and understanding consumer acceptance are crucial. Companies that sense channel demand in less than a week have double the success rate for new product introductions compared to companies that take 2 weeks or longer to sense demand, as a recent study by AMR has shown (AMR 2006). As quantified by the GfK: Sensing demand in terms of quantity and quality followed by an adequate in-store execution at the shelf can increase the NPI success rate by more than 30% (GfK ConsumerScan 2006).

By DSD, the daily presence allows a more effective new product introduction since it is imperative to better understand what consumers want. DSD enables this improved sensing of consumption patterns as well as the competitive environment as the manufacturer comes all the way down to the PoS. As picked out as a central topic before, the gathering of relevant data on-site at the respective PoS as well as the capabilities to reuse the information in products and processes is crucial.

For sensing demand in terms of quantity and quality as well as reacting appropriately, different kinds of data are necessary. This includes, but is not limited to, sales or inventory data. For example, the knowledge about the competitive situation at the respective PoS (e.g. "Is a competitor running a promotion at this location?") or other environmental factors (e.g. "Are my products properly placed and merchandized correctly?") are of major relevance.

Indeed, non-DSD suppliers do have access to sales and inventory data provided to suppliers by retailers (e.g. Wal-Mart, Metro Group) as well as syndicated data providers (such as ACNielsen or GfK) more and more. But the relevant data in terms of comprehensive and essential downstream information to improve introduction processes is not provided yet, as our researches in the Global DSD Analysis have shown.

Analyzing new product introduction over several years, 70% of North America's most successful product introductions in 2001 have been launched by DSD manufacturers (GMA 1999, p. 7).

1.3.2.6 DSD Increases the Effectiveness of Promotions

With the employment of DSD and as shown, a more flexible and quicker distribution can be implemented. Also, the supplier gains the valuable direct access to customer outlet and the shelf. Thereby, he is able to check the sales promotion everyday and monitor its success at the shelf from first hand. It can be expected, that in long-term, brand owners will gain experience in – and be able to – launch better and more effective sales promotions.

As confirmed by 71% of consumer product survey respondents, the product distribution via DSD increases the effectiveness of promotions.

1.3.2.7 DSD Increases the Profitability of Customers

DSD helps companies to get closer to the customers as it enables a direct customer access in a frequent manner while unified communication activities can be performed. Often these direct interactions are performed by the same driver every day.

Again here, the role of information and its embedding in the communication to the customer is a key success factor. By a continuous and frequent communication to the customer, information can be shared more effectively and the relation to the customer can be improved. Such frequent and open communication between a supplier and a customer boosts the customer's efficiency in using the firm's products or services. Thereby it improves the satisfaction and loyalty of the customer (Cannon and Homburg 2001, p. 29).

In fact, satisfied and loyal customers in long-term business relations do buy more and various products (cross-/up-selling) (Griffin et al. 1995), tolerate issues more easily (Homburg and Rudolph 1995), and support the set-up of a positive brand and company image (e.g. through good mouth-to-mouth marketing) (Heskett et al. 1995). The probability of redoing business with a loyal company is higher (Nieschlag et al. 1997, p. 126) and will be stabilized with increasing time of trading relations (Stahl 1998, p. 150; Griffin et al. 1995).

While understanding the true wants from the customer base and converting them into the business process, DSD suppliers are able to satisfy trading partners' demand and desires better. As shown by the GDA survey, more than 80% of CP respondents observed an increase in customers' loyalty – only 12% of retail respondents disagreed.

As of this and summarized by the subsequent figure (Fig. 1.6), companies can generate a higher profitability out of satisfied and loyal trading partners by setting up a close and one-to-one customer relationship. By this, CP companies can generate economic and competitive advantages out the customers.

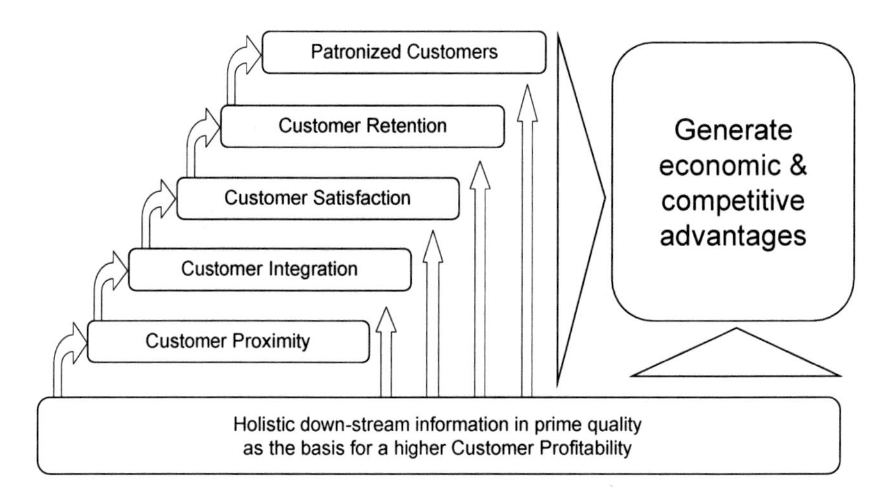

Fig. 1.6 DSD increases the profitability of customers (Adapted from Schumacher and Meyer 2004, p. 26)

1.4 Empirical Insight: How Companies Perform DSD?

In the Global DSD Analysis, the business process of DSD has been analyzed on multiple levels. Hereby, the focus of the study embraced the levels of strategy, operations and information systems. On operational level, the process was examined based on the DSD value chain and followed the single process steps. Hence, the execution of the DSD process will be discussed along the identified sub processes respectively. The subsequent illustration (Fig. 1.7) visualizes the primary process in DSD.

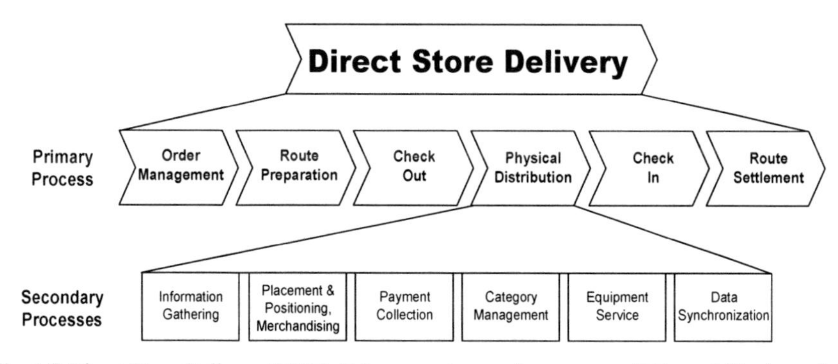

Fig. 1.7 Direct Store Delivery (DSD): Primary and secondary process (Otto and Shariatmadari 2008)

Before discussing each DSD process step on operational level, it should be stressed that there are two different approaches how to execute DSD in general. This basic question will be in the focus of the first chapter. Furthermore, a certain understanding of the process-characteristic roles is supportive to better understand its execution on process step level. Hence, both points will be discussed in prior to the analysis of DSD's primary process execution. A discussion of the secondary process steps will ensue.

1.4.1 The Basic Question: Combining or Separating Order Entry and Order Fulfillment

In terms of driving the DSD process, two basic process types exist in the business: (1) route sell (also known as spot or van sell) and (2) pre-sell (Mathews 1995). These two types differ in terms of order generation as well as in the area of order fulfillment. In the following, both types will be characterized and compared. The question of which approach is employed by the respective company may differ according to various criteria (e.g. distributor, territory, trade channel, and even account). In fact, most examined companies drive a hybrid approach and employ both types to a certain extent.

1.4.1.1 Route Sales: The Combined Approach

The first approach is known as route sales or van sales for many years in the industry and employed by the majority of firms who sell and deliver directly to individual retail outlets. The route sales approach is characterized by an individual, who performs both selling and delivery functions. This method of selling and delivery has been prevalent in industries such as beer, soft drink, snack food and baked goods for a long time. The GMA defines route sales as "a form of DSD in which the sale and delivery of product is accomplished by the same individual on the same day. In route sell, the sales person – typically the route driver – has products on the truck and replenishes each store based on immediate needs" (GMA 2002a, p. 21). In this system, the company (often the driver himself) has to forecast sales to determine the proper inventory load for the truck. The following figure (Fig. 1.8) shall illustrate the DSD route sales process model in general.

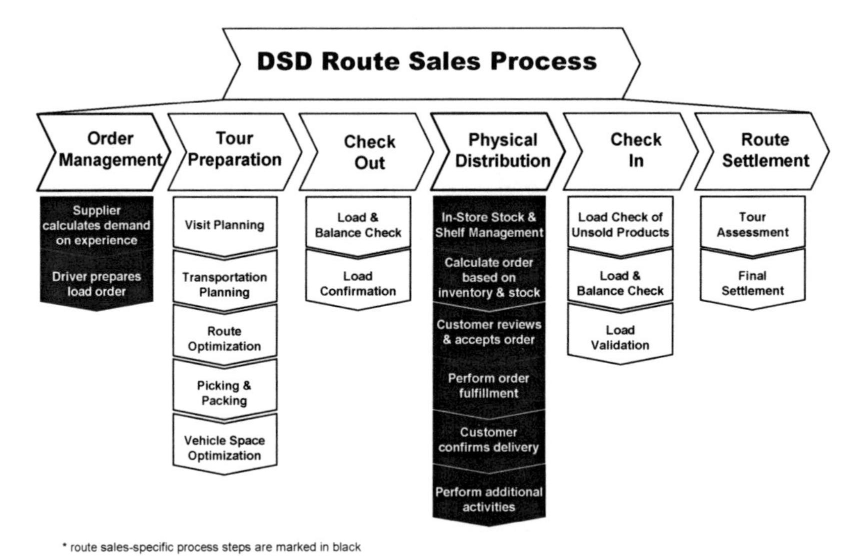

Fig. 1.8 The Direct Store Delivery (DSD) route sales process – differing process steps highlighted (Otto and Shariatmadari 2008)

But in the last years, this approach has been challenged by several impacting factors (such as an increase in distribution costs or the product proliferation in terms of brand/package combinations) (IBM 2005, p. 4). Due to this, forecasting sales has become increasingly difficult for companies. Accordingly, the mix of products loaded on the truck often did not match the demand for a given day – which resulted in both lost revenue (by not having sufficient amount of certain products on the truck) and additional costs (due to transporting and extra handling of excessive amount of wrong brand/package combinations). As a result, the need for more effective forecasting and inventory management on a truck-by-truck or route-by-route basis increased, leading to a variety of enhanced forecasting techniques with varying degrees of success (Baker and Golden 1985).

1.4.1.2 Pre-sold: Separating Order Capturing and Selling

Consequently, other approaches have been adopted by companies some times ago, separating the order capturing and selling function from the delivery function. Hereby, one individual is responsible for selling and another is responsible for delivery.

Then and typically, the selling is either done via a conventional salesman, called preseller, making personal sales calls on the business partner or by a sales person making the sales call over the phone, i.e. telephone sales or telesales. The GMA describes the pre-sell model as "a form of DSD in which order placements occur [...] prior to product delivery. Orders are typically generated by a distributor sales representative or initiated by the customer and communicated to the distributor by telephone, fax or internet. Once processed by the distributor, the order is delivered to the store within several days (typically one) following order placement" (GMA 2002a, p. 21).

Oftentimes, DSD suppliers also use merchandisers as a third entity involved in the pre-sell model to perform additional activities on-site in the store (e.g. replenish shelf and displays, pull-up product from backroom, remove out-of-date and

Alternative DSD Process Models

Order Entry Channels	Route Sale		Presales	
	Van Seller	Selling and delivering a the same time	Sales Force / Preseller	Personal, face to face selling
	Predicted Order	based on single statistics e.g. including on customer order history	Telephone Sales	Selling over the telephone
		based on multiple statistics e.g. including factors such as weather or seasonality	Internet	Selling performed via the internet
	Demand Estimation	Demand estimated by an employee e.g. the driver	EDI	Customer demand transmitted via EDI
			E-Mail / Fax / Telex	Demand transmitted via e-mail, fax or telex
	Predicted Demand		Presold Orders	

Fig. 1.9 Mapping alternative process models and typical order entry channels in DSD (Otto and Shariatmadari 2008)

damaged product, etc.). The definition and role of pre-sell may differ by company or by category.

In illustration (Fig. 1.9), the two different basic approaches have been mapped against the different order entry types.

According to the consumer products and retail respondents in the Global DSD Analysis and if employing a pre-sales model, the selling function is normally performed at least 1 day in advance to the delivery. Therefore, the trucks are loaded with the brand/package combinations that have already been sold and the issues of vehicle out-of-stock and overloads associated with the route sales system have been (for the most part) eliminated. Further and since the sales person is professionally trained and motivated to sell all brands/packages, newer and lower volume products are given the necessary attention in the selling process.

1.4.1.3 But which One is Better? – A Comparison of Both DSD Process Models

So far, it has not been proven that one process model is always more effective than another (neither by the Global DSD Analysis nor by any other known DSD examination). This indicates that each company should calculate the savings in distribution costs that would accrue to its own operations by a shift to the pre-sell system and compare these savings with the costs that the system would entail. It should be stated that many respondents report that the pre-sell system will produce higher sales volumes at lower total costs per unit sold. Actually, the share of route sales businesses steadily declined over the last years – but did not disappear completely (Business Wire 2004; Progressive Grocer 1995). Rather more, DSD companies (especially beverage companies) switched to a hybrid approach. The subsequent table (Table 1.2) below summarizes these benefits and issues of the pre-sale vs. a route sales approach. A discussion more detailed can be found at O'Neill and Bommer.

Table 1.2 Benefits and costs of the DSD pre-sales versus route sales model (Adapted from O'Neill and Bommer 1988)

Benefits	Issues
Increased sales by professional salesmen	Additional vans/cars needed
Fewer delivery trucks required	More qualified salesmen required
Fewer drivers/helpers required	Additional distance traveled
Improved truck operating efficiency	Routes generated in higher frequency
Improved loading/unloading efficiency	Increased coordination needed
Improved shelf management at retail level	

1.4.2 Roles in the DSD Process

Several roles exist in the business process of DSD. Such roles describe specific functions that are carried out by the CP manufacturer's employees. In general, roles describe a certain type of employee which receives specific, company-defined qualification and competency (Galler 1997, p. 52). Roles are used to instruct a person which expectations are made towards his action and behavior (Heidack 1983, p. 235). The respective roles are cascaded directly out of the DSD process and represent the functional scope that the respective employee should inherit (Bleicher 1991, p. 36; Rupietta 1992, p. 27). In DSD, the process-specific and for this purpose relevant roles can be differed in such with internal and external focus of activity. While internal roles take care of coordination, monitoring of external roles as well as internal order processing mostly (Otto 2004, p. 14), the focus of external roles is the physical distribution of goods, the order capturing as well as additional sales & marketing-related activities in the customer outlet (Kotler and Bliemel 1999, p. 1149; Meffert 1998, p. 608).

Table 1.3 The process-specific roles in DSD (Otto and Shariatmadari 2008)

Internal Focus	Tasks
Supervisor	Ensure actions in the distribution center to be carried out in adequate manner and appropriate productivity
	Take responsibility for work and actions of employees
	Perform checks and inspections when vehicles leave from or return to distribution center
Checker (Check in- and Check-out)	Count package groups of products together with driver
	Confirm the unloading and reloading of products
	Validate the vehicle content by signature
	Determine product and cash differences based on relevant information (e.g. initial delivery stocks, loading confirmation) and follow-up in case of differences
Settler	Analyze and process performed tours
	Reconcile inventory overages and shortages related to vehicle loading
External Focus	**Tasks**
Preseller	Negotiate and capture customer orders face-to-face at store level
	Review customer-specific sales analysis (e.g. sales history, product listings or credit status) to enhance customer ordering
Delivery Driver	Process customer delivery and manage the return of products
	Manage the delivery and clearing of empties and rental items
	Perform various customer-related tasks (e.g. gather information
Merchandiser	Carry out product-related tasks (e.g. product placement, positioning, merchandizing)
Mixed Role (e.g. Van Seller)	Perform a mixture of the above mentioned tasks by external roles

The table (Table 1.3) summarizes the relevant roles in the DSD process and aligns them on internal as well as external focus. Furthermore, other roles do surely exist in the process (e.g. picker, packer, loading persons, or scheduler). As such generic roles do appear in many other business processes, they will not be considered as process-characteristic and, hence, also not in the following.

1.4.3 The Primary Process: Order Fulfillment

On operational level and as mentioned, the process was examined based on the DSD value chain. Following the single process steps respectively, the execution of the DSD process will be discussed along the sub processes as illustrated before.

1.4.3.1 Order Management

In general, customer sales orders can be received via various channels. These order channels can be differentiated in personal (e.g. pre-selling), semi-personal (e.g. via call centers) and impersonal (e.g. via EDI, fax, internet) (Otto 2000, p. 15; Jarvenpaa and Staples 2000, p. 129; Meffert 1998, p. 820). Furthermore, customers' orders can be missing in case of a route sales process or under other circumstances. Then, the manufacturer has to predict the demand for various purposes (see the previous chapter for more details). In DSD, all of these order entry types are possible and employed manifold in the business to a different extent. In fact, most companies use a set of different types. Hereby, the implemented set of order entry channels depends on various criteria, such as the chosen DSD process model of CP companies as well as the orientation of their customers.

1.4.3.2 Tour Preparation

The process step of tour preparation (Fig. 1.10) includes all activities that are necessary to be prepared before the physical distribution to the goods addressees can be executed. This embraces all steps between the transmissions of orders received during order capturing up to the execution of goods check out in the warehouse. Especially, the following sub processes can be differed within the tour preparation for DSD.

The planning set up and management of the distribution structure is the heart of the tour preparation process. Hereby, the dilemma of the adequate customer and delivery service level versus the challenge of minimizing costs has to be harmonized (Pfohl 1996, p. 56). As known from literature, minimizing costs only is not

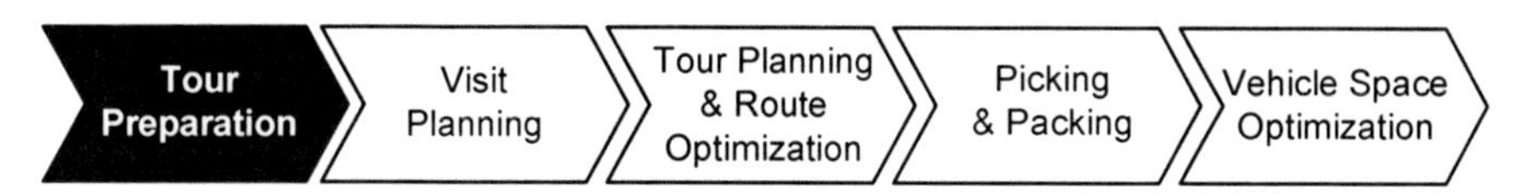

Fig. 1.10 The process of tour preparation in DSD (Otto and Shariatmadari 2008)

the appropriate answer. Rather, the appropriate trade-off between service level and costs has to be found (Stock and Lambert 2001, p. 107).

1.4.3.3 Check Out

As the DSD business is a cost-intensive business process, companies have to ensure that the physical distribution is performed in a correct manner. Thus, many companies perform an additional checking process when vehicles leave the distribution center and drive to the respective trading partners. This process is called "Check Out" Process and is meant as a confirmation process by at least one other person besides the driver. According to the respondents of the GDA, 72% of companies employ this process step.

1.4.3.4 Physical Distribution

The process of physical distribution is the core of the DSD process, as here, the direct contact with customers and consumers occurs. As shown before, DSD allows the manufacturer a direct access to customers/consumers and the product-consumer-interface on a regular basis. Consequently and during physical distribution, various activities can be performed by the manufacturers which generate a value-add to consumer product companies, as well as their trading partners. Depending on the respective role executing the customer visits, the focus of visit activities can change. Thus, they can be related to:

- Sales (e.g. a preseller negotiating and capturing new orders)
- Distribution (e.g. a driver delivering materials ordered by the customer)
- Marketing (e.g. a merchandiser presenting a new product or providing promotional materials)
- Or a mix of distribution, sales and marketing (e.g. a van seller performing several of the above).

Hence and besides Tour Maintenance, DSD's physical distribution can be differed into three sub processes: Order processing, order fulfillment, and task processing (Fig. 1.11).

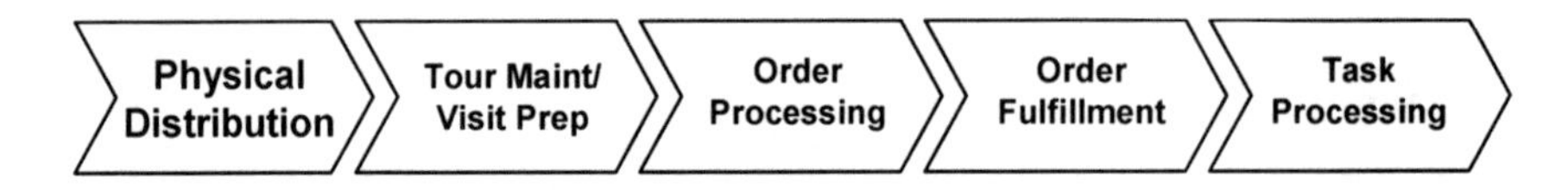

Fig. 1.11 The process step of physical distribution (Otto and Shariatmadari 2008)

1.4.3.5 Check In

After the physical distribution, the actual delivered, remaining and returned goods, as well as the received payments for sold products, have to be reconciled against the information from prior the tour. Hence and analog to the process step of check out, most of the responding DSD companies perform a checking process (meant as a confirmation process by at least one other person) when vehicles return to the distribution center. While this process step, various checks and inspections will be carried out when a vehicle returns from a tour to a warehouse or plant. This can include checking the freight, vehicle, driver, and tour documents. For example:

- Returned quantities (empties, full products returned due to over delivery, and returns)
- The tour duration
- Number of kilometers or miles driven.

1.4.3.6 Route Settlement

The route settlement is a follow-on to the tour process and also the final process step in the DSD business process. Once the field employee has returned, the settlement is to synchronize planned tour information and documents with the information from the tour that was actually executed (the actual tour).

The route settlement can be divided into the following sub processes:

1. Difference determination: The comparison of expected products and cash values with the counted values when the check-in is performed
2. Final settlement: The creation of the final documents as a result from difference determination as well as existing discrepancies between the planned and actual tour
3. Post goods issue: The posting of final documents as the final step of the tour settlement.

1.4.4 The Secondary Processes

DSD grants manufacturers direct access to customers and product-consumer-interfaces in outlets regularly. Enabled by this opportunity, consumer products manufacturers often perform further, secondary processes and activities on-site. These processes and activities are in the focus of this chapter.

While there is a very broad employment of secondary processes, its extent is company-, region- and segment-specific. Of course, the question which of the various activities is implemented for the respective customer is differing on bilateral level (i.e. depending on the respective service level agreements between manufacturer and business partner) also.

But in general and according to the customer respondents in the Global DSD Analysis, the following activities are most often performed in the industry (Fig. 1.12).

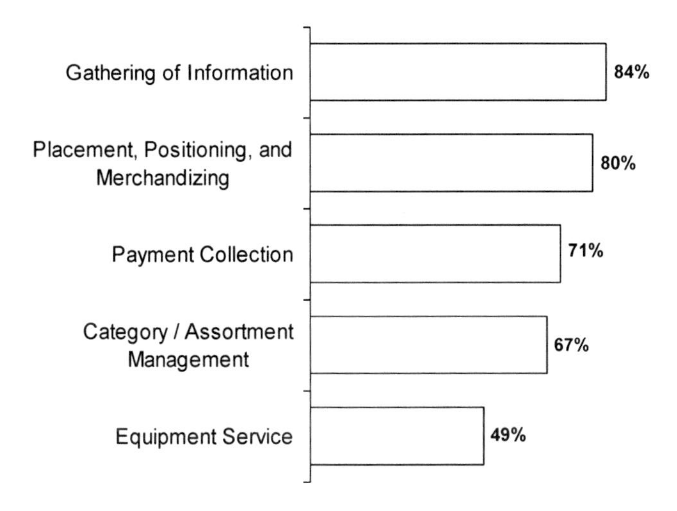

Fig. 1.12 Ranking of secondary DSD processes by importance (Otto and Shariatmadari 2008)

Further activities cited by survey respondents are the gathering of customer feedback (e.g. by capturing complaints and performing customer or consumer surveys), the execution of customer audits (such as the monitoring of service-level agreements by on-site price-control), the tracking and tracing of trade assets (e.g. vending machines or coolers), and the synchronization of data with trading partners (e.g. harmonize information such as product, price, item, promotional price, or supply to trading partner's purchasing information).

While carrying out secondary processes in the field, the extent of employment, and hence the importance, of each activity group depends on the type of goods addressee. Within DSD and as shown in the previous chapter, DSD suppliers deliver regularly to point of sales and point of consumptions, such as retail outlets, the gastronomy and HORECA business, private households and offices (i.e. home-and-office delivery), or vending machines. The following figure (Fig. 1.13) shall summarize the relevancy of each group of activity in relation to the different point of sales and point of consumptions.

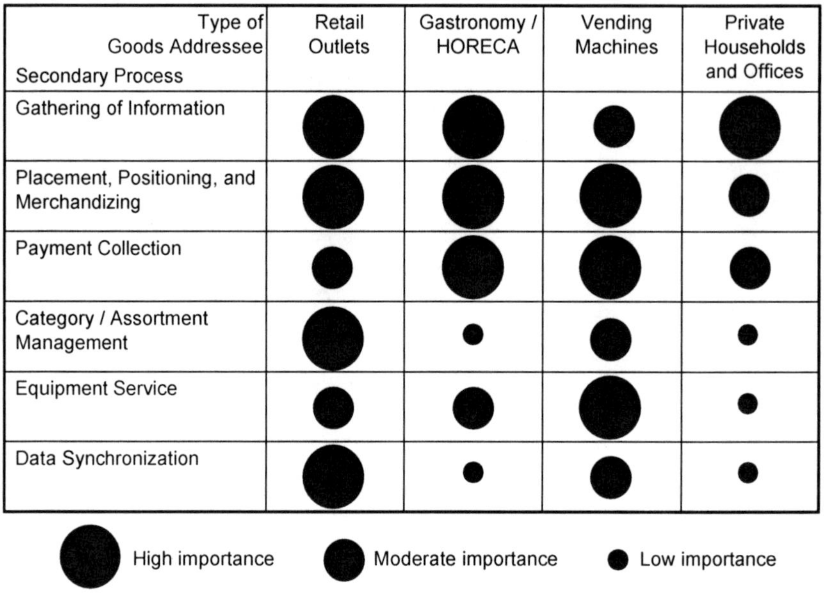

Type of Goods Addressee / Secondary Process	Retail Outlets	Gastronomy / HORECA	Vending Machines	Private Households and Offices
Gathering of Information	High	High	Moderate	High
Placement, Positioning, and Merchandizing	High	High	High	Moderate
Payment Collection	Moderate	High	High	Moderate
Category / Assortment Management	High	Low	Moderate	Low
Equipment Service	Moderate	Moderate	High	Low
Data Synchronization	High	Low	Moderate	Low

High importance Moderate importance Low importance

Fig. 1.13 Relevancy of secondary processes for selected kinds of addressees (Otto and Shariatmadari 2008)

1.4.4.1 Information Gathering

Information of market conditions represents the basis for a multitude of business decisions (Hammann and Erichson 1994, p. 7; Kinnear and Taylor 1991, p. 12). In the light of short product life cycles, fragmented and diverging consumers, as well as intensive competition, the relevancy of up-to-date, precise, and holistic downstream information is obvious. Essential for today's market success, company responsibles have to build their decisions on reliable and accurate market data. In fact, the positive impact of a systematic information management on sales- and company success has been proven by several empirical studies (Schäfer 2002; Homburg et al. 2006). The precise capturing and systematic working of such information in DSD is in the focus of this section. As the process of DSD enables direct access to customers and consumers, as well as the product-consumer-interface, it also allows companies the direct access to prime market information and its collection from first hand. Within today's competitive environment, this acts as a success-critical key differentiator from other companies.

As indicated, the gathering of information experiences an increasing role among the secondary processes in DSD. Followed by placement, position and merchandizing, payment collection, and category/assortment related activities, the collection of information is the overall top activity performed in DSD. As revealed by the GDA, 84% of consumer products respondents gather information at store level.

While numbers differ slightly in the various levels, this remains valid for regions and segments. Hereby, the gathering of information is not limited to a special kind of data. As respondents in the GDA confirmed, all kinds of downstream information are collected by the companies. Among major ones, data collection related to sales, inventory, out-of-stock, quality of product/assortment/merchandizing, competitive intelligence, and outlet structure are at top positions.

When compared to non-DSD companies in the industry, DSD-employing manufacturers receive an enormous competitive advantage by their wide-ranging access to market information and the value-add out of it. Not limited to DSD manufacturers, also their trading partners experience benefits out of the suppliers' superior know-how.

1.4.4.2 Placement, Positioning, Merchandising

Placement, positioning, and merchandising is a supply chain practice of making products in retail outlets available to consumers, primarily by stocking shelves, building up secondary placements and displays, as well as optimizing product presentation in the in-store point of sales (e.g. shelf, cooler, display). Today and on average, DSD route personnel spend 20–27% of their time stocking and merchandizing shelves in small- and large-format stores respectively (GMA Forum 2006, p. 60).

While stocking shelves and building displays are often done when the product is delivered, the activity separation gets more and more in common. In grocery stores, for example, main products delivered directly to the store from manufacturers will be stocked and positioned by the manufacturer's employee who is often a full time merchandiser. Then, the full time merchandiser is responsible for servicing an outlet for product replenishment after the product was delivered to the outlet. His main responsibilities include:

- (Re-) Filling all in-store point of sales of the customer outlet in compliance with brand owner's and its trading partner's agreements
- Cleaning all equipment and shelves that carry the brand owner's products
- Structuring and executing of special promotions (e.g. displays and tasting stands)
- Managing point of sales material (e.g. displays)
- Cleaning and condensing brand owner's products in further outlet places (e.g. backroom).

1.4.4.3 Payment Collection

Traditionally, DSD suppliers have been paid upon customer's receipt of products in-store. As indicated by Table 1.3 and predominantly, this practice receives extensive employment when delivery is done to independent organizations, such as gastronomy institutions, private households and offices, or smaller retail outlets (e.g. kiosks). Today, there are various payment methods employed in the market. Appreciating cash and checks, many DSD companies started to accept credit cards or cell phone payment methods.

Despite both manufacturers' as well as retailers' endeavors to switch widely to an electronic payment process, the traditional payment collection will remain valid in certain regions and for certain types of product destination points. Especially DSD suppliers delivering to decentralized and unorganized product recipients (e.g. kiosks, smaller gastronomy and HORECA business) will be affected by a certain extent of cash collection.

1.4.4.4 Category/Assortment Management

Due to their increased responsibility of in-store activities and higher store presence, DSD suppliers have a greater influence over outlet's assortment than warehouse-delivering manufacturers do. Very often, DSD companies are also in the position to generate additional sales opportunities and address competitive factors by performing actions on store-level.

In terms of category, the contractual arrangements captured in the trading partners' service level agreement are monitored and (if necessary) adapted by the manufacturers' DSD representatives (Ahlert and Borchert 2000, p. 97; Krause 2000, p. 124). For this, several activities can be performed in the store. Such activities can be derived from and identified based on the suppliers' product listings agreed upon as well as the dedicated sales area in the store (Günther and Mattmüller 1993, p. 79).

1.4.4.5 Equipment Service

For the distribution of consumer products, there are two main categories of manufacturer equipment at customer locations:

- Vending machines
- Trade assets.

Under equipment service, all services are subsumed that monitor and care about trade assets and equipment. Typically, monitoring and maintenance are performed together (Willerding 1987, p. 32). In DSD, service activities can be of various kinds. Anyhow, the basic needs are alike and there are four main kinds of services related to the operation of on-site equipment:

- Installing of equipment
- Maintaining and repairing equipment

- Removing equipment
- Refurbishing equipment.

1.4.4.6 Data Synchronization

"Synchronization is the process that aligns the information systems' databases of the brand owner [...] with those of their retailer customers in areas of item authorization, price and promotional programs" (GMA 2002b, p. 13). The synchronization of data is one of the main issues in the DSD process. In fact and compared to companies with alternative distribution methods, this is even more critical for DSD companies due to the following factors (GMA 2002b, p. 13):

- "The number of demand points is far greater for DSD categories than for traditional warehouse-delivered categories, since DSD companies deliver directly to store level vs. a retailer's warehouse. Many of these demand points have varying requirements and capabilities for data communication
- The number of supply points is far greater than for traditional warehouse-delivered categories. For example, the beer category alone has more than 2,500 individual companies that deliver products directly to more than 500,000 stores
- The resulting number of invoices generated by these complexities, when combined with weekly or daily store visits, is [very high]."

Hence, unsynchronized data between supplier's and retailer's system often produces many process inefficiencies in the system. Amongst others, additional work on incorrect invoices, insufficient delivery quantities, or too high transportation costs are the main results. Furthermore, data synchronization is the essential basis for many other initiatives in the industry, such as scan based trading. By efficient data synchronization and amongst others, companies will be able to speed up back-door check in processes, reduce the distribution of unauthorized items, and eliminate invoice discrepancies. While the latter typically results in invoice deductions, increased sales can be a result, too. Furthermore, synchronized data saves time for suppliers and trading partners as the management of errors and discrepancies as well as the thereof caused additional communication time (e.g. by discussing the incorrect invoice) will be eliminated.

References

Ahlert, D.; Borchert, S. (2000): Prozessmanagement im vertikalen Marketing – Efficient Consumer Response (ECR) in Konsumgüternetzen, Berlin.

AMR (2006): Three Supply Chain Actions You Can Take Today To Improve New Product Launch.

Baker, E.; Golden, B. (1985): Future Directions in Logistics Research, in: Transportation Research, (Vol. 19) 1985, No. 5/6, pp. 405–409.

Bleicher, K.: Organisation (1991): Strategien – Strukturen – Kulturen, 2nd ed., Wiesbaden 1991.
Business Wire (2004): Solid Innovation Expands Mobile Route Accounting Solutions to Include Third-Party Billing Capabilities, June 14.
Cannon, J.P.; Homburg, C. (2001): Buyer – Supplier Relationships and Customer Firm Costs, in: Journal of Marketing, (Vol. 65) 2001, No. 1, pp. 29–44.
Coca-Cola Retailing Research Council Latin America; Booz Allen Hamilton (2003): Creating value for emerging consumers in retailing.
Forrester Research (2006): Understanding Hispanics and Technology Adoption, Cambridge.
Galler (1997): Vom Geschäftsprozeßmodell zum Workflow-Modell, Wiesbaden 1997, pp. 52–58.
GfK ConsumerScan (2006): Gesellschaft für Konsumforschung: Näher am Kunden, erfolgreicher im Markt, Nürnberg.
Gjaja, M.; Vogel, H.M. (2000): The Power of Direct Store Delivery, in: Silverstein, M.J.; Stalk, G. Jr.: Breaking Compromises – Opportunities for Action in Consumer Markets from the Boston Consulting Group, New York.
Grocery Manufacturers Association (GMA) (1999): The Power of Direct Store Delivery (DSD), Washington DC.
Grocery Manufacturers Association (GMA); Roland Berger Strategy Consultants (2002): Reducing Out-Of-Stocks in the Grocery Channel – An In-Depth Look at DSD Categories, Washington DC.
Grocery Manufacturers Association (GMA) (2002a): E-Commerce Opportunities in Direct Store Delivery, Washington DC.
Grocery Manufacturers Association (GMA) (2002b): Reducing Out-Of-Stocks Will Put $6 Billion in Retail Sales into Play Annually, Washington DC.
Grocery Manufacturers Association (GMA) (2005): Unleash the Power of DSD: Driving DSD Supply Chain Efficiencies and Profitability, Washington DC.
Grocery Manufacturers Association (GMA) Forum (2006): Direct Store Delivery – Time for Retailers and Suppliers to Unleash the Power.
Gonzalez, O. (2002): Industry Analysis – Latin America's Beverage Market – Branding vs. Distribution, in: Info Americas, (Vol. 34).
Griffin, A. et al. (1995): Griffin, A.; Gleason, G.; Preiss, R.. et al.: Die besten Methoden zu mehr Kundenzufriedenheit, in: Harvard Business Manager, 1995, No. 3, pp. 65–76.
Günther, T.; Mattmüller, R. (1993): Möglichkeiten und Grenzen der Regaloptimierung, in: Marketing Zeitschrift für Forschung und Praxis, (Vol. 15) 1993, No. 2, pp. 77–86.
Hammann, P.; Erichson, B. (1994): Marktforschung, 3rd ed., Stuttgart.
Heidack, C. (1983): Betriebspsychologie, Wiesbaden.
Hennessy, T. (1994): Reaping the rewards of DSD, in: Progressive Grocer, June 1.
Hertel, J. et al. (2005): Supply-Chain-Management und Warenwirtschaftssysteme im Handel, Berlin.
Heskett, J.L. et al. (1995): Heskett, J. L.; Jones, T.O.; Loveman, G.W. et al.: Dienstleister müssen die ganze Service-Gewinn Kette nutzen, in: Harvard Business Manager, 1995, No. 4, pp. 50–61.
Homburg, C.; Rudolph, B. (1995): Wie zufrieden sind ihre Kunden eigentlich?, in: Harvard Business Manager, 1995, No. 1, pp. 43–50.
Homburg, C. et al. (2006): Homburg, C.; Schäfer, H.; Schneider, J.: Sales Excellence – Vertriebsmanagement mit System, 4th ed., Wiesbaden.
IBM (2005): Trade Promotion Management, New York.
IRI Information Resources, Inc. (IRI) (2006): Times & Trends: 2005 New Product Pacesetters – Leading New CPG Brands, Chicago.
Jarvenpaa, S.; Staples, D. (2000): The use of collaborative electronic media for information sharing: An exploratory study of determinant, in: Journal of Strategic Information Systems, (Vol. 9) 2000, No. 2–3, pp. 129–154.

Kaipia, R.; Tanskanen, K. (2003): Vendor Managed Category Management – an Outsourcing Solution in Retailing, in: Journal of Purchasing & Supply Chain Management, (Vol. 9) 2003, pp. 165–175.
Kamen, J. (1989): Price Filtering: restricting price deals to those least likely to buy without them, in: The Journal of Consumer Marketing, (Vol. 6) 1989, No. 3, pp. 37–43.
Kinnear, T.; Taylor, J.R. (1991): Marketing Research, 4th ed., New York.
Kotler, P.; Bliemel, F. (1999).: Marketing-Management – Analyse, Planung, Umsetzung und Steuerung, 9th ed., Stuttgart.
Krause, M. (2000): Computer Aided Selling in der Konsumgüterindustrie: Konzeption der Außendienstunterstützung, Wiesbaden.
Mathews, R. (1995): Understanding DSD, in: Progressive Grocer, November 1st.
Meffert, H. (1998): Marketing: Grundlagen marktorientierter Unternehmensführung: Konzepte – Instrumente – Praxisbeispiele; 8th ed., Wiesbaden.
Merkel, H. (1997): Konsumgüterdistribution – Kundenorientiertes Nachfragemanagement. Sparzwänge für Hersteller und Handel, in: Handelsblatt, September 4.
Neff, J. (2001): DSD delivers, in: Food Processing, January 18.
Nieschlag, R. et al. (1997): Nieschlag, R.; Dichtl, E.; Höschgen, H.: Marketing, 18th ed., Berlin.
O'Neill, B.F.; Bommer, M.R.W. (1988): Analysis of Alternative Distribution Strategies, in: The Logistics and Transportation Review, (Vol. 24) 1988, No. 3, pp. 237–247.
Otto, A. (2000): Auftragsabwicklung, in: Klaus, P.; Krieger, W.: Gabler Lexikon Logistik, 2nd ed., Wiesbaden 2000, pp. 14–20.
Otto, A. (2004): Auftragsabwicklung, in: Klaus, P.; Krieger, W.: Gabler Lexikon Logistik, 3rd ed., Wiesbaden 2004, pp. 14–20.
Otto, A.; Shariatmadari, R. (2008): Direct Store Delivery: Understanding DSD in Sales and Logistics, Results of the "Global DSD Analysis", Regensburg.
Pamplin, C. (2001): The Cold, Hard Facts – selling packaged ice, in: Convenience Store News, September 25.
Parlin, S. (2002): Providing personalized service: with direct store delivery, dairies get fresh with consumers, in: Dairy Field, October 1.
Peppers, D.; Rogers, M. (1997): Enterprise One to One, New York.
Pfohl, H.-C. (1996): Logistiksysteme, Berlin/Heidelberg.
Progressive Grocer (1995): How DSD fits into category management, Aug 1.
Rupietta, W. (1992): Organisationsmodellierung zur Unterstützung kooperativer Vorgangsbearbeitung, in: Wirtschaftsinformatik (Vol. 34) 1992, No. 1, pp. 26–37.
Saltzmann, H. et al. (1999): Transformation and Continuity: The U.S. Carbonated Soft Drink Bottling Industry and Antitrust Policy since 1980, Washington DC.
Schäfer, H. (2002): Die Erschließung von Kundenpotentialen durch Cross-Selling – Erfolgsfaktoren für ein Produktübergreifendes Beziehungsmanagement, Wiesbaden.
Stahl, H.K (1998): Modernes Kundenmanagement – wenn der Kunde im Mittelpunkt steht, Renningen.
Stock, J.R.; Lambert, D.M. (2001): Strategic Logistics Management, 4th ed., Boston et al.
US Federal Trade Commission (2003): Slotting Allowances in the Retail Grocery Industry: Selected Case Studies in Five Product Categories, Washington DC.
USA Today (2005): Molson Coors eyes options for Brazil unit.
Vinod, B. (2004): Retail revenue management and the new paradigm of merchandise optimization, in: Journal of Revenue & Pricing Management, (Vol. 3) 2005, No. 4, pp. 358–368.
Waller, M. et al. (1999): Waller, M.; Johnson M.E.; Davis, T.: Vendor-Managed Inventory in the Retail Supply Chain, in: Journal of Business Logistics, (Vol. 20) 1999, No 1.
Willerding, T. (1987): Gestaltungsmöglichkeiten der Kooperation im technischen Kundendienst zwischen Hersteller und Handel, Bochum 1987.

Chapter 2
Wrestling with the Restless Consumer: The Consumer Products Industry in Transition

Emiel van Schaik

Senior Vice President Consumer Industries,
SAP AG, Dietmar-Hopp-Allee 16, D-69190, Walldorf, tel.: +49 6227 761528,
e-mail: emiel.van.schaik@sap.com

Abstract

DSD can provide valuable insight into constantly changing consumer behavior. Working in conjunction with a responsive supply network, DSD enables CP manufacturers detect demand signals and quickly meet consumer expectations. At a time of diminishing consumer loyalty, this can help CP manufacturers differentiate themselves in the market place and maintain competitive advantage.

2.1 DSD in the Context of Changing Consumer Demand

As with any mode of distribution, DSD is beneficial to the extent that it helps companies meet consumer demand in an effective manner. To evaluate the viability of DSD, CP manufacturers first need to understand the changing nature of consumer behavior. This chapter helps put DSD in that larger context – with particular focus on how companies can use DSD as part of a multichannel distribution strategy to meet the constantly shifting demands of the increasingly restless consumer.

2.1.1 What Keeps the CEO Awake at Night?

In the CP industry today, no other business issue dominates the minds of CEOs more than shareholder value. In a mature industry such as CP, this is hardly surprising. Shareholders invest in CP companies with the expectation of value – and if they don't get it from the current CEO, they'll start looking for another who can deliver. Fluctuating shareholder value, in fact, is one of the leading factors contributing to the high CEO turnover rate in the CP industry today.

To drive shareholder value, CEOs need to focus on two primary areas: profitability and growth.

A. Otto et al., *Direct Store Delivery*,

DOI: 10.1007/978-3-540-77213-2_2,

In the CP industry, profitability and growth are achieved in large part by meeting consumer demand. The problem for CEOs – and this is what keeps them up at night – is that CP companies find it increasingly difficult to understand this demand. More than ever, CP companies are unable to understand who their customers are, what they want, and how they choose to get what they want. Consider the following:

- Since 2000, more than 30,000 new products have been introduced by CP companies each year (Product Scan press release 2004) – and approximately 65% of them failed (AMR 2007, p. 2). Innovating your way to profitable growth with new products – at least in the CP industry – appears to be a risky proposition. Why is it so difficult for CP companies to identify consumer wants and respond with the appropriate products?
- Less than 30% of all trade promotion programs are profitable. Yet the CP industry continues to spend an estimated $75 billion on trade promotions each year. Equally troublesome is the fact that more than 70% of CP companies fail to capture and measure their trade promotion results (IBM and SAP 2005). Why does the CP industry continue to spend so much money on nonprofitable trade promotion activities? And why the lack of metrics?
- At any given time, about 8% of the products that should be available for sale on store shelves are out of stock when consumers go to purchase them (Gruen and Corsten 2007). The lost sales due to out-of-stock items cost CP manufacturers $23 million for every $1 billion in sales. Why is it so hard for CP companies to meet demand?

These statistics – sobering enough by themselves – should also be seen in the context of a shrinking market of opportunities for CP companies in developed markets such as the United States where consumer spend growth, measured in real dollars, has slowed from 5% to 2.3% since 2004 (Information Resources 2008). With fewer and fewer obvious growth opportunities available, competition in these markets has become a zero sum game. While the situation in emerging markets, to be sure, is substantially different, CP companies should be careful there as well – a point to which we will return. In the context of developed markets, however, it seems appropriate to remark that companies must gain market share at the expense of their competitors if they want to win. This is leading to industry-wide cannibalization as companies drive margins ever lower in the effort to stand out and appeal to consumers. To make matters worse, the market is more crowded than ever before, with challenges constantly posed by players entering developed markets from emerging economies as well as by generic brands and retailer's private labels. All of this makes differentiation the name of the game in the CP industry.

2.1.2 Differentiation and the Restless Consumer

As consumers have become increasingly savvy they've also become increasingly restless – both in terms of their tolerance for and trust of corporate messaging and in terms of their loyalty to any particular brand. The linkage is obvious: less trust means less loyalty. One consumer survey conducted by Forrester found that 73.1% of respondents agreed that there is too much advertising today while 50.6% agreed that the experience they had with most products failed to equal the promises made in advertisements. At the same time, only 12% of respondents agreed that the ads they see are relevant to their personal wants and needs (Forrester Research 2007).

Today's consumers, in other words, are on their guard. As traditional advertising and promotional techniques prove less and less effective, the days of consumers passively receiving push campaigns are waning. The sheer volume of such campaigns – itself a reflection of the level competition in the CP industry – are partly to blame. Today's consumers cannot absorb all the messages coming their way. As a kind of self-defense mechanism, consumers tune out to minimize their option anxiety. Instead, they've become much more proactive. Connected to the world and much better informed, they select the products of interest to them and take the time to understand what is actually being offered. The approach is one of "Here is what I want and here is how I'm going to get it."

For the CP company that resists change, the billions of new consumers entering the market from the BRIC countries (Brazil, Russia, India, China) add little comfort. It is expected that most of these consumers will leapfrog into modern consumer culture without passing through any of the stages that marked the progression of the consumer base in earlier developed countries. These consumers, in other words, will be just as restless as their counterparts in North America, Europe, and Japan. They'll be just as bombarded with messages, just as turned off by advertising, and just as empowered by the Internet to circumvent traditional channels, zero in on the information they want, and get what they need.

2.2 Revisiting the Fundamental Questions of Consumer Demand

In light of the challenges articulated thus far, the ability of CP companies to understand the needs and wants of the restless consumer is more important than ever before. This is forcing many CP companies back to the drawing board – back to marketing fundamentals where the basic questions can be revisited. Who am I trying to sell to? What do they want? How do they want to communicate – and how, where, and when do they want to buy? The company that can answer these questions and respond effectively is the company that can best differentiate itself in the marketplace and create ongoing value for its shareholders.

2.2.1 Who and What: The Need for Better Information

In today's CP markets, a lack of understanding of who the customer is and what the customer wants has led many companies to bring the wrong products to market. The obvious antidote to this situation is more insight into demand. This is why successful CP companies have become information experts – implementing processes for gathering information and adopting the tools necessary for analyzing this information to reveal valuable consumer insights. These insights are used to drive innovation and inform the new product development and introduction (NPDI) process, so that the right products are made available to the right customers.

2.2.2 How: The Need for Better Ways to Interact with the Consumer

As already mentioned, today's consumers distrust traditional modes of marketing communications, feeling they're being "advertised to." At the same time, many consumers show a willingness to take advantage of the new opportunities available to them to be more proactive regarding how they interact with vendors. The most obvious example in this regard is the rise of online communities. Many CP companies have nurtured such communities because they lead to deeper consumer relationships, more profitable customers, and exceptionally effective ways of collecting data on consumer wants and behavior.

New modes of interacting with customers, however, are unlikely to entirely replace traditional retail-based interaction channels any time soon. This means that CP companies also have to think smart about how to make these traditional modes work more effectively. The relatively dismal state of trade promotion management, mentioned earlier, presents itself as a candidate for improvement. How can companies better measure the effectiveness of their trade promotions and determine the extent to which their customers are either motivated by specific promotions or put off?

2.2.3 Where and When: The Need for Better Demand Signaling and Improved Responsiveness

Just as market communications have grown more complex in the CP industry, so have supply chains. Today we have CP manufacturers moving into the retail business and retailers moving into manufacturing. Wholesale distributors, meanwhile, are trying to move in both directions. The smooth, linear supply chain with its clear delineation of responsibilities is disappearing. This makes it more difficult to get the right products to the right consumers where and when they want it. This is why CP companies are looking for more flexible supply networks and better ways of monitoring demand.

2.3 The Example of Procter & Gamble

As one of the leading companies in the CP industry, Procter & Gamble (P&G) has sought to improve performance across all aspects of consumer demand discussed so far. For P&G, the crux of the issue is what the company calls the *two moments of truth* (McKinsey 2005):

1. **The shelf availability moment**: When consumers buy a product because it's on the shelf at the time they want it
2. **The product quality moment**: When consumers look for and buy the product again because they liked it the first time.

By collecting, analyzing, and acting on consumer insights gathered from multiple channels, including traditional trade promotion activities, P&G has had significant success on both counts. Receiving demand signals directly from the shelf at retail locations in near real-time fashion, P&G has increased its understanding of demand dynamics and improved its ability to react almost instantaneously. This has helped the company reduce its out-of-stock ratio to approximately 5% – significantly below the industry average (Steinert-Threlkel 2004).

2.4 Responsive Supply Networks

One can summarize P&G's success with a single phrase: supply network responsiveness. One of the most frequently cited shopper frustrations is out-of-stock situations. After all, nobody likes it when they show up at a store only to learn that the product they want is unavailable. This makes higher on-the-shelf availability one of the primary areas of improvement for the CP industry. As Fig. 2.1 depicts, this is true not only for manufacturers but for retailers as well – who stand to lose just as much, if not more, when items run out of stock. By extension, we can assume that suppliers at the other end of the supply chain also stand to lose when poor product availability leads to a drop in consumption.

The point is that the answer to the challenges posed by the restless consumer requires a coordinated response from all of the key stakeholders in the consumer products ecosystem. Success, in other words, depends on the ability to collaborate. Today, no CP company can afford to act alone. Instead companies need to build responsive supply networks together with key partners to more effectively meet shifts in demand and keep pace with an increasingly fickle consumer base.

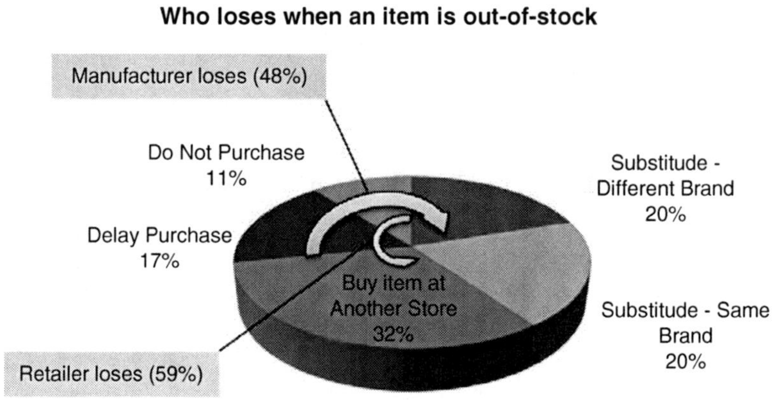

Fig. 2.1 Impact of out-of-stock in a store

But what exactly is a responsive supply network? Simply put, a responsive supply network is a supply chain that's oriented to the fluctuating demand and high product complexity that characterizes today's CP markets. A 2005 study by The Economist Intelligence Unit shows that 80% of surveyed executives expect demand, not supply, to drive the production of goods and services in the future (*The Economist* 2005). In such an environment, instead of a linear supply chain that depends on often inaccurate long-term forecasting to meet demand, CP companies need a responsive supply network that can sense and respond faster and smarter to demand and supply dynamics across a globally distributed environment. By gathering and sharing insights into consumer demand and acting on demand fluctuations on a near real-time basis, all participants in the responsive supply network stand to increase revenues and ensure growth under increasingly challenging

Table 2.1 Improvements based on better demand sensing (AMR Research, 2008)

Benefit category	Percentage that think improvement is possible	What improvement is possible?		
		High percentage	Median percentage	Low percentage
Shrinkage	40–50%	75%	18%	0%
Out of stock	50–60%	100%	20%	3%
Returns management	40–50%	50%	20%	2%
Margins	70% or greater	6%	4%	2%
Sales	50–60%	100%	7%	0%
Labor costs	50–60%	70%	5%	0%
Restock	50–60%	75%	25%	0%

market conditions. The business case is persuasive. According to AMR Research, the most advanced demand-sensing companies have 15% less inventory, 17% better order performance, and a 35% shorter cash-to-cash cycle time (AMR 2008).

2.5 The Importance of Being Direct

How does all this relate to direct store delivery? How does a mode of distribution – a process traditionally associated with the world of logistics – help companies more effectively address the shifting demand of the restless consumer? The answer, of course, has a lot to do with the fact that today DSD can be much more than drivers in trucks dropping off goods at the back door of a given retail outlet. The value of DSD as a mode of distribution is that it's exceptionally close to consumption – and to better meet consumer demand, that's exactly where CP companies need to be.

Supported by best practices and augmented with proper monitoring tools and data gathering technology, DSD moves from a narrow focus on logistics to a larger process that can help companies address a wide range of issues in the context of the fundamental questions of consumer demand discussed earlier. While many of these issues are discussed at greater length in the opening chapter of this book and elsewhere, they are worth reviewing here, if only briefly.

To the issue of gathering information to get at the who and what of consumer demand, CP companies can use DSD to generate critical insights on consumer behavior. Because DSD brings organizations so close to consumption, it's easier to gather accurate information over time and observe long-term trends. It's also easier to monitor shifts in demand and react in something approximating real time. With order-to-delivery lead times that are sometimes less than 24 h, DSD can play a critical role in supporting the responsiveness CP companies need to compete more effectively (Otto and Shariatmadari 2008).

CP companies can also use data and insight gleaned from the DSD process to improve customer interaction and deliver what consumers want. Part of what makes this possible is the close collaboration and communication with the retail outlet where the goods are sold. CP companies can work with retail outlets to fine-tune issues such as product presentation, pricing, and trade promotion details – and then monitor results to understand what works and what consumer desire.

Finally, DSD can be a highly effective process for detecting demand signals. When manufacturers own distribution up to the point of sale and consumption, it's easier to see what's moving and match demand quickly. With DSD, CP companies can speed replenishment cycles, reduce inventory levels and minimize out of stock situations. Ultimately, as Fig. 2.2 summarizes, DSD can play a critical role in helping CP companies not only understand consumer demand but to consistently act on it as well.

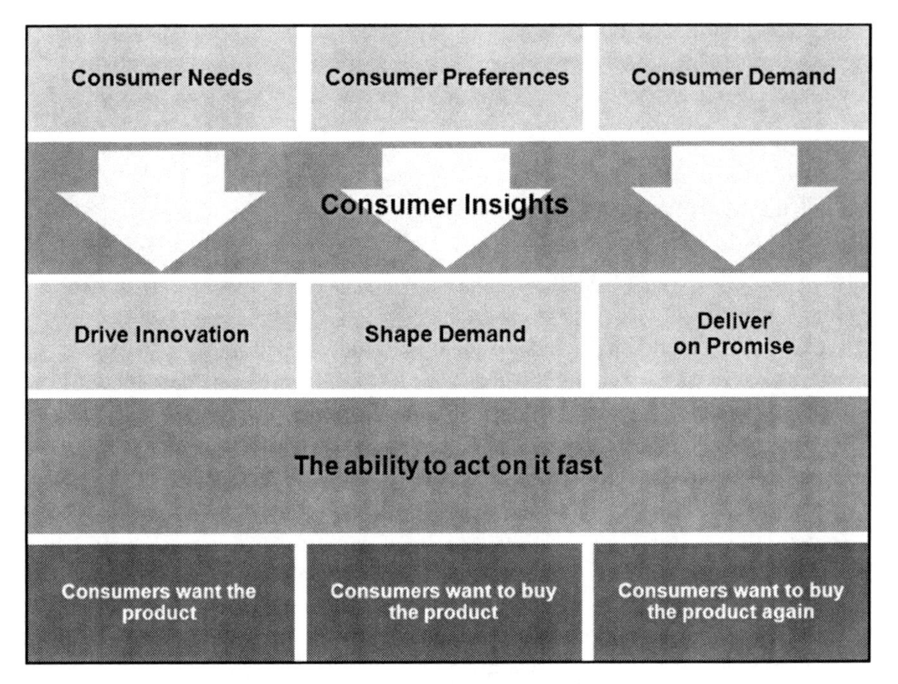

Fig. 2.2 Consumer insights and the ability to act fast (SAP AG 2008)

To broaden the scope slightly, CP companies would be well served to also consider DSD in the context of other, emerging forms of direct distribution. Take, for example, some interesting developments in the area of store-independent vending machines. These vending machines are becoming smarter and increasingly able to deliver the critical point-of-sale data required to help organizations respond most effectively to consumer demand. At the same time, the smart vending machine space is giving way to modern virtual store technologies such as multimedia kiosks and smart phones – already a reality in Japan – that have the potential to make data, people, and objects accessible everywhere and immediately.

Direct distribution is also critical for any online business dependent on direct home delivery. The Global Commerce Initiative predicts that home shopping will account for somewhere between 15% and 25% of all shopping by the year 2016 (GCI 2006). If manufacturers want a piece of this business, they'll need to adjust. Here, the challenges will focus on issues of order picking and fulfillment (in store, at the back of the store, separate local distribution centers). How well companies adapt will depend on the success each has in implementing distributed production with integrated logistics. Based on the opportunities available, it is expected that neighborhood distribution covering the "last mile" to the home will improve significantly. In some areas convergence will take place between home shopping and neighborhood distribution, with convenience stores acting as central pick-up locations. At the same time, rising energy costs may also spark the emergence of bundled demand and bundled transport/delivery in the form of a "single mailman" who delivers complete household needs – groceries, restaurant meals, pharmaceuticals – in one drop-off.

The point here is not to enumerate all of the areas in which direct distribution will come into play in the world of consumer products. Nobody can predict the future. At the same, however, it does appear that modes of direct distribution are becoming increasingly important as consumer behavior shifts. Companies that cut their teeth and gain experience in one mode of direct distribution – such as DSD, where the process is mature and the benefits clear – may find themselves in a better position to expand to other modes as business opportunities emerge.

References

AMR Research (2007): Predicting Total Business Impact To Achieve Maximum Product Lifecycle Value, p. 2, August.

AMR Research (2008): Above the Noise, Supply Chain Leadership Matter, February 25.

Forrester Research (2007): North American Technographics® Technology, Media, and Marketing Benchmark Survey, Q3.

Gruen, T.W.; Corsten, D. (2007): A Comprehensive Guide To Retail Out-of-Stock Reduction, in the Fast-Moving Consumer Goods Industry, Grocery Manufacturers Association (GMA), Food Marketing Institute (FMI), National Association of Chain Drug Stores (NACDS), The Procter & Gamble Company (P&G), The University of Colorado at Colorado Springs, Washington, DC.

IBM and SAP (2005): Trade Promotion Management: Regain Control Over Trade Funds Spending.

Information Resources Inc. (2008): Times & Trends, CPG 2007 Year in Review, Emerging Trends Shaping 2008 Opportunity, January.

McKinsey & Company (2005): Leading Change: An Interview with the CEO of P&G, *McKinsey Quarterly*, July.

Otto, A.; Shariatmadari, R. (2008): Direct Store Delivery: Understanding DSD in Sales and Logistics, Results of the "Global DSD Analysis", University of Regensburg, Regensburg, Germany.

ProductScan press release (2004): "Build a Better Mousetrap" New Product Innovations of the Year.

Steinert-Threlkel (2004): Procter & Gamble: Delivering Goods, Baseline magazine http://www.baselinemag.com/c/a/Projects-Supply-Chain/Procter-Gamble-Delivering-Goods [03-28-2008].

The Economist (2005): Economist Intelligence Unit, Business 2010 in Asia-Pacific: Embracing the Challenge of Change, 2005, p. 8.

The Global Commerce Initiative, 2016 (2006): The Future Value Chain.

Chapter 3
Insights: Getting Closer to Consumers

DSD operations heavily rely on robust technology since it takes place in the field beyond the borders of protected production and logistics facilities. This paper attempts to present the state of the art DSD technology and its application into practice with a focus on hardware covering handheld computers, data capture devices, peripherals and communication devices.

Recent research and practice clearly reveal that consumer behavior becomes more and more difficult to understand and predict. Consumers are less brand loyal thus they switch brands more frequently, and make product purchase decisions when they are actually looking at the product in a store. Large numbers of products are introduced each year into the consumer products market, however the flop rate is very high. Despite investments in technology and logistics, out-of-stock rates have not decreased over the years. Especially promotion fill rates are behind the expectations.

As a consequence, market research gains importance. Companies need to get closer to consumers, need real time and unobscured insights into consumer behavior. Understanding consumers buying patterns, i.e. which products they will buy where, when, and why, becomes more important – but also more difficult. This holds true for retailers, but much more for manufacturers. Large retailing chains with increasing market shares block access to the end consumer making market research more difficult. It is this environment, DSD sets in. The underlying statement of this chapter, covering the next three papers, is that DSD is a powerful market research instrument. **Preddy, Rigney, and Gogos of The Nielsen Company** open up the discussion: DSD distribution systems help to read PoS changes in real time and to adapt quickly. DSD manufacturers collect store-level shipment data and observational data about the store environment. Combined with the daily presence of the DSD reps in stores, DSD enables manufacturers to adapt their offerings to the specific store need, run promotions and product introductions, manage inventory and provide faster sensing of out-of-stocks.

Seen from a marketing perspective, DSD is a particular type of marketing channel. Selecting a channel properly is complex and multi-criteria task. As **Kotzab of Copenhagen Business School** shows in his paper, many scholars have allocated a great deal of attention towards this problem. In any case, the channel decision is a trade-off. It is essential to appreciate the channel decisions of DSD companies in the light of the market research capabilities of DSD. DSD is more expensive and it reduces logistics efficiencies. If one can witness such a high acceptance of DSD, it is through a change in the underlying trade off: from efficiency to market research, to innovation, and finally to increased sales. **Thomas, de Starke, and Pieters of Deloitte** stress that DSD represent a shift in focus; it helps to move beyond efficiency to innovation.

A. Otto et al., *Direct Store Delivery*,
DOI: 10.1007/978-3-540-77213-2_3,

Chapter 4
Conceptual Understanding: DSD in the Light of Supplier–Retailer Relationships in the CP Industry

Herbert Kotzab

Department of Operations Management, Copenhagen Business School, Solbjerg Plads 3, DK-2000, Frederiksberg, tel.: +45 3815 2450, e-mail: hk.om@cbs.dk

Abstract

DSD is a marketing channel which is used by manufacturers to sell and to distribute goods directly to retail stores bypassing any intermediate logistics system. The paper positions DSD within the framework of marketing channels and shows how relationships between the members of the marketing channels are impacted by DSD.

4.1 Introduction

Especially within in the grocery industry, brand and product managers are facing markets affected by the information age, more demanding consumers, and new retail formats (PWC 2000; Clarke 2000), distribution is embedded in a dynamic environment. In the past, while most of the dynamics in the grocery industry related to the establishment of innovative retail store formats and e-tailing, logistics also recently become an attractive instrument for distribution innovations (Kotzab and Bjerre 2005). Large retailers set up their own sophisticated, IT-driven logistics systems in order to continuously replenish their outlets. In addition, manufacturers have further developed their own distribution activities, which had been known in the past as sales persons or sales truck drivers, but have been now transformed to a modern way of direct distribution, acknowledged as DSD. Kinsey (2000, p. 1127) estimates that approx. 30% of all food is delivered in a DSD-mode to retail stores and the share of DSD in Europe is around 3–15% (ECR-Europe 1999, p. 27). Today, with approx. half a billion DSD deliveries to food retailers a year, DSD is "an important part of food distribution" (Theodore 2006, p. 4).

The aim of this paper is to conceptualize DSD from a marketing channel point of view and to show the peculiarities of this direct mode of distribution. The paper is divided into the following sections. First, marketing channels and distribution will be defined and it will be shown how marketing channels develop in general.

A. Otto et al., *Direct Store Delivery*,

DOI: 10.1007/978-3-540-77213-2_4,

Next, DSD will be defined, and the advantages and disadvantages of DSD will be discussed. Finally it will be shown how relationships between the members of a marketing channel will change due to the upcoming of DSD. The paper closes with an outlook for the future challenges of DSD.

4.2 Marketing Channels and Distribution

4.2.1 Defining Marketing Channels and Distribution

Distribution can be defined as the total sum of all activities and related institutions, which are necessary to guarantee a successful connection between production and consumption. The sequence of firms performing the movement of ownership, the negotiation of title and the physical movement of products is defined as a marketing channel (Mallen 1970, p. 3).

Marketing channels are the routes which lead products and services to the desired locations and include as Coughlan et al. (2006, p. 2) define "a set of interdependent organizations involved in the process of making a product available for use or consumption".

Mallen (1970, p. 4) include thereby producers, service and limited-function wholesalers, retailers and intermediaries as members of a marketing channel. Looking at the distribution process itself, it can be understood (Chopra and Meindl 2007, p. 74) as the necessary steps which are taken to move and store products from a supplier stage to a customer stage. As distribution costs are also quite high, the role of distribution for supply chain profitability is consequently crucial (Chopra and Meindl 2007, p. 74).

The dimensions of a marketing channel also include the length of a channel, which is a question of the number of layers, the breadth, which is a question of the number of middlemen at a given layer and the multiplicity, which is a question of the total number of channels to the ultimate customer.

The function of a marketing channel is to close certain discrepancies which refer to differences in time, quality, quantity and space. The performance or outcome of a marketing channel is measured by how the channel achieves the level of convenience as expected by customers in terms of quantity (break-bulking), spatial convenience, waiting and delivery time and product variety (Coughlan et al. 2006, p. 43) which is also known, according to Bucklin (1966), as service output levels. The two fundamental problem areas of distribution relate to acquisition or sales management (= how to obtain orders) and to physical distribution or logistics (= how to execute orders).

Marketing channel activities are flow and exchange activities that basically refer to three flows: the flow of goods, the flow of information and the flow of nominal goods (money) (e.g. Kotzab and Bjerre 2005, p. 18). The exchange processes can be distinguished into:

- Marketing processes that include all activities that provide a customized set of products/services as demanded by customers/consumers
- Logistics processes including all activities that help to transfer this specific set of products/services to the markets
- Easing processes, which refer to all activities that facilitate the purchase.

These processes will occur in any circumstance, no matter how many partners are involved in the functioning of a marketing channel. All members of a marketing channel can combine the generic distribution functions in many ways to create effective marketing channels (Coughlan et al. 2006, p. 14). The number of possible marketing channels or channel formats is unlimited and marketing channels develop continuously mainly due to technological changes.

4.2.2 Development and Design of Marketing Channels

Marketing channels are crucial for the success of manufacturers and therefore of strategic importance (Rosenbloom 2004, p. 4 or Cespedes 1988). Coughlan et al. (2006, p. 33) or Rosenbloom (2004, p. 32) differ between the following classes of marketing channels:

1. ***Manufacturer-based channel formats*** such as manufacturer direct, manufacturer-owned full service wholesaler-distribution, company stores, license, broker or locker stock (e.g. the distribution systems of Revlon, Levi Strauss, Athletic Footware, Mattel)
2. ***Retailer-based channel formats*** such as franchise, dealer direct, buying club, warehouse clubs, mail order, food retailers, department stores, mass merchandisers, specialty stores, category killers, convenience stores, hypermarkets (e.g. Blockbuster Video, McDonalds, Sam's Club, Land's End, Safeway, J.C. Penney, The Gap, Carrefour, 7-Eleven)
3. ***Service provider-based channel formats*** such as contract warehousing, sub-processor, cross docking, intermodal, roller freight, stack trains and road railers, direct mailer, value-added resellers (e.g. Caterpillar Logistics Services);
4. ***Door-to-door channel formats*** such as route, home party, multi-level-marketing, rack jobbing (e.g. Tupperware, Electrolux)
5. ***Buyer-initiated channel formats*** such as co-op, dealer-owned co-op, buying groups (e.g. Topco, AMC)
6. ***Point-of-consumption merchandising channel formats*** such as kiosks, vending machines, computer access information
7. ***Catalog and technology aided channel formats*** such as specialty catalogs, business-to-business catalogs, TV-/Home-shopping, trade shows, e-tailing (e.g. QVC)

8. ***Wholesale-based channel formats*** such as merchant wholesalers, agents, brokers and commission merchants.

Keh and Park (1997, p. 840) or King and Phumpiu (1996, p. 1182) identify three basic possibilities when it comes to physical distribution in the grocery industry:

1. Via distribution centers owned by retailers (= self distributing retailer)
2. Via distribution centers owned by wholesalers (= wholesales supplied)
3. Via distribution centers owned by suppliers (= manufacturer direct store deliveries).

The overall design of a distribution network is impacted by the specific customer service as well as cost related factors (Chopra and Meindl 2007, p. 93):

- Customer-service related factors including:
  - Response time which is the amount of time it takes for a customer to receive an order
  - Product variety which is the number of different products/configurations that are offered by the distribution network
  - Product availability defined as the probability of having a product in stock when a customer order arrives
  - Customer experience which includes the ease with which customers can place and receive orders as well as the extent to which this experience is customized
  - Time to market defined as the time it takes to bring new products to the market
  - Order visibility which is the ability of customers to track their orders from placement to delivery
  - Returnability or the ease of with which a customer can return unsatisfactory merchandise and the ability of the network to handle such returns.

- Distribution costs related factors including: Inventory costs which are the costs for reducing the mismatch between demand and supply by having a product available when a customer wants it. Inventory costs can be reduced by consolidation and by limiting the number of facilities in the network
  - Transportation costs defined as the costs which are incurred in bringing material into a facility (= inbound transportation costs) as well as the cots of sending material out of a facility (= outbound transportation costs). Outbound transportation costs are typically higher as the load units are smaller
  - Facilities and handling costs defined as the costs for having and operating physical locations in the supply chain network. Facility costs decrease when the number of facilities is reduced and increase when inbound lot sizes tend to be very small;

– Information costs or the costs for having data and analysis concerning the other cost drivers. Information provides the opportunity to design supply chains more responsive and more efficient.

Chopra and Meindl (2007, p. 93) combine these factors to six generic distribution network structures – (a) retail storage with customer pickup, (b) manufacturer storage with direct shipping, (c) manufacturer storage with in-transit merge, (d) distributor storage with package carrier delivery, (e) distributor storage with last mile delivery and (f) manufacturer storage with pickup. Each of these options has their specific strengths and weaknesses in relation to the network design factors. Table 4.1 presents the results of comparing the options to each other (Chopra and Meindl 2007, p. 93).

However, this multitude of possible marketing channel formats and ways of physical distribution can be fundamentally differentiated between direct or indirect distribution, depending on the number of intermediate stages between production and consumption.

The most efficient structure of a marketing channel – seen from a manufacturer's point of view – can be found on a continuum between market and hierarchy, on whether a manufacturer keeps distribution in-house (= DSD) or outsources marketing channel activities partly or totally (= intermediaries delivery) (see Fig. 4.1).

Table 4.1 Comparative Performance of Distribution Network Structures where 1 indicates the strongest performance and 6 the weakest performance (Reading example: Retail storage with customer pickup has the strongest performance in response time as compared to the other distribution network design options) (Chopra and Meindl 2007)

	Retail storage with customer pickup	Manufacturer storage with direct shipping	Manufacturer storage with in-transit merge	Distributor storage with package carrier delivery	Distributor storage with last mile delivery	Manufacturer storage with pickup
Response time	1	4	4	3	2	4
Product variety	4	1	1	2	3	1
Product availability	4	1	1	2	3	1
Customer experience	5	4	3	2	1	5
Order visibility	1	5	4	3	2	6
Returnability	1	5	5	4	3	2
Inventory	4	1	1	2	3	1
Transportation	1	4	3	2	5	1
Facility & Handling	6	1	2	3	4	5
Information	1	4	4	3	2	5

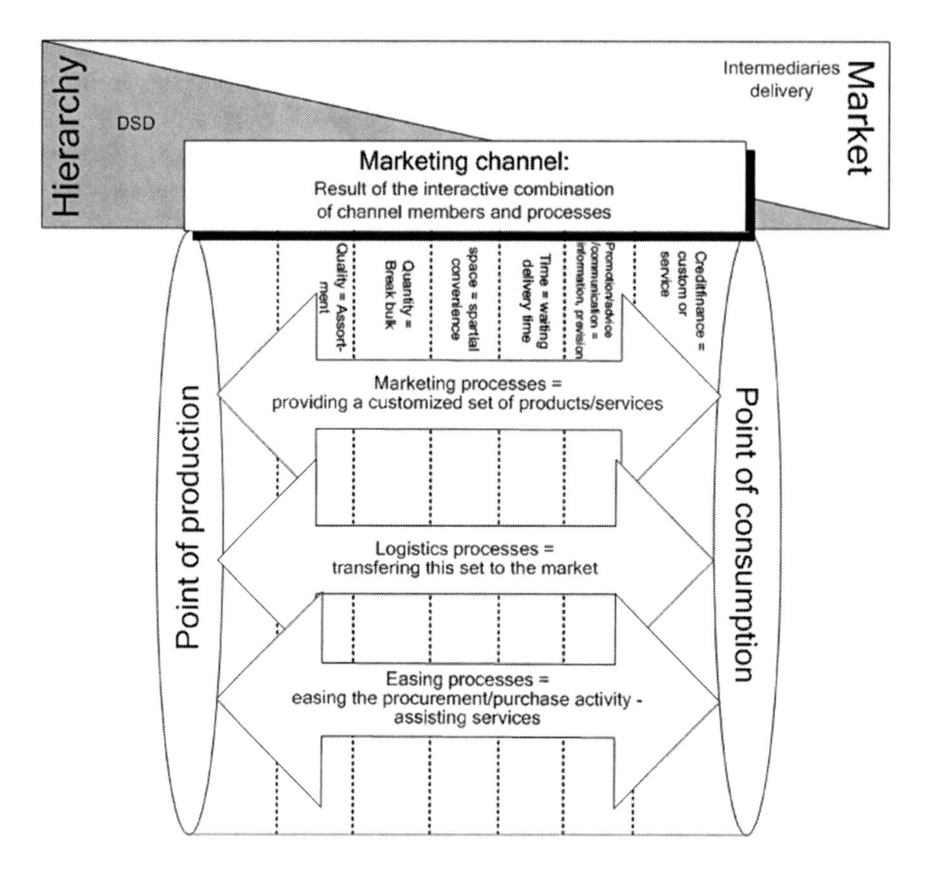

Fig. 4.1 Efficient marketing channel structure on a continuum between market and hierarchy

4.3 Characterization of Direct Store Delivery from a Marketing Channel Perspective

4.3.1 Definition of Direct Store Delivery

DSD is defined as a business process that manufacturers use to both sell and distribute goods directly to the point of sales (PoS) or point of consumption (PoC) including additional product and market related services such as merchandising, information gathering or equipment service and bypassing any retailer or wholesaler logistics (see Chapter 1).

Based on the general presentation of marketing channels, DSD can be characterized as follows:

- DSD is a direct, manufacturer-based marketing channel format and direct mode of physical distribution which aims to directly deliver products and services to a point-of-sale (PoS)
- As compared to the various options which are offered for distribution network design by Chopra/Meindl (2007, p. 93; Table 4.1), DSD can be characterized as hybrid model as it includes characteristics of the 'manufacturer storage with direct shipment and in-transit merge' as well as of the 'retail storage with customer pickup'-model
- DSD is further a vertical system where a manufacturer can get more access to the customer as compared to traditional systems and DSD compresses the total marketing channel (Anderson et al. 1997, p. 63)
- DSD refers to the movement of finished products from a supplier stage to the stage of a retail outlet[1]
- The range of activities goes from simple direct logistics up to shelf-management. There is no special focus on specific product groups or retail store formats with a high affinity to DSD, although business practice has shown that beverages, snacks, cookies/crackers and backed goods are the most DSD-delivered goods to supermarkets and to convenience stores (GMA 2002, p. 1 or 33; Kinsey 2000, p. 1127).

Such as any other distribution channel too, DSD also aims to maximize profits and to maximize the channel goodwill, which indicates whether the middlemen cooperate and support the manufacturer's product in relation to the remaining assortment, as well as the channel control, which is the ability of the manufacturer to see that the recommended marketing policies are carried out within the marketing channel (Mallen 1970). DSD as a direct distribution channel is rather expensive but allows maximal channel control.

For Keh and Park (1997, p. 841), product categories such as branded products where freshness is critical, branded products with large movement volumes and products which need extensive in-store inventory management, are the most prominent DSD-product categories. It seems though that especially products with very short shelf life seem to be very appropriate for DSD as additional distribution stages cannot be afforded (Huppertz 1999, p. 72).

The common body of literature refers to the elimination of wholesale and retail storage and delivery activities. Kurnia and Johnston (2001) as well as Kurnia et al. (1998) identify a close relationship between DSD and cross docking operations as both concepts can be considered as flow through activities which enhance lead times in the grocery supply chain.

Previous forms of DSD have existed for many decades however under a different 'brand'. Thomas and Thiede (1992, p. 54) introduce the concept of truck wholesalers or route sales-persons who were delivering merchandise such as beer, soft drinks, potato chips, bread and mild directly to the retail outlets.

One can also argue that DSD is another form of drop shipment or third-party-deal which "is an arrangement whereby the retailer forwards customers' orders to the wholesaler, distributor, or manufacturer, that fills customer orders directly from its own inventory" (Randall et al. 2006, p. 567) and where the retailer's profit refers to the difference between the wholesale and retail price (Michigan State 2007). However, while drop shipments are initiated by retailers, DSD is initiated by manufacturers.

4.3.2 Advantages and Disadvantages of Direct Store Delivery

As sales execution at the PoS-level becomes increasingly important, DSD seems to be the most efficient distribution mode or even a marketing tool for a manufacturer to cope with these challenges (Beverage Industry 2006, p. 13; Food Logistics 2007, p. 12).

The application of DSD allows manufacturers to streamline their supply chains and to reduce stock levels in the system (Kinsey 2000, p. 1127). If a vendor has direct access to the shelves, they can be replenished at any time directly in the store. This allows them to speed up cycle times and to decrease specific labor hours for a retailer (GMA 2002, p. 2). Kinsey (2000, p. 1128) reports on savings of 95–100 labor hours a week.

A study of the GMA (2005) also showed that stock levels at stores of DSD-delivered goods turn three times faster than warehouse delivered goods (Casper 2006, p. 14).

DSD is however increasing the number of transports with smaller shipments (LTL) and is increasing the 'vendor traffic' in a store. A typical large food retailer receives today 1,100 DSD deliveries or approx. three million items while a small food retailer gets 12,000 DSD deliveries with approx. 80,000 items a year (Theodore 2006, p. 4).

A recent study of the GMA (2005) has shown that certain store formats in the U.S. receive 225 DSD deliveries per week and which each receipt will take 10–14 min to process. This means that at least 45 h of DSD receiving time needs to be calculated (Casper 2006, p. 15). It is therefore necessary to perform DSD in a very efficient manner in order to exploit the cost-cutting effects of DSD completely (Huppertz 1999, p. 72 or GMA 2005). The challenge thereby is to consider the optimal delivery size per drop as there is a trend to reduce PoS inventory and to utilize the different load capacities of the used trucks as ECRE (1999, p. 28) indicates.

The efficiency of DSD can be improved by four techniques as suggested by ECRE (1999, p. 28):

1. One stop – direct delivery from one shipping point of a manufacturer to one drop point of a retailer

2. Multi-drop – direct delivery from one shipping point of a manufacturer to multiple drop points of one retailer
3. Multi-pick – deliveries are loaded from multiple manufacturer loading points and shipped to one drop point of a retailer
4. Multi-pick-and-drop – deliveries are loaded from multiple manufacturer loading points and shipped to multiple drop points.

The fourth possibility is an especially cost-intense way of DSD and is therefore suggested to be outsourced to a logistics service provider (ECRE 1999, p. 28), this is also known as a three-tier DSD model as compared to the two-tier DSD model with no logistics service provider involved (GMA 2002, p. 4).

The DSD efficiency study of the GMA (2005, p. 9) has shown tremendous improvement possibilities as DSD deliveries to stores are 10–30 times more frequent than retail-warehouse deliveries, and DSD products' inventory turns three times faster than brands delivered from retail warehouses.

The study also showed that the average DSD delivery takes 36 min for smaller retail stores and 84 min for larger retail stores. The supplier time can be split up in the following activities (see Table 4.2).

Table 4.2 DSD supplier time by activity and in percentage of time (GMA 2005, p. 17)

Activity	Small format (min/%)		Large format	
	min	in %	min	in %
In-store merchandising	7.4	20	22.6	27
Backroom inventory management	3.8	10	5.6	7
Check-in verification	5.7	16	12.9	15
Prepare and print invoice	2.1	6	2.9	3
Select and stage order	6.7	18	12.2	15
Pull and process credit returns	2.7	8	11.7	14
Backdoor delay	5.8	16	13.6	16
Closeout delivery	2.1	6	2.6	3
Total	36.3	100	84.1	100

The typical processes of sales people need to be re-engineered, especially in-store activities such as order-generation processes, shelf-control and shelf-management (Hjort 2000, p. 58). The DSD personnel spend on average 20–27% of their time on stocking and for merchandising shelves, but unfortunately also the same amount of time waiting (GMA 2005, p. 17). Table 4.3 shows the differences between efficient and inefficient DSD deliveries in terms of time devoted for DSD activities.

Table 4.3 Inefficient versus efficient deliveries in percentage on the basis of 60 min (GMA 2005, p. 18)

	Efficient deliveries	Inefficient deliveries	Difference between efficient and inefficient deliveries
In-store merchandising	50	27	13.8 min more
Backroom inventory management	5	7	3.8 min fewer
Check-in verification	10	15	3.0 min fewer
Prepare and print invoice	4	3	0.6 min more
Select and stage order	19	15	2.4 min more
Pull and process credit returns	7	14	4.2 min fewer
Backdoor delay	4	16	7.2 min fewer
Closeout delivery	1	3	1.2 min fewer

In order to complete DSD in an efficient manner, manufacturers have to convince their retail partners to provide flexible receiving windows, to devote backroom space for specific products such as weekly promoted items and to provide prompt resolution to invoice differences (GMA 2005, p. 25).

4.4 Changing Relationships Between the Marketing Channel Partners Due to Direct Store Delivery

The continuous development of marketing channels affects the exchange relations between the channel partners, which, for many years, have been purely market exchange oriented, meaning that the competencies amongst both parties had been clearly disseminated: Manufacturers produce, wholesalers distribute to retail, retailers distribute to end-users.

However, the emergence of DSD shows that manufacturers are taking over activities which had been in the past performed by retailers and in particular by wholesalers. DSD leads to a different structure of the marketing channel and as the marketing channel functions are now performed differently, and also to a different service output level: Manufacturers produce and distribute to retail, retailers distribute to end-users. In such a setting, no wholesale is required as manufacturers take over their responsibilities. The range of DSD activities for a manufacturer would include (GMA 2002, p. 2):

- Space management
- Conducting and execution of in-store merchandising
- Handling of store-level category management
- Store-level inventory management.

Manufacturers should be aware of the following issues which negatively affect the working relationships with their DSD retail partners (Lofstock et al. 2007, p. 20):

- ***Lower margins for retail partners*** as manufacturers pre-price their items. In most of the cases, DSD products have already a price label attached which cannot be changed anymore. Manufacturers are therefore called upon to fair pricing based on the real cost savings by DSD in order to maintain relationships with their retail partner
- ***Loss of control*** as products are directly delivered onto the shelves and retail partners need to accept what is shipped to the store and when it is getting there. Manufacturers need to deliver even faster than the retailer's own logistics system and require paying attention to the DSD-staff and their execution of DSD activities at the PoS. Retail partners perceive differences in the daily DSD-operation which leads to overstocking, unauthorized deliveries and violations of space restrictions and placing. These differences often refer to the experience of the manufacturer's DSD-staff.

Additional hurdles refer also to various industry-specific and geographic legal restrictions, complicated data synchronization needs and multiple company systems (GMA 2002, p. 2).

4.5 Key Factors for the Design of DSD Networks

Companies which are in the phase of choosing DSD need to rely on such design principles which are in line up with their competitive strategy and performance objectives (Anderson et al. 1997, p. 59). The most important forces for changing a distribution system are, according to Anderson et al. (1997, p. 59):

- ***Proliferation of customer needs***, which is especially in emerging markets an issue where DSD allows a direct control of the selling, serving and pricing of their products
- ***Expanding capabilities for addressability and variety***, where DSD allows direct communication with the customers and therefore a possibility for differentiation
- ***Channel diversity***, where DSD replaces centralized batch distribution to localized one-at-a-time distribution
- ***Customer expectations***, as DSD increases availability of products as there are rapidly replenished.

Mallen (1970) understands the selection of a distribution channel as a multi-stage process which includes decision areas, guidelines, determinants, figures, the decision itself and the channel review and evaluation. When it comes to the decision of establishing a DSD channel, the following questions can be posed (see Tables 4.4 and 4.5).

Table 4.4 Decision areas for distribution channel set up (Mallen 1970)

Decision areas when setting up distribution channels	
Question	Which means for DSD…
What degree of directness should the company's channel structure have?	… very direct which shortens the length of the channel and increases control
How selective should the channel be?	… no middleman's logistics in between and as many final distribution points as possible
What type of middlemen are to be selected?	… if middleman are required for logistics than only facilitating intermediaries and retailers are providing their outlets
How many channels should be established for a given product?	… DSD is an additional distribution alternative to the existing channel mix
How shall the individual middlemen be chosen to fill the slots created?	…. DSD requires intensive distribution, so as many distribution points as possible

Table 4.5 Performance of distribution network options for different product/customer characteristics. Scale from +2 to –2 where +2 = very suitable, +1 = somewhat suitable, 0 = neutral, –1 = somewhat unsuitable, –2 = very unsuitable (Chopra and Meindl 2007, p. 94)

	Retail storage with customer pickup	Manufacturer storage with direct shipping	Manufacturer storage with in-transit merge	Distributor storage with package carrier delivery	Distributor storage with last mile delivery	Manufacturer storage with pickup
High demand product	+2	–2	–1	0	+1	–1
Medium demand product	+1	–1	0	+1	0	0
Low demand product	–1	+1	0	+1	–1	+1
Very low demand product	–2	+2	+1	0	–2	+1
Many product sources	+1	–1	–1	+2	+1	0
High product value	–1	+2	+1	+1	0	–2
Quick desired response	+2	–2	–2	–1	+1	–2
High product variety	–1	+2	0	+1	0	+2
Low customer effort	–2	+1	+2	+2	+2	–1

The overall question for the channel decision areas can be posed as: "What degree of directness should the company's channel structure have?" (Mallen 1970, p. 50). In case of DSD, the answer is 'very direct' which allows shorter channel structures, however it may also be a question of product and customer characteristics (Chopra and Meindl 2007, p. 92).

The current forms of DSD in the FMCG-industry however challenge the evaluation results of Chopra and Meindl (2007) as successful DSD-models are applied for high demand products. This also means that the successful implementation of DSD depends on the market dynamics, the environment of the channel as well as of the existing resources of the manufacturer (Mallen 1970).

4.6 Outlook

Manufacturers in the grocery industry have realized the power of having access to PoS-activities. DSD is one possibility to reach the end-user directly and to streamline the supply chains. Although retailers recognize the danger of loosing control of their store, several studies have shown that DSD replenishes shelves faster which helps to avoid out-of-stock situations and increases the shopping frequency at the store. Much of the presented discussion focused on markets of the Western Hemisphere. Most of the efforts for DSD in those markets are driven by efficiency issues as the western markets in general are very saturated. From a logistics point of view, DSD competes in these markets also with a given logistics infrastructure of intermediaries.

The growth markets of the grocery industry are however in other regions, such as the BRIC-countries, where the retail infrastructure is not that developed as in Western Europe or in the U.S. manufacturers are therefore obliged to use DSD due to lacking retail warehouses and delivery systems. The successful establishment of DSD will so secure market position. It is therefore recommended to further investigate the consequences of DSD under such market conditions.

References

Anderson, E.; Day, G.; Rangan, V. (1997): Strategic channel design, in: Sloan Management Review (Vol. 38) 1997, No. 4, pp. 59–69.

Beverage Industry (2006): DSD strategies highlights changes, opportunities in distribution, in: Beverage Industry, May, pp. 8–10.

Bucklin, L. (1966): A theory of distribution channel structure, IBER Special Publication, Berkely, CA.

Casper, C. (2006): Uncovering the Benefits of DSD, Food Logistics (Vol. 86) 2006, May 15, pp. 14–16.

Cespedes, F. (1988): Channel management is general management, in: California Management Review (Vol. 31) 1988, No. 1, pp. 98–120.

Chopra, S.; Meindl, P. (2007): Supply Chain Management: Strategy, Planning and Operations, 3rd edition, Prentice-Hall, Upper Saddle River, NJ.

Clarke, I. (2000): Retail power, competition and local consumer choice in the UK grocery sector, European Journal of Marketing (Vol. 34) 2000, No. 8, pp. 975–1002.
Coughlan, A. et al. (2006): Coughlan, A., Anderson E., Stern, L. and El-Ansary, A.: Marketing Channels, 7th edition, Pearson/Prentice Hall, Upper Saddle River, NJ.
Efficient Consumer Response Europe (ECRE) (1999): "Working Three-gether" – transport consolidation with the involvement of logistics service providers. Efficient replenishment project Phase II, Roland Berger & Partner GmbH, Opwijk, Belgium.
Food Logistics (2007): GMA to study better ways to use DSD, in: Food Logistics, June, p. 12
Grocery Manufacturers of America (GMA) (2002): E-commerce opportunities in Direct Store Deliveries. A white paper. GMA, Washington, DC.
Grocery Manufacturers of America (GMA) (2005): Driving DSD supply chain efficiencies and profitability. Unleash the Power of DSD. GMA, Washington DC.
Hjort, J. (2000): The changing role of beverage sales people, in: Beverage Industry, June, p. 58
Huppertz, P. (1999): Market changes require new supply chain thinking, in: Transportation & Distribution, March, pp. 70–74.
Keh, H.T.; Park, S.Y. (1997): To market, to market: the changing face of grocery retailing, in: Long Range Planning (Vol. 30) 1997, No. 6, pp. 836–846.
King, R.; Phumpiu, P. (1996): Reengineering the food supply chain: The ECR initiative in the grocery industry, in: American Journal of Agricultural Economics (Vol. 78) 1996, December, pp. 1181–1186.
Kinsey, J. (2000): A faster, leaner, supply chain: New uses of information technology, in: American Journal of Agricultural Economics (Vol. 82) 2000, No. 5, pp. 1123–1129.
Kotzab, H.; Bjerre, M. (2005): Retailing in a SCM-Perspective, CBS Press, Copenhagen.
Kurnia, S.; Johnston, R. (2001): Adoption of efficient consumer response: the issue of mutuality, in: Supply Chain Management: An International Journal (Vol. 6) 2001, No. 5, pp. 230–241.
Kurnia, S. et al. (1998): Kurnia, S., Swatman, P. and Schauder, D.: Efficient Consumer Response: A preliminary comparison of U.S. and European experiences, 11th International Conference on Electronic Commerce, Bled, Slovenia, June 8–10, pp. 126–143.
Lofstock, J. et al. (2007): Lofstock, J.; Quackenbush, K. and Sharrah, K.: Wholesale change, in: Convenience Store Decisions, February, pp. 20–22.
Mallen, B. (1970): Selecting channels of distribution: a multi-stage process, in: International Journal of Physical Distribution (Vol. 1) 1970, No. 1, pp. 50–56.
Michigan State (2007): Home business scam, http://www.michigan.gov/cybersecurity/0,1607,7-217-34396-108704--,00.html, 2007-07-20.
PriceWaterhouseCooper (PwC): Europan Retailing 2010. http.//www.ideabeat.com/ResLib/pricewaterhouse/euroretail2010/page1.htm, 2000, accessed June 24, 2000.
Randall, T. et al. (2006): Randall, T., Netessine, S. and Rudi, N.: An empirical examination of the decision to invest in fulfillment capabilities: A study of internet retailers, in: Management Science (Vol. 52) 2006, No. 4, pp. 567–580.
Rosenbloom, B. (2004): Marketing Channels. A Management View, 7th edition, Thompson, Ohio.
Theodore, S. (2006): New strategies for distribution, in: Beverage Industry, January, p. 4.
Thomas, J.; Thiede, L. (1992): Computer fraud perpetrated against small independent food retailers during the direct store delivery process, in: Journal of Small Business Management, October, pp. 52–61.

Endnotes

[1] Here, Chopra and Meindl (2007, p. 75) refer to the DSD activities of Procter & Gamble, who however limit their DSD to large supermarket chains.

Chapter 5
Using DSD for Prime Market Research

Neil Preddy, Wayne Rigney, and Paris Gogos

The Nielsen Company, 200 W. Jackson Boulevard, Suite 2500, Chicago, IL 60606, USA,
tel.: +1 479-273-9977, e-mail: requests.dme@nielsen.com

Abstract

Market research offers a wide range of techniques for understanding consumers' actions and attitudes. DSD distribution systems differ from traditional warehouse-based distribution systems in both generating and executing actionable insights through market research. DSD systems give CP manufacturers store-level shipments data and observational data about the store environment. This information, combined with the regular presence of the DSD representatives in stores, enables manufacturers to cost-effectively: tailor their assortment to the specific store audience, manage live events such as promotions and new product introductions, manage inventory for faster turns and higher availability and provide faster alerts of execution problems such as out-of-stocks. DSD systems enable more precise demand signaling which improves efficiency and lowers costs throughout the entire supply chain. DSD manufacturers and retailers more effectively serve consumers and shareholders by combining high value insights with the ability to act quickly and directly to capitalize on opportunities and solve problems at the store.

5.1 Market Research in the Changing Consumer Goods Environment

> "The world is changing. We see it in the news, in neighborhoods, and on grocery shelves. And perhaps more so than any time in our world's history, we are able to identify and understand the shifts in the environment, the global economy and in the rapidly developing markets" (ACNielsen 2006, p. 3).

Market research is about understanding the changes in our world and how they impact our lives, including our attitudes and our behavior. The decisions we make as individual consumers reflect our preferences in a given situation. Market research helps companies understand change so they can present desirable choices to consumers, capitalize on the opportunities and avoid problems that result from failure to adapt. The primary goal of market research is to deliver actionable insights that enable companies to effectively serve consumers and shareholders.

A. Otto et al., *Direct Store Delivery*,

DOI: 10.1007/978-3-540-77213-2_5,

In this chapter, we will consider how DSD distribution systems differ from traditional warehouse-based distribution systems in both generating and executing actionable insights through market research.

5.1.1 From Theory to Practice

Nielsen research indicates that, as much as possible, consumers worldwide want food, beverages and other products that:

- Are healthful and beneficial to them
- Make their lives easier
- Are offered at a good value.

Around the world, companies try to satisfy those needs in relevant ways. Although the big ideas are global, how they translate into consumer action is very individual by country, local market, consumer segment and product function. Thus, a "healthy" drink may mean water to some people and diet sodas to others. A "good value" in Greece may be a luxury in Guatemala. Today, market research drives business activities that implement "micro marketing" rather than "mass marketing" strategies. To serve consumers effectively, the operational strategies, such as the distribution systems employed, must be aligned with the business and marketing strategies (ACNielsen 2006, p. 3).

We see these big trends demonstrated when we consider the example of a U.S. consumer, Douglas[1] as he shops at his neighborhood grocery store. A native of the U.K., Douglas now lives in River Park, an affluent suburb of Chicago with his wife and two children. River Park has a highly educated population with a high percentage of professionals. The population is predominantly white with a mix of ethnic backgrounds. The suburb is home to two small church-affiliated universities with residential and commuter student populations.

Douglas and his wife both work so he regularly does the family grocery shopping at the large DiamondMart grocery and drugstore a few blocks from his home. He occasionally shops at the NaturalMart store nearby for a few specialty items like vitamins, artisan bread and cheeses, wine and bulk muesli. Every 4–6 weeks, Douglas and his wife travel together 10 miles to the nearest BigBuy store, an upscale warehouse store where they stock up on bottled water and soda, paper goods, laundry detergent, fresh meats, snack foods, batteries and other items. BigBuy carries a very limited selection in each category and items are packaged in double or triple quantities. Douglas's purchase decisions are based on the price, quantity-consumption ratio and brand when his preferred brand is available or he has no preference.

Several years ago the River Park DiamondMart renovated and expanded the store space. The store expanded its specialty foods offerings, dramatically increasing the number of SKUs stocked. Since then additional sections have been added or expanded for organic/health foods, specialty cheeses, international foods and more. Fresh or short shelf life products such as milk, yogurt, eggs, cheese, deli meats, fresh fruits and vegetables dominate Douglas's regular purchases from DiamondMart. DiamondMart is Douglas's main source for non-perishables such as canned goods, staples, baking supplies, cleaning supplies, for frozen vegetables, ice cream and pizza, cereals and for occasional ready-to-eat and prepared foods. The family favors fresh and minimally processed foods, minimizes transfat and sodium and generally shops close to home. They try to keep the number of store trips to a minimum by purchasing in sufficient quantities while balancing spoilage and storage space limitations, brand preferences and promotional offers. Douglas's biggest complaint about the store is that certain items that are staples for his family are frequently out of stock – and that it is pointless to shop at his preferred time of Sunday evening because too many items are unavailable.

Douglas's shopping habits are not unusual for his neighborhood but are very different from those of customers at the Melwood Park DiamondMart a few miles west of River Park. There the store shelves reflect the preferences and buying patterns of the working class African-American, Hispanic and Eastern European shoppers who live nearby. These shoppers visit the store more often but spend less per visit. The store is located near several large format retailers including consumer electronics, home improvement and office supplies stores. Occasionally Douglas stops in the Melwood Park DiamondMart location to pick up a few items after a visit to the nearby SuperElectronics store. Douglas notices that some individual items are priced lower but there is less variety in fresh produce. It takes him longer to find the items he is looking for this less familiar store layout so he prefers his "home" store.

5.1.2 Market Research in Action: Better Insight Delivers Higher Profits

To be successful, micro marketing requires the ability to serve targeted consumers at the store – or to target the consumers served by the store. What Douglas purchases will have similarities – and differences – from his neighbors down the block and across the Chicago region. Localized micro strategies require strong understanding of consumer demand at the store level and an agile supply chain that can deliver the right assortment of products to the right location at the right time. Insight into consumer preferences and behavior is more essential than ever for consumer goods and retail success in our complex and rapidly changing world. For example, Nielsen research indicates that the number of new products introduced in the U.S. annually has skyrocketed from 2,899 in 1980 to 10,651 in 2005 (Mooth and ACNielsen 2007, p. 1). Similarly, the number of stock keeping units (SKU) on the shelves of any format retail store has increased dramatically so that managing retail operations cannot be based solely upon "knowing the products" but requires both automation of business transactions and tools for "managing by exception" in order to keep the right products available on the shelves. Together market research and DSD distribution create a powerful integrated approach to micro marketing. In combination, they give you:

- Actionable insights into opportunities and problems
- Ability to act on them quickly and effectively
- At the store with the consumer.

5.1.3 Market Research and Business Intelligence

Who is buying? What are they buying? Why are they buying? What causes them to buy more? What prevents them from buying?

Understanding who buys and why is essential for successful consumer goods manufacturers and retailers. Various methods are employed to generate answers – or at least insights – into consumer buying behavior. Generally we think of *market research* as activities that create or collect new data to answer our questions. A variety of market research techniques are used individually and in combination to develop relevant insights into current and future purchases. Techniques include activities such as surveys, focus groups, panels, usability studies, diaries and collecting market (syndicated) data. The purpose is to develop actionable insights that inform business decisions from investment priorities to R&D goals, new product development to channel tactics and creative strategies.

More recently, the term *business intelligence* (BI) has also come into use describing techniques to analyze data created in the course of business operations to gain insights about business performance and opportunities to improve it. Business intelligence activities include analyzing productivity of individual products, customers, sales people, distribution centers, promotional activities, etc. BI also opens the door to understanding consumer behavior in the context of the company's actions. Did consumers not buy a product because it was not available on the store shelf? Why was it unavailable? Was the promotion effective because the inventory was accurately allocated to the retailers and stores that best serve the target consumers? Was the increased demand for flavor A the result of flavor B being unavailable?

The data employed in BI is typically captured in the transactional or support systems of the company: orders, shipments, returns, promotions, sales activity etc. It can also come from business infrastructure such as the corporate phone switch, computer networks, fleet vehicles and other electronic components. As businesses have become more automated, more data has become accessible for analysis. Business analysts can evaluate the effectiveness of the company's DSD representatives not just from the orders they write but also from their time-in-store, route effectiveness, and other business systems metrics. Business analysts now delve more easily into revenue and profitability by customer, by sales territory, by product line, by SKU, by time period. They can compare performance over time and can evaluate the impact of strategies employed to build revenue.

Over time, the sources of data have evolved. Some information that was previously unavailable or only available through proxies such as surveys or audits is now captured automatically in the business systems. Similarly, as the questions change and the perspective shifts, much of what market researchers would like to know must be developed externally through data collection activities. Systems change and become more effective. Some of the lines blur as collaboration increases data sharing between manufacturers and retailers. Manufacturers are gaining increased access to actual consumer demand information for their products through syndicated or retailer-shared PoS data, through scan-based trading data and through distribution systems. As a result, they have less need to approximate this information through survey or interview techniques. For example, shopper diaries may provide insight into the number and variety of shopping destinations but are not necessary for market basket analysis when the checkout scanner captures an objective record of exactly what was purchased in each store trip.

There is still an important need to put the information about individuals or smaller groups into the broader market context in order to understand which conclusions can be generalized across the broader market and which are specific to smaller segments or local areas. Syndicated market data continues to play an important role in describing the overall category and market performance. The combination of internal and external data is required for benchmarking and gap analysis that shows how the individual product or store is performing compared to the category or market as a whole.

Since the goals of market research and business intelligence are the same and the boundaries between internal and external data are constantly changing, we will simplify for purposes of this discussion and refer simply to "market research" rather than trying to maintain a distinction between traditional market research and BI. The distinction disappears anyway when we keep the focus on developing objective actionable information to increase productivity and profitability. And, in most cases a combination of activities is required to answer the key questions of consumer behavior and product performance effectively.

5.2 Warehouse Versus DSD Distribution – Product and Data Flow

What is different about the data generated in a DSD system? Is the data telling us anything more or different? Does it enable any different action? What has changed?

Data is at the core of actionable market research. From a data perspective, there are some important differences between warehouse-based distribution systems and DSD distribution systems. Data is recorded in business transaction systems at each step of the process that goods change location and/or ownership. Since the flow of products is different, the points where data is created or collected are different. Although a manufacturer will usually employ a single distribution strategy across a brand, the retailer is working with both warehoused and DSD products and perhaps variants on each system. When Douglas visits DiamondMart, he is unconcerned with how the products reach the shelves. His goal is to find the items on his list and complete his purchase quickly. He may be willing to purchase additional items that attract his interest and he will be frustrated if too many of the things he needs are out of stock. The retailer and manufacturer have different levels of insight and ability to act to satisfy Douglas and keep him as a loyal shopper.

5.2.1 Warehouse Distribution

In warehouse-based distribution systems, there are actually two separate but connected supply chains belonging to the manufacturer and the retailer (as shown in Fig. 5.1). The manufacturer's supply chain flows from the manufacturing plant upstream to materials suppliers and downstream to the manufacturer's warehouse(s). From there, goods are shipped to the retailers' distribution centers and at that point, the manufacturer loses visibility into the location or movement of its products until individual units are scanned at the cash register recording a consumer's purchase.

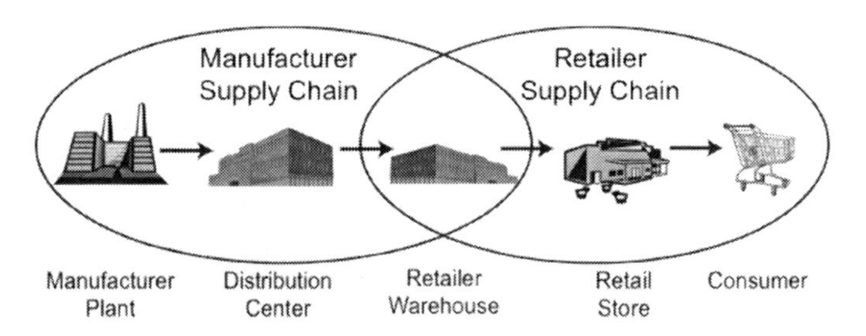

Fig. 5.1 Warehouse delivery system. In a warehouse-based distribution system, the manufacturer and retailer supply chains are distinct, but intersecting. The manufacturer is driven by *orders*, not *consumer demand*

The demand signal generated from within the manufacturer's supply chain reflects orders from the retailer for delivery to each of its distribution centers on behalf of all of the stores serviced. The manufacturer can calculate store level demand from point-of-sale PoS data to improve its demand forecast but this approach has some obstacles because it requires cross-functional communication, clarification and cooperation to add value to the forecast. More importantly, the manufacturer loses insight into store level inventory allocation, especially for promotions and new product introductions, making it more difficult to ensure promotional effectiveness. Without visibility into individual store orders or inventory, manufacturers can calculate some store effectiveness measures such as out-of-stocks (OOS) or stores-not-selling a promoted item but only after the fact and not in time to react to the problems.

5.2.2 Direct Store Delivery (DSD) Distribution

By contrast when a manufacturer invests in DSD distribution, it creates and controls a single demand-driven supply chain (as shown in Fig. 5.2). The supply chain from upstream suppliers to the manufacturing plant is the same as in the warehouse distribution system. From the plant, inventory moves to the manufacturer's distribution centers where it is loaded on trucks headed directly for retail stores. The manufacturer's deliveries create a transaction record of shipments to each individual store. This data directly reflects individual store demand and can be used to calculate consumer demand during a window of time in specific locations. Different approaches to DSD generate different data items, particularly relative to the frequency of deliveries and level of transaction automation. When retailers and manufacturers collaborate to implement scan-based trading, several transactions – and therefore several layers of data – are eliminated as inventory remains the property of the manufacturing vendor until it is scanned at the point of consumer purchase (Willard Bishop Consulting 2007). In this case, less data is more meaningful since it requires less consolidation and reconciliation to reflect what was actually sold.

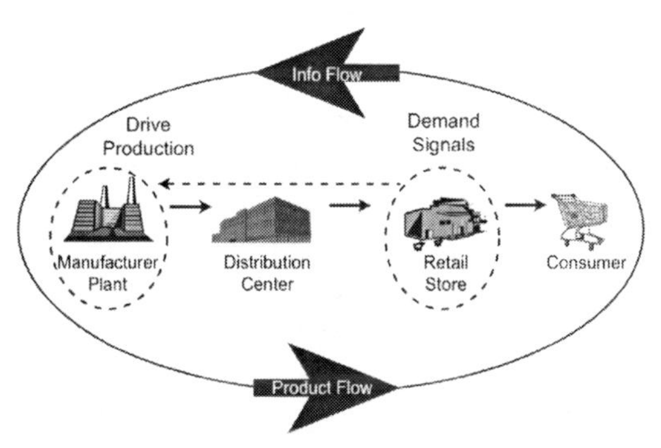

Fig. 5.2 DSD supply chain. In a DSD distribution system, the manufacturer and retailer supply chains are integrated. The manufacturer is driven by consumer demand

From the manufacturer's perspective, DSD brings an added level of control to the availability and presentation of products in the store. The manufacturer has a physical presence in the store on a regular basis. Depending on the DSD implementation, they may have one representative or several different people handling the tasks of checking the stock, writing orders, delivering goods, stocking shelves, creating displays and interacting with store personnel to communicate plans, troubleshoot problems and build relationships. Today's DSD teams are equipped with handheld devices that can record inventory levels for each SKU. These devices can also be loaded with the historical and forecast sales for each item. Putting the data at the DSD team's fingertips while they are in the store gives them the immediate ability to spot likely overstocks or threatened out-of-stocks, particularly during promotions when the risk is high. This level of visibility into availability helps the manufacturer capture more sales and helps keep Douglas happy because he is able to purchase the products he wants.

In addition to working with data directly in servicing the store shelf, the DSD team is able to capture additional data that will be used in future planning and execution. When HappyYogurt runs a 10 for $5.00 promotion, the DSD team records for each store whether the promotion was featured in an end cap or only on the regular shelf space and any other relevant store factors. Next quarter, when the promotion runs again, inventory allocation by store will be more accurate than if it were based strictly on historical sales data without taking the display environment into consideration.

5.2.3 Both Systems Utilize PoS Data

In the consumer products world, there is now a high degree of equality between manufacturers using DSD and warehouse distribution when it comes to accessing and analyzing PoS data. In the past, DSD companies had better access to store level data because of the direct product flow and their close relationship with the stores. Today, Nielsen makes available PoS data from approximately 50,000 stores in the U.S. with about 30,000 of those stores sharing daily data. Nielsen has created an analytical environment where the data is both accessible and insightful for clients. Clients focus strictly on understanding product movement and consumer behavior because Nielsen does all the complex and time-consuming work of transforming and harmonizing the data so that it is ready for analysis. The data is widely used by manufacturers and retailers alike in evaluating performance and planning for the future.

PoS data is also available to manufacturers directly from retailers in some circumstances. With integrated scan-based trading, the manufacturer gets the relevant PoS data immediately by store, directly from the retailer. Some retailers provide all of their vendors access to PoS data for the vendor's own products only. Access is usually through a portal system that requires the manufacturer to download their slice of the data in a format determined by the retailer. This data might be available daily but usually it is on a weekly basis. Manufacturers must invest the resources to access and download the data from their various retail customers. Then they must convert each data file into a common format to merge and harmonize the data before they can begin to analyze product movement, promotional effectiveness and store performance across retail accounts, trade areas, etc. In some cases, the manufacturer is required to present the retailer regular reports on product performance based upon the retailer's PoS data.

Since manufacturers using DSD historically have had better access to PoS data, they have evolved to a higher level of sophistication in utilizing the data in decision-making. Success in systematically finding and acting upon insights found in the data promotes a culture of data-driven decision-making to improve business results. Having "feet in the stores" capable of intervening to capture sales or prevent lost sales provides a significant motivation to identify the opportunities and threats. Once identified, they can be prioritized based upon their value to the company and the immediacy of a solution. Knowing the revenue impact of an out-of-stock can create urgency in replenishing the inventory. In the normal course of business, the DSD supplier will have a truck with stock at the store the next day or within a few days. It is possible and even practical to adjust the delivery schedule and/or the stock to fill costly shelf gaps sooner.

For warehouse-based manufacturers, the path from insight to action is more indirect. Manufacturers may only have a person in the store every few weeks and even then, that person has less latitude to step in and solve a problem or even to consult directly with the store staff on a solution. In the warehouse-based distribution model, manufacturers bring insights and recommendations to the retailer's corporate staff to influence action at the store level. The field representative calling on stores may be able to observe and highlight availability problems but doesn't typically travel with stock in her car to fill the gap on the spot.

5.3 Information Content in Direct Delivery Data

The market research value of PoS data comes in accurately knowing exactly what was purchased by day, by store, by shopper. This detailed view of consumer action provides the basis for both "big picture" trend analysis and specific product and consumer dynamics. Depending on the granularity and scope of the data and your analytical interests you can explore questions like:

- Sales by day of week or time of day
- Units purchased per consumer
- Product share of category by store
- Product share of total market
- Product share of shopping cart
- Complementary products in shopping cart
- Change in sales velocity during promotion
- Stores not selling an item the store agreed to carry.

The additional data available from DSD distribution opens additional insights. The DSD-specific data is:

- Store-level
- Low latency – e.g. daily, biweekly, or weekly
- Shipment-based or observational – e.g. environmental factors.

These characteristics make DSD data a powerful tool for driving retail execution and understanding consumer demand.

5.3.1 Store-Based Analysis

Using the store instead of the distribution center as the unit of analysis enables quick and efficient analysis at every level of the organization. Stores can easily be aggregated by region, size, demographics or other characteristics while preserving the ability to "drill down" to investigate the makeup of the group or specific stores with performance outside the norm for the group. When the unit of analysis is the distribution center, the detail is lost and cannot be recovered. A store-level view assists each front-line store manager and merchandiser in fixing problems and capitalizing on opportunities. Instead of trying to determine how overall trends play out in a specific location, they can look at what's happening in their own "laboratory" given its particular characteristics of size, location and, most importantly, consumer demographics. When aggregated, store-level data provides useful insights to brand and category managers who need bigger picture information. To understand the value of DiamondMart as a customer, looking at the retailer as a whole is satisfactory. But for assortment and planogram decisions, the differences between the neighborhoods the individual stores serve are important.

5.3.2 Latency

DSD data reduces the time between consumer action and corporate understanding. DSD data is generated based upon delivery schedule frequency so is typically available faster and in finer "slices" of time than distribution center orders. The time period is driven by the shelf life, volume and storage requirements of the product category along with the manufacturer's brand strategy. DiamondMart receives daily products with a very short shelf life such as daily newspapers and bread. Time intervals may be aggregated up for a broader view when the initial unit of time is small, but collecting data on a monthly or quarterly basis precludes more detailed analysis. Understanding that DiamondMart sells four times more beer Thursday through Saturday than Sunday through Wednesday improves availability all week long without the costs or risk of holding excess inventory.

5.3.3 Shipments

DSD data measures shipments to the store. Before writing an order, the DSD representative checks the shelf for out-of-stock and expired stock so there is immediate visibility into where inventory was too low – or too high. DSD shipments match actual consumer purchases more closely in time and quantity than shipments to DC centers. Order quantities are agreed based upon current sales rates and expected demand and are adjusted based upon actual shelf stock.

5.3.4 Observations

DSD systems enable representatives to record observations of environmental and causal factors in the store such as out-of-stock items, point-of-purchase materials, special promotion displays and locations. These observations provide powerful explanatory data that is used in adjusting forecasts and inventory allocation. For example, if when the SuperIceCream Company ran a 2-for-1 promotion at DiamondMart in July, the DSD representatives recorded observations at 75 of the stores that they stocked both the regular freezer case location and the freezer end cap display. Then when planning inventory allocations for a similar promotion the following July, SuperIceCream Co. will consider both sales history and the display space factor to avoid allocating too much inventory to the stores that have not committed to the end cap again.

5.4 Putting the Information to Work

> Without question, the DSD supply chain represents a unique and powerful system that places highly motivated, well-trained and professional category experts in stores every day, advancing the sales of some of America's best-selling brands. Retailers who leverage these DSD category experts also unleash years of experience at store level to provide a level of category and consumer focus that can mean the difference between success or failure. The net result of increased collaboration is a supply chain system that consistently produces above-average growth rates, exceptional product turns, unequaled new item speed-to-shelf, and store-by-store assortments and replenishment, while delivering greater consumer value every day (GMA 2005).

DSD data opens opportunities to improve productivity and profitability when the information it provides is actually ***used*** to make better decisions. It is not sufficient to have the data, or even the knowledge that can be gained from the data. It is necessary for the information to reach the people who can act on it. And, they must have the power and the resources to do so. Certainly the store manager can be more effective, especially in managing by exception with the objective insights provided by market research. But the impact is far wider. By eliminating time waiting to make a delivery, reconciling invoices, entering receiving data, etc., the DSD system increases the available time in-store for merchandising, selling, and other revenue-generating activities by the vendor team. A Willard Bishop Consulting study of DSD efficiencies for the GMA documented that an average small-format store benefits from nearly 700 h per year of in-store labor from its DSD suppliers; a large format store receives 17,000 labor hours per year. This boost in store resources pays off for the manufacturer, retailer and consumer (GMA 2005, p. 16).

To take full advantage of the time in-store, suppliers using DSD rely on data, not just perceptions, to detect, diagnose and define key leverage points for improving sales productivity. Because they have both the pressure and the power of people in the field daily, companies using DSD supply chains tend to be more mature in their use of data-driven decision making to address issues and opportunities through:

- Sales and category management
- Event management
- Inventory management
- Alerts
- Demand management.

5.4.1 Sales and Category Management

Category management has become a key battleground for manufacturers and retailers trying to improve profitability and meet consumer demand. Major manufacturers are developing more in-depth assortment planning to match their product mix on the shelf to the consumer base and physical arrangement of the store. A leading beverage company is reported to develop 60,000 planograms a year to specifically target their assortment to individual stores. Market research identifies the preferred consumer profile for each product line and identifies the shopper base for each store. Instead of allocating product by store size or historical sales, manufacturers using DSD can allocate based on the shopper base. They can even fine-tune in the field to account for temporary fluctuations in the local market.

At the River Park DiamondMart, HappyBeer delivers and merchandises its flagship HappyBeer in combination with its premium beer lines, a wide range of imported and specialty labels and a large display of non-alcoholic energy drinks sold mainly to teens. The smaller Melwood Park store features an assortment dominated by the HappyBeer label accompanied by single facings for several of the premium beers and energy drinks and deeper stock in four of the imported labels and two specialty beers. The basic plans for the stores are determined by the store size and shopper base but they are regularly adapted to fluctuating local demand influences by the DSD team. For example, a middle school located a block away from a convenience store generates high walk-in traffic for snack foods during the school year that drops dramatically during severely inclement weather, winter break, spring break and the gap between summer school and start of the school year. DiamondMart is close to the River Park high school and athletic fields so during lunch and after school hours it gets teen traffic that varies with the school calendar. When HappyBeer schedules an in-store energy drink promotion for the week of the high school's spring break, the River Park store manager and DSD team agree to shift it a week later to coincide with mid-term exams instead of the school holiday and they feature instead a display of specialty beers targeted at professional adults who are not influenced by the school schedule. The result is better sales and higher customer loyalty in both consumer segments.

5.4.2 Event Management

Event management encompasses planning and execution of promotions, new product introductions, closeouts, etc. Event management includes planning, stocking and monitoring to ensure availability or, in the case of discontinued products, selling out and switching smoothly to the replacement SKU. With the benefit of data on store level shipments and sales and on environmental/causal factors, DSD vendors and their retail customers are able to plan and execute events more accurately and to adjust more quickly when the demand is higher (or lower) than expected.

5.4.2.1 Dynamic Event Management with DSD

Many successful DSD vendors now download inventory and forecast data for each store they visit into the handheld devices of drivers and merchandisers. On site, they can compare the store's current stock position and recommend additional stock be moved to the store when the store is more successful on particular SKUs. Rather than risk an out-of-stock situation on an advertised, promotional, or new product item, the store team can review the sales velocity two or three days into the event and adjust the timing of orders and stock levels. This is particularly important when a promotion is more successful than anticipated and stock will run short before it ends unless there is an intervention. Similarly, if an event is underperforming, there may be options available to adjust the displays or other execution details or to release stock allocated so that it is available for over-performing stores.

When the event execution at a store or a group of stores results in stellar performance, that success can be immediately identified in the DSD system because of the shorter timeframes for analysis and more granular data. But the benefit does not have to be limited to the store(s) that find the key to success. DSD vendors and retailers are able to carry the successful practices to other stores within a day or a few days, amplifying the success of the event right away rather than waiting for the next event to spread the innovation widely. In the dynamic, fast-changing world of consumer demand, it is better to capitalize on opportunities immediately, particularly since preferences might have changed before the lessons could be applied to the next series of similar events. Demand shocks are difficult to relate to order and inventory data, but the immediacy of store shipments and inventory data enables the DSD teams to focus on store-level derived sales or consumer demand information. An event affected by local weather patterns near the store, such as a tropical storm warning issued during a bottled water promotion, can set up demand shocks that are amplified through the system and affect planning on future events disproportionately. Similarly, beer purchases in some Florida communities during college spring break weeks are significantly higher than other weeks in the season. Knowing how external events impact local stores is essential to having adequate supply – and avoiding over-supply at other periods in the future. Having the ability to interpret the data in light of conditions local to a store or group of stores reduces the distortion that is fed into the supply chain system. This capacity is much more readily available in a DSD supply chain than in a warehouse supply chain.

5.4.2.2 Responding to Local Events

Store-level planning and execution in the DSD system enables stores to respond more dynamically to local events that create short-term demand fluctuations. In summer 2008, the U.S. Swimming Olympic Trials will bring more than 20,000 swimmers, their families, coaches and fans to Omaha, Nebraska for 8 days of competition. It will be the first time Omaha has hosted the event which smashed all previous attendance records when it was held in 2004. Demand for energy drinks, bottled water, portable foods, healthy snacks, suntan lotion and many other products will surge, particularly in neighborhoods in close proximity to the venue and team hotels. Consumer goods manufacturers and retailers will do their best to anticipate demand and prepare accordingly. Manufacturers using DSD systems will be able to leverage the demand history of stores near the Long Beach, California venue in 2004 including the causal/environmental observations to forecast the Omaha demand spikes more accurately. But with shifting tastes and tens of thousands of new product introductions over the 4-year interim, there will still be plenty of uncertainty in the demand forecasts. DSD systems will be prepared to read and respond to the situation in the stores in time to capture potential demand as efficiently – and profitably – as possible. The benefits of combining market research and DSD are realized by manufacturers and retailers across a wide range of micro-bursts demand disturbances caused everywhere by planned and unplanned forces including weather and natural disasters, festivals and sporting events, social and political disturbances, cultural and educational institutions and many others.

5.4.3 Inventory Management

Retailing research for over a decade has documented the importance of product availability at the shelf (e.g. CCRRC 1996; GMA, FMI and CIES 2002; GMA 2005; Willard Bishop Consulting 2007). The cost of out-of-stocks is high and impacts profitability at both manufacturers and retailers as it affects immediate purchases, brand loyalty and store preference by the consumer (CCRRC 1996, pp. 8–11). Given all the work and investment that goes into bringing consumers into the store, the most important goal of inventory management is efficiently keeping availability high so that consumers are served while costs are kept in control.

DSD best practices recommend managing inventory and replenishment by monitoring a list of high velocity, advertised, promoted, traffic-generating and high-risk SKUs. Paying particular attention to these items which are most likely to go out of stock and/or most costly to have unavailable and replenishing them more frequently is much easier in the DSD system. Using color-coded shelf tags and eliminating the practice of filling shelf holes with other items makes ordering more accurate. The ability of the DSD representative to walk into the store with a precise list of SKUs that should be on the shelf along with store-specific shipments, inventory and forecast data is a powerful tool for managing inventory to ensure availability, even despite unforeseen demand shocks (Willard Bishop Consulting 2007). Manufacturers can identify shrinkage and phantom stock problems more easily when they combine store-level SKU data for shipments, items-not-scanning, and out-of-stock events.

5.4.3.1 Improved Promotion Inventory Allocation

A comparison of inventory allocation methods illustrates how more accurate allocation results in better product availability and promotion efficiency. The simplest approach is allocating equal inventory across all stores (see Fig. 5.3). This approach may not be used in practice but it shows the impact at the store level of misallocation by highlighting the extremes in over- and under-stock. In this example, 29 stores go out-of-stock while 42 stores have excess inventory. The gaps between allocated and demanded inventory are very large for many individual stores. The cost in lost sales due to availability problems is high. Allocation of inventory by store size (shown in Fig. 5.4) appears to cut the gaps somewhat but now results in 41 stores out-of-stock and 34 with excess inventory. The revenue result may be

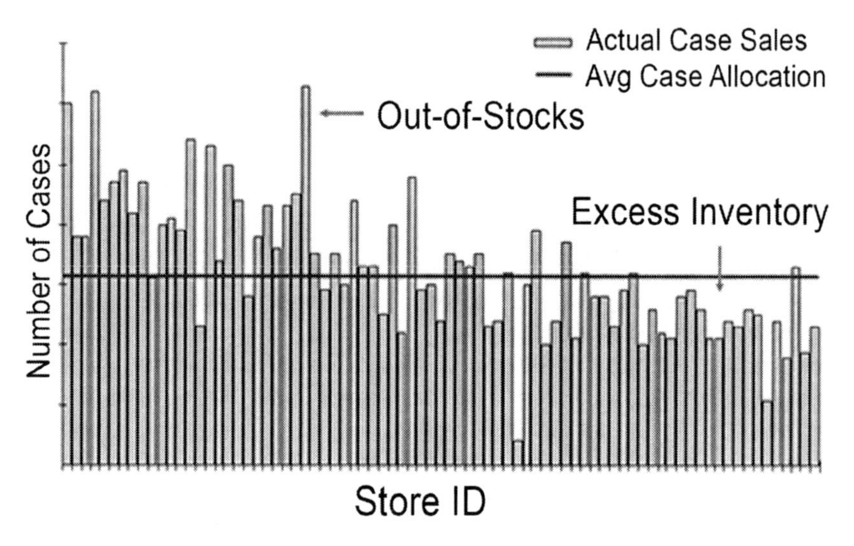

Fig. 5.3 Store allocation: equal to all stores. How stock of items on promotion is allocated by store impacts the store's ability to meet consumer demand while avoiding excess inventory. When stock is equally distributed to all stores, some stores run out of stock and others have too much

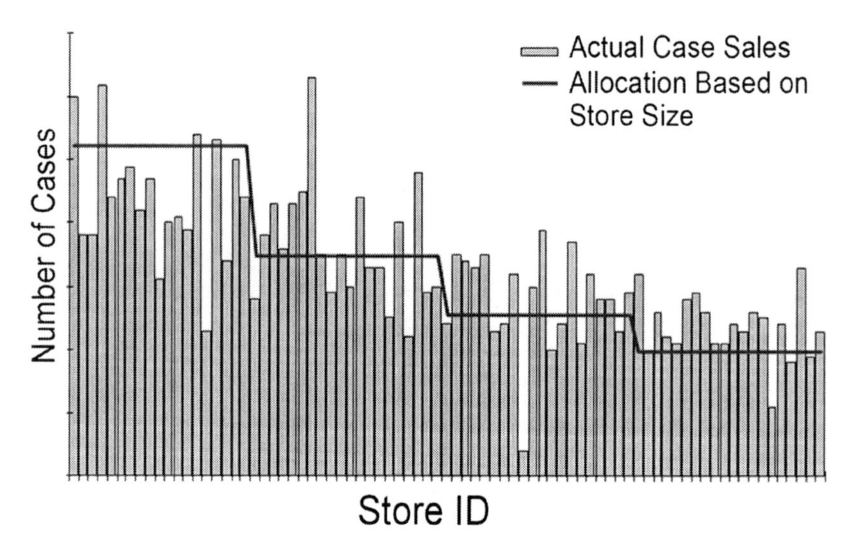

Fig. 5.4 Store allocation: distributed by store size. When more stock is allocated to larger stores, stock-outs and excess inventory can occur due to shopper differences and other variables

slightly improved but does not reach close to the full revenue potential with some stores wasting shelf/backroom space with inventory that will not sell during the promotion event while other stores sit with empty shelves.

Analyzing category sales by store to allocate inventory improves availability somewhat (shown in Fig. 5.5). By grouping stores into quartiles based on their success with the category, we come closer to approximating the stores' demand patterns with 38 stores going out-of-stock, 36 with excess inventory and smaller cumulative gaps. Unfortunately, category demand overall cannot accurately estimate the demand for all the lines in the category. For example, Store A in a suburban neighborhood with young families performs in the fourth quartile of sales for cold and cough remedies while Store B in an urban neighborhood dominated by young working adults ranks in the first quartile. If FamilyCareProducts Company allocates inventory on a promotion of their baby and infant products using the whole category as the reference, they will be out-of-stock at Store A and overstocked at Store B. The promotion will not deliver the planned results because the target consumers cannot find the products on shelves where they shop.

With the store data and causal factors, a manufacturer using DSD can more accurately allocate promotional inventory by individual store demand forecast. In Fig. 5.6, we see the number of out-of-stock stores drops to 18 but now most of the gaps between demand and inventory are small. Most stores will sell through their inventory just as the promotion ends. With a small number of more moderate misallocations, the DSD teams are motivated and able to correct the problems by

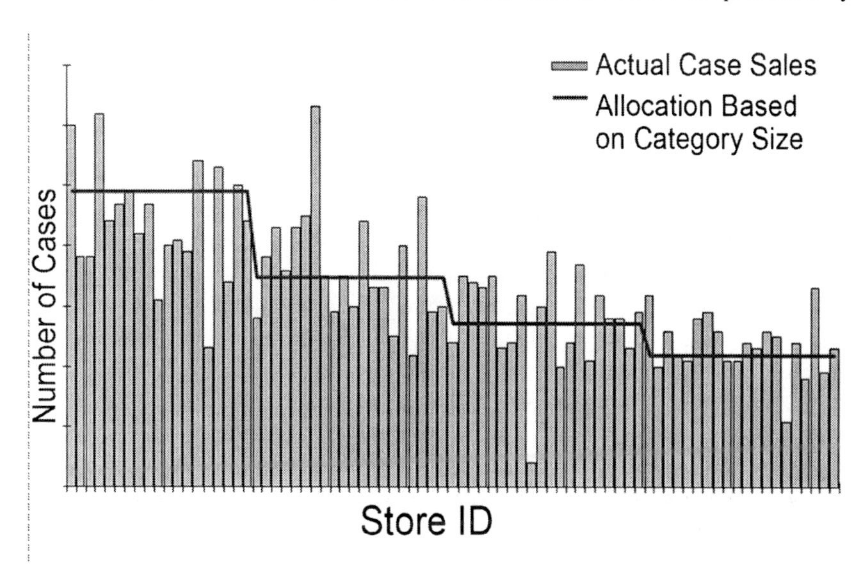

Fig. 5.5 Store allocation: distributed by category size. Analyzing category sales by store to allocate inventory improves availability somewhat. By grouping stores into quartiles based on their success with the category, we come closer to approximating the stores' demand

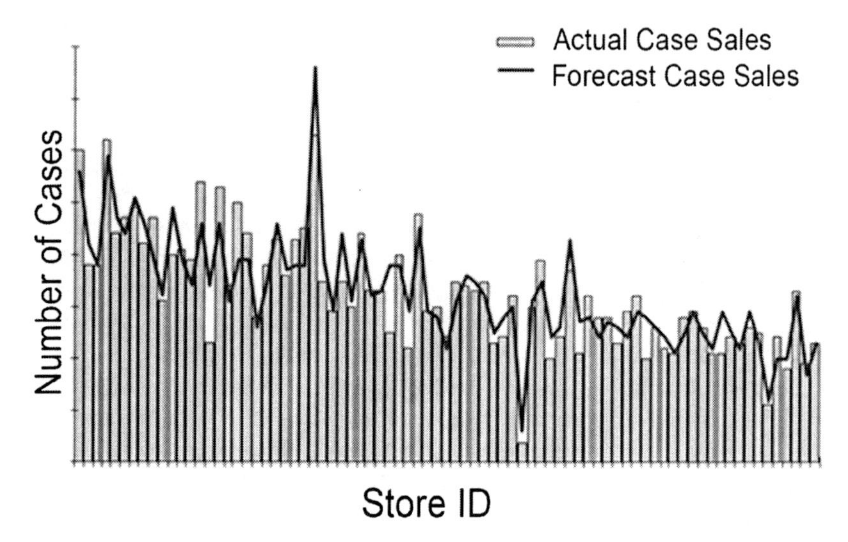

Fig. 5.6 Store allocation: distributed by store level demand. Allocating stock by each store's demand is the most accurate way to avoid disappointing consumers while minimizing inventory

reallocating stock to stores that are experiencing greater than expected demand. The manufacturer and the retailer benefit from a more successful promotion, less forward-buy impact on future sales and consumers who are satisfied instead of frustrated.

5.4.4 Alerts

Alerts provide current and predictive warnings of situations that need correction. Alerts are most often used for availability issues, events, and noncompliance such as on pricing, promotions or new product introductions. With thousands or hundreds of thousands of SKUs in each of thousands or tens of thousands of stores, it is not feasible to generate alerts by walking around, even with lists of items to monitor such as high velocity, promoted, advertised, or high risk items.

Alerts are used to notify brand managers, store managers, and DSD representatives of conditions that impact store performance including out-of-stocks and higher than expected response to promotions. Alerts are also used to notify regional or corporate managers of exceptions to programs, policies and events such as traited stores not selling, competitive pricing, delays in new product introductions and more.

Alerts are only valuable if they can be generated soon enough to be relevant and if they can be acted upon. The DSD system enables faster reactions by the store or DSD vendor who are the frontline team working for success. Douglas likes to make milkshakes and desserts and snacks for his kids from premium brand

SuperIceCream because of the nutritional value, particularly compared to some of the snack and dessert offerings available. At Douglas's house, kids are welcome to ice cream after school, after meals and at bedtime – as long as there's some in the freezer- which means they run out regularly. When SuperIceCream offers a 2-for-1 promotion, Douglas will buy several extra cartons – if it's available. Too often, DiamondMart runs out of vanilla – Douglas's only flavor option – and instead he buys nothing at all. He's frustrated and the kids are disappointed but they will not eat a different flavor. Since SuperIceCream uses DSD, the field rep logs the OOS flavor each time it happens. The OOS event can alert the DSD distribution center of the immediate need to increase vanilla units and to schedule extra stock onto a truck for River Park the next day. With a series of OOS flavor events logged against various stores, the planning team is alerted of the need to review the flavor mix for some stores. In the short term they can adjust the forecasts and shelf space allocations for the affected stores and in the longer term, they can conduct further market research to see if they are receiving "early warning" of some larger trends in flavor consumption. Alerts make it easier to tune into changes and stay in synch with consumer demand.

5.4.5 Demand Signaling

In most supply chain systems, signaling consumer demand is not a primary responsibility of the store, yet the store is where consumer demand is met – or not. In many consumer goods companies, the demand forecast is developed with little input or interaction from the departments creating consumer demand or interacting with the stores where that demand is satisfied. The brand managers who are funding and executing demand generation activities such as advertising, promotions, and new product introductions may provide information on how successful they hope to be in building consumer demand, perhaps even by region and time period. But neither brand managers nor supply chain managers are accustomed to focusing on the store and its specific needs. Nor are they primed to take advantage of the insights into consumer demand that are available from direct PoS data, DSD shipment data, in-store event logs and other demand indicators recorded close to the consumer purchase. There is a challenge in feeding this data to departments that do not traditionally use it.

The signals from store shipments and derived consumer purchases are stronger, clearer and more accurate than distribution center orders/shipments because the measurements are taken closest to the actual consumer demand both in time and location. Direct data is more complete and removes inaccuracy factors such as forward-buying and inventory level changes from the demand forecast input. Using DSD store data in demand signaling enables you to be truly demand driven.

5.5 Tools for Market Research

In evaluating potential market research and business intelligence activities, the primary considerations should be:

- What questions can be answered
- What is the value of the insight
- What resources are required (time, cost, skills, tools, and data)
- What actions can be taken as a result
- What is the expected return from the activity.

Evaluating a range of activities will enable you to select those with the most value to your organization, both strategically and tactically. Over time certain activities may come to be baseline practices which are required for efficient and effective operation of the business. This is particularly true in the consumer goods and retail sectors where consumer tastes and preferences are continually shifting. Because DSD vendors are closer to the consumer purchases and are able to respond quickly to consumer action, they generally place more of a premium on using the data to gain insights and direct action. Companies mature over time in their level of sophistication in analyzing data and incorporating data-driven decision-making into their operations.

The complements to DSD shipment data include:

- Syndicated PoS data that puts those local shipments in the context of the broader market
- Store demographic profiles that inform micro-strategies that appeal to the relevant demographic groups served by each store outlet
- Software designed with the power to dig into the data and the speed and ease to deliver answers quickly and easily.

Tools designed specifically for the job give you the ability to learn faster and then to take action based upon your knowledge. The direct PoS and shipments data in the consumer products sector is high volume and highly dynamic. At the same time, there is wide variety in the analytical requirements of the business users depending upon their role in the organization. To be most useful, the analytics system needs to be highly portable so that it can be utilized at the points of leverage and collaboration.

When adopting tools for analyzing and reporting on the direct shipments data, DSD companies need systems that are capable of:

- Providing fast speed-to-answer for high productivity by all users through ease of use and appropriate design for the specific tasks required
- Delivering built-in intelligence with CP-specific analytics to save time, increase accuracy and promote greater insight
- Supporting the right data structures with flexibility to organize data for all the different users and applications

- Integrating and harmonizing the data with other data sources to enable benchmarking and improve market coverage and delivering a scalable solution across all levels of the enterprise
- Complementing other business systems such as SAP by interfacing easily to streamline the workflow
- Offering low total cost of ownership through rapid deployment, minimal impact on IT, no need for custom coding and easy-to-use data management tools.

Applying the right tools to get the most out of the data takes the pain and effort out of the analysis and concentrates the energy and brainpower on the resulting decisions and actions.

5.6 Information into Action

The primary goal of market research is always informed action. Both manufacturers and retailers can make profitable decisions, limit risk and build consumer loyalty using DSD supply chain data. DSD data gives better insights than warehouse shipment data because it offers:

- Visibility to store shipments
- Visibility to product availability and out-of-stocks
- Ability to collect and integrate additional store level causal factors.

In a warehouse-based distribution system, manufacturers lose visibility into product movement from delivery to the retailer's distribution center until consumer purchase. Without transparency, collaboration to improve retail execution and serve consumers is more difficult.

DSD distribution creates a system where people are in place to act on information, respond to opportunities and trouble-shoot challenges right away. To make the most of a DSD system, companies must collect and analyze the data that is available and provide insights to the people who are in position to act in time for them to have an impact. Tools like Decisions Made Easy software make it easy to pull together the consumer products data available in a variety of disparate systems and harmonize it for analysis across time periods, stores and store groups, geographic periods, categories, sales teams, or any other dimension of interest. These tools help manufacturers and retailers understand product performance and consumer behavior at the store level and to push information out to the field for more effective retail execution (Decisions Made Easy 2007, pp. 7–9).

Market research in the DSD system gives manufacturers and retailers the ability to understand and act to improve availability and profitability both immediately and longer term through more insightful:

- Sales and category management
- Event management

- Inventory management
- Alerts
- Demand signaling.

The DSD supply chain delivers manufacturers and retailers more insights into the success or failure of their efforts. It opens the door for more fact-based selling and more effective collaboration to take advantage of opportunities and solve the challenges they face. The net result is a system that is more responsive to consumers and more productive for manufacturers and retailers. The result is more satisfied and loyal consumers like Douglas who find the products they want on the shelf and are open to trying the new products developed to give him healthy and convenient products that deliver value.

References

AC Nielsen (2006): What's Hot Around the Globe: Insights on Growth in Food & Beverages. New York.

Mooth, Rob; AC Nielsen (2007): Beating the Fragmented Odds: Food Launch Rules of the Road. Consumer Insight Magazine http://www.nielsen.com/consumer_insight/ci_story2.html. Accessed 14 August.

Coca-Cola Retailing Research Council (CCRRC) (1996): The Retail Problem of Out-of-Stock Merchandise: Where to Look for Incremental Sales Gains. Atlanta, GA.

Decisions Made Easy; The Nielsen Company (2007): Attacking Stock-Outs: Improving Availability at the Shelf Using Direct Data. Chicago, IL.

Grocery Manufacturers Association (GMA) (2005): Unleash the Power of DSD: Driving DSD Supply Chain Efficiencies and Profitability. Washington, DC.

GMA, FMI, and CIES (2002): Retail Out-of-Stocks: A Worldwide Examination of Extent, Causes and Consumer Responses. Washington, DC.

Willard Bishop Consulting (2007): "Capturing the Full Benefit of DSD Strategies" webinar presentation. Prescient Applied Intelligence. Accessed 22 March 2007.

Suggested Further Reading:

Anderson, Doug; Nielsen Homescan & Spectra (2007): Population Churn (Part 1): Business as Usual for the U.S.? Consumer Insight Magazine. http://www.nielsen.com/consumer_insight/ci_topline_article1.html. Accessed 14 August 2007.

Gartner Group (2006): Managing the Shelf: A Collaborative Outlook on Category Management from the Consumer Goods and Retail Industries Consumer Goods Technology, Retail Information Systems News. Randolph, NJ.

Endnotes

[1] The consumer, Douglas and his family are fictitious personas used to demonstrate the concepts presented. All place, store and brand names referenced are invented for illustration only.

Chapter 6
Trends and Developments in DSD

Alan Thomas[1], Koen De Starke[2], and Leon Pieters[3]

[1] Deloitte, 200 Clarendon St., Boston, MA 02116, USA, tel.: +1 617 437 2765, e-mail: alathomas@deloitte.com

[2] Deloitte, Berkenlaan 8B, B-1831, Diegem, tel.: +32 2749 59 12, e-mail: kdestaerke@deloitte.com

[3] Deloitte, Laan van Kronenburg 2, Postbus 300 (P.O. Box), NL-1180 AH Amstelveen, tel.: +31 652672524, e-mail: leonpieters@deloitte.com

Abstract

In spite of widespread adoption of the DSD process in the food and beverage industries, and despite many recent technological advances, there is still untapped value in how, when, where and why DSD gets deployed within its traditional channels – and even beyond them. While DSD does not address every consumer-oriented situation, we believe that, with some effort to adapt the distribution process and technology enablers, DSD has enormous potential to deliver even greater value to retailers and suppliers. To fully tap this potential and differentiate themselves, food and beverage companies in particular will need to capitalize on several key trends that are shaping the DSD process. The leaders of the future will not be content to merely react to business dynamics created by these consumer and retailer mega-trends; rather, they will position themselves ahead of them and leverage value into market share in the highly competitive DSD environment.

6.1 The Convergence of Direct and Indirect Store Delivery

There is a common misperception that Indirect Store Delivery (ISD) and Direct Store Delivery (DSD) are incompatible with one another. However, in today's world, where channels, routes-to-market and supply chains are converging in evermore complex ways, it is increasingly evident that in many supply chains the one-size-fits-all approach no longer applies. In the coming years we are likely to see the best from both worlds converging into Direct Store Management (DSM).

When replenishing outlets with products, the supply chain system is traditionally defined as an Indirect Store Delivery or a Direct Store Delivery operating model. According to the ISD concept, orders are submitted centrally from the outlet via the retailer's headquarters to the supplier's central order desk. In most cases

A. Otto et al., *Direct Store Delivery*,
DOI: 10.1007/978-3-540-77213-2_6,

the supplier does not know the order details at the outlet level but receives one consolidated order for the entire retail chain. The supplier does the order picking and delivers the products directly to the retailer's central, and sometimes regional, warehouse. This is where the supplier's responsibility ends. It then is the task of the retailer to split the consolidated order into the individual outlet orders and to deploy these orders via its own distribution network to the outlets. In essence, the retailer's central warehouse services the needs of the individual retail outlets with their own resources and on their own schedule.

Variations to this textbook definition of ISD have also developed in recent years:

- *Vendor Managed ISD*: instead of delivering based on actual orders from the retailer, the supplier manages the inventories at the central – and in some cases regional or local – level of the retailer. In this model, minimum preset inventory levels are the trigger for replenishment to the retailer's central/regional warehouse. The vendor services the account as a benefit to the retailer, perhaps with certain pre-set volumes, as a way of helping the retailer become more streamlined and cost efficient
- *Daily Replenishment ISD*: using the Point of Sale information from the retailer (when possible at the outlet level, but this could also be on a consolidated level), the sold quantities are replenished on a daily basis to the retailer's central location. This is often used in situations where large volume or quantities move from producer/bottlers into the retail channel and present very real logistical distribution challenges, e.g. in soft drink beverages, beer, or bottled water. In some cases a variant combination with cross-dock ISD is also possible
- *Cross-dock ISD*: in this model the supplier plans or picks orders by region or outlet in such a way as to send the order to the retailer in one truckload. Once in the retailer's facility these orders are split and sent directly via the retailer's truck fleet to the individual regions or outlets.

When the retail outlet has its products directly replenished by the supplier plant or distribution center, we are generally talking about Direct Store Delivery. In this model the orders are captured by the outlet owner himself, sent via the retail headquarters to the supplier, or captured by a sales representative from the supplier/distributor as a service to the retailer. In both cases, the supplier is responsible for delivering the goods at the point-of-sales, either to the retail establishment itself or, in many cases, directly onto the shelves of the retail outlet.

In the Direct Store Management concept, order capturing and merchandising operations are handled in a traditional DSD mode, but the delivery is handled according to a "direct supplier-to-retail-outlet" concept or an "indirect supplier-to-retail-outlet" concept. Based on the characteristics of different customer channels/route-to-markets, the characteristics of the product itself, and the infrastructure of the supplier and retailer, a combination of ISD and DSD is used. In fact the route to market in any particular replenishment situation may change depending on variables that arise such as stock-out, promotion and event driven marketing.

Sophisticated capability to plan and evaluate the impact of the replenishment method will provide distributors and retailers of the future much more capability to meet the consumer's needs than the static route based scenario of today.

6.2 The Focus Shifts from Logistics to Sales and Marketing

The term 'Direct Store Delivery' does not do justice to the richness and potential value of this way of going to the market. The term tends to draw attention to the delivery aspect, whereas the DSD process of the future may in fact bear little resemblance to the route-based process of today. Positioning for that future will require deeper understanding of customer needs, near real-time knowledge of demand changes, innovative business processes, and a partnership between retailer and DSD distributor that differs from the relationship of today.

Historically, factors such as 'bulkiness of goods' or 'freshness of produce' have been the primary drivers for this way that consumer package goods companies do business. However, the access DSD provides to the consumer/shopper at the point-of-sale can potentially offer huge strategic advantages – provided that the information about the consumer can be captured, analyzed and exploited. To understand how DSD facilitates access to this information, we should first distinguish between the following processes that are executed through different business cycles:

- Selling/Order-taking
- Delivering
- Merchandising.

In reality, the three processes are not always executed at the point of sale, and several tasks can be combined during the same visit. The profile and skills set of the individual executing the task varies of course, depending on the activity being performed.

6.2.1 Selling/Order-Taking

The fact that a salesperson has regular contact with the store manager (or at least the category manager responsible for that product or segment) at the point of sale can be very valuable, but the value heavily depends on the commercial degree of freedom a retail manager has. For instance, when he or she has limited flexibility in deciding whether particular long-running standard products and sizes can be sold at that outlet, attractive new products introduced or whether an extra point of sale display can be placed and the terms under which that takes place, the 'selling' effort is very constrained. And the reality today is that because of retailers' increasing globalization more decisions are made at 'headquarters', while local on-site sales personnel have decreasing influence on the transactions taking place.

However, when evaluation criteria of store managers include broader metrics such as revenues and profits at the outlet level – which they should – it might be wise for headquarters to leave a degree of freedom to the stores – that, after all, is where the local knowledge of the shopper/consumer resides. Consider, for example, the relevance of a national grocery chain introducing particular products in just a couple of its stores with a shopper population attracted to those products. Clearly the success or failure of a product in a given locale can be driven by the specific demographics or wealth of a given area.

In many cases today, the order for a particular outlet is driven by the central supply chain organization of the headquarters looking at sell through data, margin and price points of a huge (and ever growing) selection of products. The harsh reality is that a delicate balance exists between having a minimal stock level/ investment at all locations (both central, as in the outlet's local warehouse) and selling out or in the terms of the trade "out-of-stocks". The best central planning and execution can still result in a loss of sales and a portion of consumer mind-share when these stock-outs occur. We can contrast this with a situation in which even if the local store manager has limited influence on local commercial activities, the fact that sales people from the manufacturers and distributors communicate and service the outlet directly at that location can surely give additional insight into expected sales volume of commercial activities, reducing the risks for out-of-stocks.

There is significant benefit to all parties in servicing the local retailer, gathering specific local market data, and combining that data with more powerful and mobile sales intelligence reporting capability. Trends and learnings are shared, as are the possibilities of sales growth between the retailer, the national chain, and the distributor. All will benefit as the consumers needs are met more precisely on the retailer's shelf.

6.2.2 Delivering

This is the process that typically comes to mind today when discussing DSD. Oddly enough, however, delivery is often the process with least value, driven as it is by pure operational (read *cost*) considerations and not by revenue growth. As such, who delivers the goods to the store does not really matter as long as it is done in a cost-effective, efficient, and timely manner. Manufacturer and retailer need to look at the total supply chain and optimize its efficiency; this will drive the decision as to which party is best placed for executing this process. Third-party logistics parties might be a far better option to perform this task than for manufacturers to do it themselves.

Here again, some forward-thinking distributors are trying to counter-balance this by empowering their delivery drivers to become the eyes and ears of the sales force at the retail outlet. Today's more innovative organizations encourage, and in many cases train, delivery personnel in customer service techniques. They expect them to sell from inventory on the truck, note competitor stock-out situations and promotions, conduct in-store surveys, and in general gather intelligence from the grocer's floor. This activity typically crosses over to merchandising, which in some cases may be provided by separate personnel in addition to the delivery personnel. Such activity has market intelligence-gathering potential if it is made a part of the responsibility and compensation structure.

A recent landmark study by the Grocery Manufacturers of America (GMA) on the logistics of delivering and stocking product clearly points to the areas with potential benefit to both distributors and retailers. The study analyzes activities during a typical DSD delivery visit and contrasts efficient and inefficient DSD processes and the percentage of time utilized by each step in the process. As dramatically shown in the chart, for the DSD delivery process to become more efficient, changes need to be made to the steps and activities required of the driver and the retailer. We believe these changes need to be not only technological but also oriented toward business process as well (Fig. 6.1).

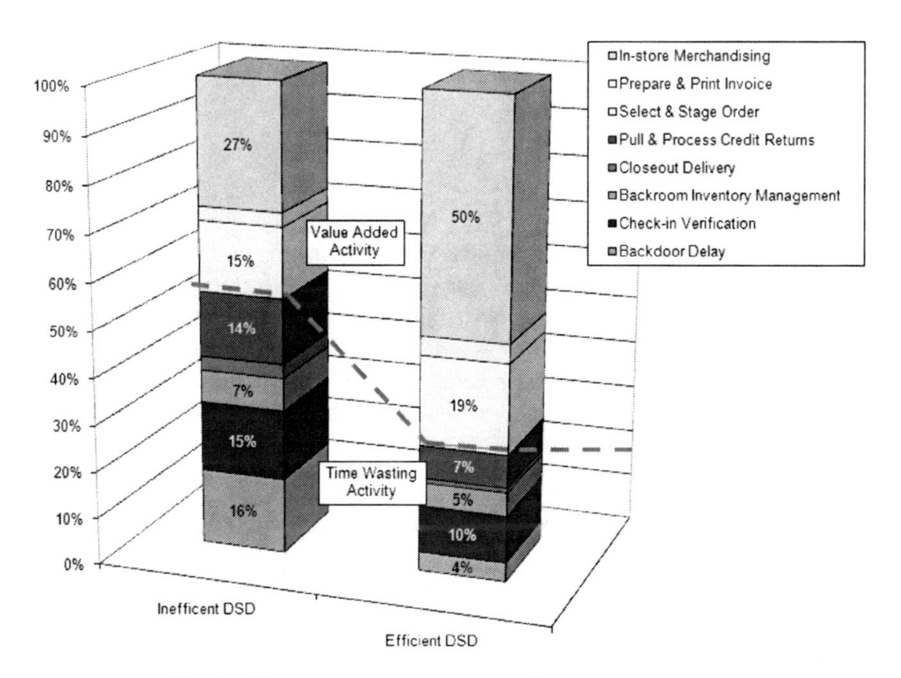

Fig. 6.1 Chart based on GMA study of efficient DSD (GMA 2005)

The biggest time-wasters in the delivery cycle were activities related to wait time at the receiving location of the retailer, the pull and process activities related to credit returns, the tasks related to inventory management and check-in as well as close-out delivery activities. The difference in these activities between an inefficient and an efficient delivery could total as much as 17 min of time spent onsite.

The steps and activities identified as providing enhanced value and customer satisfaction were those supporting error-free delivery, such as selecting and staging the orders and preparing and presenting the invoice. By far the largest value-added activity was around in-store merchandising and retailer relationship development. An efficient DSD delivery will spend the valuable 17 min on-site in these types of activities.

It is easy enough to analyze today's data into these categories and state the potential benefits. However, it is important to consider how rapidly the business environment is changing and the highly competitive nature of the DSD marketplace. For instance, to dramatically change the delivery dynamics described by the GMA may require setting pre-determined service levels, and developing a sophisticated optimized and synchronized schedule of availability between the retail outlet and the delivery route that is flexible yet cost effective for all parties. Technology and automation of course will play a part in addressing the pain points of inaccurate and time-wasting activities like receiving, order preparation and pulling but the real value will come from a mutual partnership between distributor and retailer leading to increased profitable sales for all parties.

6.2.3 Merchandising

The actual merchandising involves the shelving, facing of the products and, potentially, the building of displays. Correct execution is extremely important to increase impulse buying at the point-of-sale. A merchandiser or manufacturer's representative will naturally be inclined to position its brands in the best possible way. A retailer must therefore clearly define the boundaries within which merchandising can be performed. This is a very time-consuming and labor intensive process, and is hence very costly. A retailer needs to balance the risks of allowing a particular brand to be pushed with the high cost of doing it internally, or not doing it at all.

In a DSD environment, selling and merchandising activities are typically performed by people who are commercially driven or "incentivized" and who are backed by the manufacturer's sales and marketing organization. By bringing the retailer's insights together with those of the manufacturers at the point of sale, it is possible to gather a unique understanding of the shopper.

The profile of a particular shopper – often known from the prevalent loyalty cards if this information is shared between retailer and distributor – combined with a deep understanding of the full portfolio of the manufacturers' brands, allows for a targeted commercial marketing activity at the point-of-sales: the right products, at the right time at the right price and supported by the right promotions. This enhanced understanding benefits both retailer and manufacturer and is greatly facilitated by regular contact between store managers and key account managers.

DSD is an ideal way to institutionalize this process, provided that all parties use it to maximize value and do not view it as a way to simply shift costs onto each other.

6.3 More Use of DSD to Capitalize on Local Opportunities

Occasion-based marketing (OBM) focuses on the moment of consumption and analyzes the market environment (percent market share, competition factors and incentives, promotional packages, etc.) at a particular occasion or event. Much research is still needed in this area, since traditional retail behavior analysis focuses primarily on linking channels to market with consumer behavior and not at the occasions that drive that consumer behavior. However, occasion is an important factor in the buyer's complex decision-making process that manufacturers and distributors will need to better understand and exploit.

Some factors are now better understood, and successful manufacturers and distributors of consumer packaged goods are beginning to assimilate them into their market and sale tactics. For instance, we observe that for a typical consumer packaged product, somewhere between three to five occasions represent as much as 70–80% of the annual business. Being able to link the occasion and the association with the product provides a better indicator of market maker success than traditional market analysis, which typically analyzes over 50 sales channels in a relatively static fashion without factoring in the element of timing/occasion.

We believe that a good understanding of the occasion tied to the consumption event drives a better understanding of the shopper (who quite literally wants the product or brand best identified with that particular occasion) and hence produces a highly valuable and strategic view of the right channels to getting the right marketing mix at the point of sales. In fact, on certain occasions, that consumer is much less likely to be motivated by price or promotion than by product availability and format. The better a producer/distributor can target the product a particular consumer is likely to need for a specific occasion and plan its related packaging, pricing, promotion, etc., the more successful and profitable the sales tied to that occasion will be.

However, the occasion-driven consumer is also highly time-sensitive. This means that it is almost impossible to sell Christmas baked goods after that holiday has passed or, to take an example in the US, to sell corned beef and cabbage after the March 17 St. Patrick's Day holiday. Therefore the inventory at the retailer and in the distribution channel must be clearly understood in relation to the event driving the spike in purchases. The potential consequences are a sharp drop-off on sale of the product, fire-sale promotions, or returns.

It is widely accepted now that better exploiting the information that can provide insight into shopper behavior has a potentially tremendous impact on the performance of both the retailer and manufacturer. This is a "win-win" in the most fundamental way.

DSD offers a unique growth vehicle for both retailer and manufacturer, but this is not always because of its cost efficiencies. Rather, it brings a depth and breath of understanding about both the marketplace and the end consumer which ultimately leads to the Holy Grail of increased sales. It is a symbiotic, practical approach to retailer-manufacturer collaboration that provides the market intelligence necessary for making key investments.

6.4 DSD Technology Moves beyond Efficiency to Innovation

Technology is a key tool for handling the repetitive and time-sensitive transactions that make up a modern route-based distribution system. But the ease and availability of mobility processing is only the beginning of that impact. New ways of deploying technology in conjunction with streamlined and enhanced DSD processes can lead to as-yet untapped value for both retailers and distributors.

It is true that at its simplest level (and this is in fact still common in many regions of the world), paper-based Direct Store Delivery handles the basics of pre-sales order taking, sales delivery preparation, recording empties/returnables activities, and static retailer invoicing. Even where more sophisticated back-office systems currently exist to plan routes, assemble and dispatch orders, and calculate settlement and route accounting, the paper-based system can and does work for many organizations lacking the technical sophistication, capital investment, or commercial curiosity to see the potential benefits provided by mobilizing their DSD workforce. Whatever the degree of technology currently implemented, the trend will be for all DSD processes to be further enabled by advancing technology. The simple paper-based routes of today will no doubt use mobility enablers that make route sales and delivery more efficient without requiring a higher degree of sophisticated technological layers. Today's more advanced DSD technology users will also no doubt enhance and adopt the newer technologies coming to distributors and retailers that will continue to give them the sophistication and competitive advantage that they seek in their particular markets.

Technology providers have been mobilizing the DSD workforce for the past two decades and have expanded and extended technical options to the industry. Simple automation of order taking, delivery and invoicing on a hand-held device in some form undeniably speeds up the route stop and provides a more fool-proof record of a day's route-based activities away from the distribution center. But the latest iterations of technology enablement now extend to real-time synchronization via a multitude of connectivity options, mobile "revise and print on demand" capabilities, and digital exchange of information between the distributor and retailer. But merely giving mobile capability to pre-sellers or DSD delivery drivers doesn't comprehensively address the true needs of the increasingly complex requirements of food and beverage distribution.

Standardized electronic transactions sets, such as DEX (Direct Exchange/EDI 894) and NEX (Network Exchange) have been around for several years. In particular markets and geographies they have, to some degree, helped expedite the transmission of vendor invoice data to the retailer. While this standardization of electronic information protocol certainly helps reduce unauthorized items and quickly identify cost discrepancies between retailer and supplier systems, it does not fix the underlying data integrity issues or significantly reduce the time it takes to receive deliveries at the store.

Electronic transmission of invoice information at the store level has little value if high levels of data discrepancies exist between distributors and retailers. Resolving cost disputes and discrepancies is a continuous challenge for trading partners and in many cases this adds significant time to the receiving process and back-office functions. A single cost discrepancy on an item may delay every single delivery at the store level. For these reasons, joint-industry efforts are presently underway to develop global data synchronization standards that will streamline the DSD process and facilitate the flow of information and products between vendors and their retail partners.

Through the increased use of global data synchronization, consumer packaged companies and retailers have been able to drastically increase the accuracy of information at multiple levels. Data sync has traditionally focused on item setup/ authorization and basic cost information. However, it has quickly developed into additional areas such as party creation and maintenance (i.e. store location information) as well as more complex promotional pricing collaboration efforts. A common format allows manufacturers to reduce need for proprietary solutions and mapping to each retailer. Global data sync will continue to gain momentum as companies continue to implement and adopt standardized data sharing protocols and realize the value of their initial investments.

In addition to using global data synchronization, some national retailers are redesigning their vendor websites and creating standard workflows to effectively manage DSD processes with smaller distributors that do not have data sync capabilities. An ongoing industry trend has been moving the resolution of invoice cost discrepancies away from the stores to centralized departments such as merchandising or finance so that only item quantities are validated during the delivery process. On the front-end, data synchronization efforts aim to minimize disruptions; on the back-end, standardized workflows aim to help resolve receiving and discrepancies.

Forward-thinking retailers are currently investing in systems that allow them to track delivery accuracy based on audit algorithms that randomly select invoice line items on each delivery to validate quantities and build vendor certification programs based on store-specific performance history. The main objective of these efforts is to minimize receiving time while maintaining an adequate control and delivery integrity.

One of the biggest challenges for retailers regarding DSD vendors has to do with inventory data integrity. Due to loose receiving processes and lack of controls, balance-on-hand (BOH) information is often inaccurate for many DSD categories. Without accurate inventory information, retailers in many cases are unable to leverage actual PoS information to generate recommended order quantities automatically in a timely fashion. For the most part, CPG companies have mobile hand-held technology that allows their sales representatives to enter order quantities based on store delivery history as well as current inventory levels.

Emerging replenishment solutions aim to leverage retailers' PoS data together with demand creation factors (e.g. promotional data, special events, weather conditions, etc.) to generate accurate sales forecasts and link this information to vendor ordering devices to provide enhanced visibility and ordering support. Additional inventory validation is required for selected SKUs on a regular basis to ensure data integrity and accurate order quantities.

While the uses of mobile technology mentioned above are key enablers of the DSD process, some companies, notably in the beverage industry, are planning even more innovative approaches. A DSD sales route of the future may encompass real-time order taking with a mobile device that both shows available-to-promise inventory and interacts dynamically with production schedules to ensure a more tightly linked supply chain. But this may only be half of the DSD ordering process of the future. For outlets and products enabled by RFID, true scan-based trading will literally account for product and reorder it as the product is transacted at the point of sale in a highly synchronized "pull" supply scenario.

Inventory placed at the outlet on consignment and tagged with RFID identifiers will financially change hands between the distributor and retailer when the consumer pays for it at the register. In addition to electronically transferring funds, a reorder signal will then be transmitted to both the distribution and the production groups in a pull-through of inventory into the supply chain.

From a logistics perspective, cost and resource optimization can potentially take place against the constant flow of orders, assessing the geo-coded outlet locations, on-line reorder requirements, availability of trucks and drivers with the required product, thus breaking the traditional boundaries of fixed geographic routes. With the intersection of the wireless internet and the enhanced processing capability of ERP/mobility systems, such factors as weight, traffic conditions, and delivery restrictions can be processed into a smooth reordering stream that takes into account much more than a delivery today can possibly manage.

Merchandisers of the future will use enhanced technology as well. Predefined product placement plans and optimized real-time promotion planning will enhance and streamline the time spent in store assessing the point of sale situation, restocking activities, and managing promotional materials. Enhanced handheld CRM devices with embedded cameras, voice note recording and built-in retailer and consumer surveys will guide and assist in the gathering of precious marketing information about competitors, local outlet conditions, and even observable consumer behavior.

The value of that point of sale market intelligence, though, lies not so much in the gathering of it as it does in translating it into specific action plans at the account and SKU level. Back-office CRM fed with this mobile data and with the ability to identify trends, conduct simulations, model financial impacts and recommend better solutions in a near real-time environment will become the standard by which DSD distributors succeed or fail. The valuable minutes that the distributor's sales, delivery or merchandising people spent onsite with the retailer requires them to act extremely efficiently and that their actions benefit both the distributor and the retailer.

6.5 The Greening of DSD

Ever since Al Gore shook the world with his environmental wake-up call "An Inconvenient Truth," the focus of many consumers and companies has been on "going green." For the first time in history, companies are considering en-masse if they have made the right business choices in the interests of environmental responsibility. Whether they are doing so because of a deep commitment to the environment or because of concerns about marketing and perception is irrelevant: every consumer business company needs to take this into account as it has become one of the criteria of choice for the consumer. This trend will increasingly require retailers and suppliers to factor in the impact of their "carbon footprint" when deciding between ISD and DSD/ DSM.

6.5.1 DSD's "Carbon Footprint"

In the textbook definition of DSD there are three touch points with the retail outlet, each of which has an impact on the total carbon footprint:

1. Order capturing by the sales representative
2. Delivery of the products to the shelf
3. Handling the merchandising at the outlet level.

Touch points 1 and 3, for example, are combined when sales representatives cross the country in their vehicles, thus contributing to the carbon footprint. That said, the largest carbon footprint is caused when multiple trucks, on a daily basis, deliver products from different suppliers to a single outlet which, among other things, causes congestion in densely populated areas.

The ISD concept, in which all deliveries are combined and the outlet receives its deliveries from a single truck, may on the surface seem far "greener" than the many individual trucks required by the DSD concept. However, the situation is more complicated. True, the ISD truck might replace the many DSD trucks and therefore could have an impact on carbon footprint and congestion, but it will by default be a much larger truck spewing more exhaust. It is also easier to replace the gasoline engines in small trucks with electric or hybrid engines than it is to do so for bigger trucks. The fact that goods will be first brought to one central location and then back to an outlet (hub-and-spoke system) might also create more miles than direct delivery. This situation often occurs, for example, when a retail outlet to be serviced is located near the supplier's plant and could receive delivery with minimum mileage according to a DSD concept; by contrast, consider a "locked-in" ISD concept, where the retailer's distribution center is at the other side of the state from the producer's location. The bottom line is that a thorough calculation of the end-to-end carbon footprint needs to be done to define the impact of any given supply chain concept, whether ISD or DSD.

6.5.2 The Carbon Footprint and Locally Produced Products

Today's consumers, with their heightened awareness of social and environmental issues and an increasing number of choices available to them, are driving some of the fundamental changes in the food and beverage supply chain. The very processes that enabled mass-marketing, high-volume production and wide-spread distribution of products could also sacrifice quality and lower the standards of food safety and traceability. More affluent consumers now see the value in buying and supporting local products in a movement to higher quality, fresher products. Consumers across the globe, experiencing an increasingly complicated and technology-dependent existence may also be yearning for simpler times and products, which are often provided by local brands and producers. These local products may also be marketed in smaller portions and in simpler packaging since the consumer value drivers are no longer just those of price point and durable long-term packaging.

Food and beverage producers and distributors are also seeing value and profit in meeting these consumer needs for locally produced fresher products. Whether from a keen desire to reduce the environmental impact of transportation or simply from a financial cost/benefit perspective, producers are re-evaluating their supply chains and their networks of producing and packaging facilities. This trend towards local products has a direct impact on the distribution model for products that make their way onto the shelves of today's retailers, and it is a factor in considering the future of DSD as a distribution method. After all, in its simplest form that hearkens back to its origins, DSD represents the one-to-one marketing, sales and delivery of products to the channel.

In a trend likely to expand globally to address growing environmental and health concerns, some UK retail chains are putting product mileage on their shelves. Retailers in other countries are following this trend and, in fact, environmentally aware consumers are starting to make choices based on this simple "size of the carbon footprint" differentiator. Such consumers will increasingly drive many aspects of the distribution method based on how they perceive the ecological impact of a purchase.

Consumers may assume that close proximity between a grower and a retailer makes for a greener product. Viewed strictly in terms of mileage this might be correct, but this perspective does not address the total lifecycle of the product. For instance, was the crop grown in the sun (requiring less carbon to produce it) or in a greenhouse (requiring more carbon to produce it)? Such factors complicate the relatively simple calculation highlighted in the previous paragraph regarding the ISD-versus-DSD carbon footprint. Standardization of the calculation, simplifying the representation of a carbon footprint, and clearly identifying the consumer's "green" choices are likely to become prevalent in the near future.

Although price point, brand, and quality continue to be the primary criteria for choosing a product, mileage is likely to become an important criterion. It is important to remember, however, that an accurate understanding of the real green factor of products in the marketplace requires a total green-index that considers the front-end to back-end cycle and the recycling and reuse policies of the producers and distributors.

As the total-green-index grows in importance over the next decade, companies will have to develop the delivery concept that is most sustainable. This decision might be affected by the company's own Corporate Responsibility platform, future legislation by local/central authorities (e.g. only access to city centers in certain timeframes) and consumer perceptions.

Because of this, it is likely that new transportation modes will be developed and implemented. In some European cities dispatch of deliveries in city centre outlets is operated by ordinary light rail in the form of trams rebuilt for transporting goods. Other cities are testing electric and hybrid transportation systems. In all cases the objective is to reduce the number of trucks in the city and minimize the carbon footprint.

Although new technologies will never completely replace human interaction – which is, after all, the critical success factor in DSM – it is likely that some technologies such as webcams and real-time information via the internet will greatly reduce the number of outlet visits by sales representatives.

Growing emphasis on environmental and social issues means that more retailers will demand a distribution concept that complies with their Corporate Responsibility charters and that more consumers will demand that the products they buy come from a "green" supply chain. Suppliers and retailers would be wise to start assessing the environmental impact of their supply chain today in order to be fit for the future – whether they choose ISD, DSD, DSM or a combination of these approaches.

6.6 Smaller Formats, Shorter Cycles? The Role of Geography

Not surprisingly, DSD processes differ subtly in various regions of the world. Some of these nuances may give us a look into the consumer trends of the future that DSD will have to address. These differences are driven by the buying habits ingrained in the particular cultures, their demographics, and/or their geographic circumstances. Japanese consumers, for instance, live in a densely populated country and have relatively small homes and apartments which require small storage and refrigerator size. They are also very focused on quality and freshness, and retailers and producers are aware and cater to these criteria. As a result of these factors, the majority of Japanese consumers tend to purchase their grocery and food supplies in one- to two-day increments. They continue to do so even though Costco and other large "warehouse stores" have entered the market offering larger format packaging and value.

Since the US introduced the convenience store business model to Japan more than 20 years ago, such stores have become one of the most influential entities for food and beverage manufacturers in Japan. For instance, the top three major players such as 7-Eleven, Lawson and Family Marts have more than 27,000 shops nationwide. Some of the business requirements for convenience stores are high; which includes multiple deliveries per day since each convenience store has limited space. And also Japanese consumers are so sensitive for expiration dates. This has also led to close integration with the manufacturers, distributors, and stores which is especially valid for co-promotion to reflect the sell-through data to the food and beverage manufacturers for better production planning. Lessons learned in this type of high turn, high touch environment may lead to success in the consumer shopping experience of the future irregardless of region of the world.

Vending machines have also penetrated many urban and rural areas. There are 5.6 million vending machines in total which represent nationwide revenues of 62 billion USD. Beverages share about 48% and account for 30 billion USD. All the major beverage manufacturers such as Coca-Cola, Kirin and Asahi have their own distribution subsidiaries for vending machines to manage their supply chain by optimizing distribution routes and planning replenishment. Some major companies use mobile phone technology to adapt vending machines to monitor consumption volume per vending machine. That data is synchronized with their logistics systems and linked to their manufacturing sites of parent company.

These trends by consumers in a bellwether country could indicate the future in a larger global sense as consumers become more focused on smaller format, shorter duration buying periods and a demand for fresher, locally produced products. The self-service concept of vending appeals to these types of consumers who dictate, when, where, and how much they will purchase and consume. In some test markets, including Japan, Intelligent Vending is already in place regulating and reporting pricing, sell-through and replenishment needs wirelessly direct to producers and distributors.

Servicing the ever-growing number of vending and self-service locations in ever-smaller formats in shorter replenishment cycles will require DSD to adapt from its traditional route-based approach. It will likely need to become a more dynamic and responsive business process enabled by technology that supports the goal of right product, right price, right time that consumers will demand in the future.

6.7 Getting a Grasp on the Future

The reality of today's multi-trillion dollar food and beverage industry is that success depends on driving down direct production costs by efficient mass production techniques, and on daily commodity-based arbitrage and hedging of key product ingredients. Meanwhile, mass-media marketing must be exploited to its fullest for better return on the marketing dollar. In addition, new markets are being driven by far-reaching geographic sales and the relative ease and convenience of product distribution via a multitude of interchangeable transportation modes. The significant advancements in food and beverage preservative techniques and bottling/packaging improvements further enable today's proto-typical high-volume, mass-market supply chain. Yet despite these modern conveniences and enhancements to basic food and beverage preparation and distribution techniques, over the past ten years we have started to see a reversal in some of these trends back to smaller formats, preference for local – fresh and greener choices among products, and a trend to self-service.

We also see greater awareness among distributors, retailers and producers that the benefits of agility in distribution and the growing social acceptance of smaller-volume, local products typical of DSD-delivered food and beverage products might be extended to most high-volume consumer products such as cosmetics, clothing, and consumer electronics. Potentially the DSD model will evolve into the primary means of small lot size replenishment at many more localized retail points as a convenience to consumers.

Industry leaders of the future will differentiate themselves by providing retail outlets with enhanced services such as extended merchandising and flexible and individualized promotions; in doing so, they will better understand the buying habits of their customers. In addition, organizations that understand their products' positioning and price points in the broader contexts of Corporate Responsibility, ecological/green considerations, and the health and food safety agenda will reap the rewards of both profits and customer loyalty.

References

Grocery Manufacturers Association (GMA) (2005): Driving DSD Supply Chain Efficiencies and Profitability, Washington DC.

Chapter 7
Growth: Supporting Product Distribution

DSD is not a one size fits all distribution model. Because of its high cost, it is particularly important to understand the specific situation in which to use DSD. This chapter extends the understanding. Whereas the previous chapter stressed DSD's market research capabilities, this chapter draws the attention to the simple "distribution" task. The main argument is that there are situations in which DSD is chosen because there are simply no realistic alternatives.

As **Natu of Empresas Polar** shows, emerging markets, like many consumer goods markets in South America, are typical DSD markets. They have a high share of unorganized retail which is dominated by mom and pop shops. These shops offer consumers a limited product range for daily shopping and daily consuming and do not have their own logistics. Manufacturers either invest in DSD or delegate the distribution to institutional distributors/wholesalers. In this environment, DSD allows the manufacturers to keep the distribution under control and to secure higher margins as opposed to the alternative of supplying the organized retailing chains. Unorganized retailing suffers from poor ordering and displays a propensity to do business on a cash basis only. Leaving the distribution to institutional distributors is also not a viable solution since their poor logistics operations cause products to reach the point of sale with only a shortened shelf life. DSD can address most of these issues. In developed markets with efficient retailer driven logistics, DSD primarily supports market research and customer insights. In emerging markets, DSD ensures the bare and fresh availability of products in "the field" and protects higher margins.

Pucelik of PPAS and **Zamora of Movilitas** confirm this argument for a particular industry through examples. The beverage business in the Czech Republic is 80% based on cash deliveries where DSD is particularly helpful. Furthermore, the business profits from a high quota of ad-hoc ordering can actively increase sales.

Certainly, the costs of DSD can become too high. As **Amrit of Wipro Research** explains, the Indian retailing landscape is not ready for DSD because the average volume per shop is too low. In India, shopping is dominated by rural farmers markets. Organized trade is just beginning to emerge. Thus, distributors still dominate the markets. Bypassing the distributors via DSD is the next development step in India.

A. Otto et al., *Direct Store Delivery*,

DOI: 10.1007/978-3-540-77213-2_7,

Chapter 8
Regional DSD – The Latin American Perspective

Vinay Natu

Empresas Polar, 2 da Ave. de los Cortijos de Lourdes, Edificio Centro Empresarial Polar, Caracas, Venezuela 5474, tel.: +58 212 202 3019, fax: +58 212 202 3027, e-mail: vinay.natu@empresas-polar.com

Abstract

DSD as a service model is a traditional way of doing business for a number of consumer goods manufacturers, while representing a large fixed cost base for others which sometimes means no profits. This divergence regarding DSD has taken a winding path towards its maturing, and the debate resurges as customer power shifts take place. This paper reflects on the Latin American perspective, discussing the relevant considerations and issues that contribute to DSD effectiveness, and its evolution. It reviews the intrinsic shopper and customer factors, as well as variations in local/regional and multinational manufacturer perspectives regarding the opportunity and cost implications. As well as the impact that availability of market related information has on DSD management.

8.1 Introduction

DSD's coming of age within the mainstream software industry is indeed a welcome development for those who have been a part of it over the years. The path to this maturing has been a winding one in the different parts of the world where DSD service models have been in operation. This paper reflects on the Latin American perspective, discussing the relevant considerations and issues that contribute to DSD effectiveness, and its evolution.

8.1.1 DSD's Evolution in Latin America

Latin America's commercial world over the recent past has been dominated by distributors with the occasional yet highly emblematic DSD service models (e.g. brewers, carbonated beverages, salty snacks and tobacco). Many consumer goods

A. Otto et al., *Direct Store Delivery*,

DOI: 10.1007/978-3-540-77213-2_8,

manufacturers have sought to enjoy the better margins covering mom and pop customers, either directly or predominantly through Distributors. Protectionist legal environments have favored a perpetuation of the distributor model, due to high switching costs, reduction of fixed costs for manufacturers and lack of a viable alternative. The use of DSD as a service model has been preferred by a few industries. Some with high margins to sustain the model, and others with category and consumer consumption needs that made DSD a necessary response. PoS execution and control being the common enabler for both goals.

8.1.2 Customer Make-Up

A diversified customer base is characteristic of the Latin American markets. Organized trade or large retailers today comprise around 50% of the Mexican market, yet coexist with roughly 800,000 mom and pop stores who continue to grow in number. In other words despite the consolidation via these retailers, the small store segment is here to stay, and is a means to serve a large base of consumers while being a source of good margins for manufacturers. This situation repeats itself in a number of the other markets. In Venezuela for instance there are approximately 325,000 small stores which thrive alongside large retailers who make up between 5% to 25% (depending on the categories) of the sales of consumer goods manufacturers (Table 8.1).

Table 8.1 Customers in Latin America

Country	Approximate population	Approximate number of small stores
Colombia	44 million	400.000
Brazil	180 million	1.000,000
Mexico	100 million	800,000
Venezuela	26 million	325,000

This coexistence is based on shopper behavior, particularly amongst those at the bottom of the pyramid. Lower income consumers and shoppers do so frequently, and at neighborhood stores. As an example, a beer shopper may go to the corner store to pick up a large bottle for consumption at home. This very same shopper may go to another neighborhood store later in the day, to socialize and play dominoes with his friends and share a six-pack. More often than not, the store owner is also a friend who lives close by, and gives credit when needed without collateral.

Given the scale of large retailers they have tended to be at distances that require a car or need transportation. This makes access difficult for economic reasons as well as those to do with security concerns, and the physical limitations of carrying a number of bags over distances. Furthermore in a number of cases, these neighborhood small stores tend to be informal and pay no taxes.

The challenge and opportunity then has been to serve this diversified base and meet consumer needs, while surmounting inevitable pressures from large retailers.

8.1.3 Challenges

One of the first challenges is the recognition that there is a large base of consumers who have wants and need serving, that are beyond the obvious and immediate horizon of large retailers. Due to the scarcity of reliable information, identifying the size and segments within this consumer and customer base is a difficult task, and often subject to dismissal for this reason alone. Traditional sources such as vendors who sell customer census information are often inadequate and out of date given the shorter life cycles of the smaller stores. The only recourse often is to conduct a census, measuring the variables that interest each manufacturer. Focus groups too help in segmenting consumers.

One approach that has worked involves the creation of an internal group and infrastructure, which is focused on obtaining and maintaining customer information and segmentation. This with the purpose of reviewing customer segments periodically, and monitoring continually the relevance of customer service models (i.e. go-to-market models) works best when it is distinct from the trade marketing group, while being a part of the sales organization. This approach and role is discussed in greater detail towards the end of this paper.

Once past the step of identifying segments of sufficient size and separation, the next challenge stems from choosing the most appropriate means to serve the targeted segments. Within the DSD option, these range from being those that are completely controlled by manufacturers to others that rely on third parties. This is where often tradition and/or risk aversion comes into play, and differences between multinational and local firms are most evident. For the categories mentioned earlier, tradition is most pressing for categories such as tobacco, beverages and snacks, even for multinationals. Often moving away from global execution standards is not an option, and requires overcoming many obstacles.

Controlling in-store execution is a challenge that cuts across categories and service models. For DSD as a model and supported by appropriate software this is an area that has yet to reach its full potential. Some of this has to do with the automation and control orientation towards DSD, as well as a lack of clarity and creativity in how to make this happen.

Hardware and software capital and operational costs are often factors that need to be overcome in the design of DSD models for the range of activities that can be supported and enhanced. While the range is wide, not all the activities create differentiation and/or add value to the manufacturer or customer served.

8.2 DSD Perspectives and Approaches

8.2.1 Global Multinational

Global brands and consistent sales execution make for a potent force that drives DSD initiatives. This is a well established driver for categories such as tobacco, beverages and snacks. However for other categories within the Latin American context, adapting these imperatives to locally diverse conditions makes for a creative and often irreverent exercise. Given that multinational headquarters are primarily located in more developed economies, and where organized trade and large retailers have a strong presence, there is frequently little support for dealing with a wide variety of relevant customer segments and particularly those dominated by mom and pop stores.

Furthermore, the higher fixed cost that may be associated with a direct DSD service model makes it a harder sell to headquarters. Which is why distributors become a relatively easy sell, promising some of the benefits of DSD, while providing for a more variable sales cost structure. Undoubtedly, there is a price to be paid in terms of lower visibility and consistency of execution through distributors. Often the greatest creative opportunities lie in devising a low cost direct DSD scheme, that seeks to achieve more consistent and focused sales execution for the categories, while minimizing fixed costs and capital investment.

Clearly a multinational is well positioned to be able to leverage consolidated software and hardware global development and purchasing agreements, as well as their support.

8.2.2 Regional and Local

While free of some of the imperatives of global brand standards, regional companies do have similar standards that need to be met. The difference arises from the fact that regional economies may be more in synch with each other, than in the case of a globally aware multinational. And hence adjustments to service models to meet category and brand needs are better understood by regional players. Regional manufacturers do have certain efficiencies of scale, though they may be less than those for global multinationals.

Local manufacturers are perhaps best able to move quickly and make DSD service model enhancements with changing market conditions. Particularly when it comes to dealing with weaker market conditions, and being able to preserve at least some of the essential elements of the DSD service model. This being preferred to having to make structural changes and migrate from a direct to an indirect service model.

Affecting all are security aspects, particularly for payment methods. The use of cash tends to be the dominant mode, and there is ample room for banks and telephone companies to work in a concerted manner, to implement safer handling of funds via cellular phones or cash cards. The challenge here tends to arise from the fact that a large part of the target population served by small customers, does not have any banking experience or relationship. And view such formalization as increasing their exposure to being taxed by their governments. In addition, there is reluctance amongst the banks and telephone companies to work together in the hope of greater success and profit in going-it alone.

In a number of cases, small customers are willing to make direct deposits to manufacturers bank accounts for credit invoices due. But this is a minority, and does not work for all categories.

8.3 The Evolution of Organized Trade and its Implications for DSD

8.3.1 Evolution of Organized Trade

A growing presence of organized trade has been a trend that has accompanied the growth of Latin American economies over the past decade. There was undoubtedly a shift in consumption towards this retail format, as purchasing power increased. This led manufacturers to lower their focus on the traditional mom and pop stores that were the mainstay earlier on, and develop capabilities to manage the inherently more complex relationship with organized trade. The pendulum had indeed swung the other way.

However, this seemed to reach a plateau towards the early 2000s, and the trend slowed to a crawl if not a standstill. Argentina at one end of the spectrum saw close to 70% of its consumption move towards organized trade and hold, while Mexico and Brazil seemed to be stuck at around the 50% mark. Furthermore, manufacturer margins came under real pressure due to the intense negotiations with organized trade. An example of this was the increasing reliance on back margins to bolster the bottom lines of retailers, while manufacturers tried to steer more spending towards consumer programs and initiatives.

In essence manufacturers have begun to discover the downside of putting all their eggs into the organized trade basket. This has led to some reflection on how to segment the diverse array of customers, and seek out creative ways in which to serve them and consumers.

8.3.2 Centralized Reception

To minimize shelf stock-out, centralized reception of manufacturer shipments has been growing in popularity for retailers. This allows them to ensure that each retail outlet receives the required quantity of each item, based on close tracking of shelf inventory and sell-out patterns. In Latin America, this has been the objective as well, however it has tended to be used more for extracting margin concessions from manufacturers. Furthermore in relevant categories, management of items whose expiry dates ("good for consumption till") are short, has led retailers to demand greater concessions to cover higher losses for stale product. In other words, manufacturers find themselves incurring higher costs, for reducing retailer shelf stock-outs through centralized shipments.

DSD service models are a good counterbalance and alternative to these pressures, as they enable a close follow-up of shelf movement, as well ensure the freshest product being available to the shopper.

8.3.3 Category Specific Considerations

There are inherent reasons where the DSD service model remains the one of choice for certain categories, and makes them less prone to the centralized reception trend. As mentioned earlier, "sell by" dates for certain categories are critical, and manufacturers are loath to leave this rotation of inventory to the whims of retailers' consolidated shipments to their outlets. The DSD service model allows for rotation amongst outlets by manufacturers, ensuring that there are very few "stales".

Furthermore, merchandizing needs for high rotation items make it essential that manufacturers rely on the DSD service model. This allows them to adjust shelf space inventory according to demand on a very frequent basis, and adjust store orders and inventory as well. Examples from the dairy and bakery industry are highly illustrative of this.

Sometimes categories have highly seasonal patterns, and this makes it imperative for a rapid refreshment of shelf inventory.

8.3.4 Channel Strategies

Given the wide array and changing consumption and shopping behaviors, across varied customer types it is essential that manufacturers constantly monitor and adjust channel strategies.

Channel strategies for manufacturers in Latin America implies questioning their status quo of how they "go to market", in ways that are independent yet cognizant of the volatility of some of the markets. This gets more pronounced for some categories as compared to others. The focus here is on looking for a balance between maintaining profitability and growth of existing channels, and developing new modes of serving consumers where clear benefits are delivered to them, as well as for manufacturers and the clients they serve. Often the benefits of improved service are not visible nor appreciated by the intended audience, and it is in the interest of manufacturers to monitor the relevance of their service models, even through insufficient point of sale information.

These strategies can swing between those inclined towards a low cost approach for mass market reach, or others who focus on some very specific segments, to those that customize their strategies depending on the priority of their segments of interest. Including DSD service models in their portfolio of options is natural to some, while prohibitively expensive for others. What is certain is that this multi-fronted approach makes for a more complex operating environment, where technology plays a stellar role in achieving and maintaining focus.

8.3.5 DSD Strengths in a Changing Channel Mix

DSD service models, when utilized judiciously, offer a number of advantages that need to be taken into consideration by manufacturers.

Without attempting to provide an exhaustive list, some of the salient advantages are as follows:

- Physical presence at the point of sale provides an excellent means to read on a regular basis the true sell-out of a manufacturer's products. With technology to assist in this reading they can truly leverage this presence. This frequent reading by customer enables a better understanding of market dynamics, which would otherwise be subject to revisions on traditional monthly cycles in synch with financial closings. In Latin America, systems still have a strong internal control bias, where inventory reconciliation wins over visibility of product rotation
- Successful point of sale execution to serve a wide array of consumption and shopping behaviors, across varied customer types is the cornerstone of a successful go to market strategy. DSD service models are effective in bringing about consistency in this execution
- In the developing and sometimes volatile economies in Latin America, where product supply can be an important variable, simply having stock available for sale on the truck can make for a potent value proposition
- Given the important presence of mom and pop stores within the Latin American customer mix, DSD service models provide a counterbalance to the pressures

of organized trade. Allowing manufacturers to be creative and proactive in providing innovative solutions to consumers, with often a higher degree of co-operation from this small store segment.

8.4 Economic Considerations in Latin America

Similar to other emerging markets, Latin America has had a history of volatility and growth. It is over the last 5 years that there has been a more consistent pattern with lower inflation rates and GDP growth. With the leftward slant in some countries, there are dark clouds on the horizon once again. Particularly since buoyant oil and commodity revenues are misconstrued to be a result of sound economic policies. How does one then plan for, invest in and maximize the value of DSD service models in this type of environment?

8.4.1 Volatility

Volatility in Latin America manifests itself in many ways. Disposable income being the source of most consumption is to begin with a factor that affects some categories more than others. Reactions to variability in disposable income have been diverse geographically speaking. Those along the coastal areas with temperate climates tend to enjoy the boom times, with less regard for saving for a rainy day. Whereas those in the mountains who tend to endure harsher weather, are more conscious of the need for restocking the cupboard.

In addition, electoral spending has a cyclical effect that is more pronounced with populist governments. As such revenues tend to swing, with higher fixed costs becoming a burden for maintaining flexibility. The challenge then is to build flexibility as a bulwark against volatility.

8.4.2 Indirect or Direct Service Models

In the face of such volatility, for a number of multinational manufacturers safety wins over developing the business opportunity. This typically implies a reliance on indirect service models. These range from Distributors (exclusive and non-exclusive), to wholesalers who are attended by a dedicated sales force or by the Distributors themselves.

Regional and local manufacturers on the other hand tend to depend on indirect service models, due to capital and scale constraints. Their choice of direct DSD service models tends to be steadfast over time, and once set up a switch to an indirect mode is rarely made. The competitive advantage gained from direct service models, is addictive, and manufacturers look to maintain it by cutting costs. It is only in a financial crisis or similar difficulties that cause manufacturers to make a drastic change in their go to market strategies.

In certain markets due to overly restrictive labor regulations, manufacturers have relied on one-man distributors to achieve some of the benefits of DSD execution, while at the same time retaining the variability of selling expenses. Often the route to this service model is via a direct approach initially, where execution standards are established, and a subsequent switch to one-man distributors is made with the intention of making selling costs variable.

Hand Held Technology to accompany either model, makes for relatively similar investments, but with very different focus in terms of use. Basic internal controls are desired for both models, but higher order point of sale oriented functions which are a logical extension in direct models, require additional negotiations for the indirect model. Quite often, 'manufacturers' and 'distributors' strategic interests are not aligned, and unless there is such alignment, technology investments can become a tussle that often leaves both parties unsatisfied with their return on investment.

An important aspect of this decision making process, revolves around splitting customer attention from the physical delivery of products. Often this split is treated superficially when it comes to making decisions about service models, and they are viewed as part of the same decision by manufacturers.

8.4.3 Hybrid Models

A combination of indirect and direct service models is often the "middle of the road" approach that manufacturers take to mitigate the risks of "going it alone".

This is done by aligning costs to consistency and predictability of revenue streams. In other words, a more direct approach is taken where customer segment revenues are more predictable and profitable, whereas an indirect approach is taken when there is high variability of customer revenues.

While this may sound straightforward in practice, it is quite an art form to segment your customers when dependable information is scarce. Often the only way to obtain this information involves conducting a customized census of current and potential customers, and their relevant attributes. This segmentation is crucial to migrating high revenue variability customers (particularly smaller ones) to a more stable stream over a period of time (through increasing portfolio penetration etc.). This may mean a transition over time of customers being served indirectly migrating to a more direct form, with a corresponding increasing in cost. The difficulty in making this transition arises from switching costs, particularly in countries where legislation mandates a high indemnity for severing distributor relationships.

Manufacturers, who are capable of executing this balancing act, will find themselves with a competitive advantage that is effective and long lasting.

8.5 Vision for the Future – DSD in Latin America

Thus far trends that characterize market conditions in the developed world, have dominated forums/literature of different types. Prominent is the case of managing complex relationships with organized trade. Business leaders amongst manufacturers have thus been inclined favorably towards them, while attempting to reconcile the differences between local realities and strategies that derive from these trends. In other words, local realities often are at odds with these trends that get a large share of space in various forums.

In the years to come DSD as an option will be revisited more often than in the past for many reasons:

- Real growth opportunities in the small store segments, particularly with convenience and total cost of purchase being important considerations
- Counterbalance to the influence of organized trade
- Capability to execute effectively the growing pipeline of innovations in products and services being created for shoppers and consumers.

8.5.1 Overcoming Customer Information Obstacles

The paucity of reliable customer information for smaller stores in Latin America, is a given and needs to be addressed with imagination and thought. Achieving success in this effort is vital to exploit the opportunity that exists. Roles within manufacturers' commercial organizations will have to created or adjusted to allow for this to assume the necessary importance.

There are incipient efforts by industry associations in some countries (GS1 in Colombia), to increase this visibility and order. It is in the interest of manufacturers to foster success in these endeavors. However, for the majority of the countries, the onus is on individual manufacturers to conceive and implement an internal infrastructure and field sales support process to achieve this visibility. As a consequence for manufacturers, a role will be needed to oversee the upkeep of this asset, and be constantly focused on updating effectiveness of service models (DSD and others), in synch with a changing customer mix. Such a role rarely exists in current commercial organizations, and is a combination of capabilities that may be present today in sales administration groups and other sales functions. In other words a "Go-To-Market" conscience needs to be built, that is based on constantly updated and improving customer information.

More often than not typical commercial organizations do not contemplate such a role. It is becoming increasingly apparent that current oversight of customer information and service models is insufficient in the face of the growing opportunity in the small store segment in Latin America.

8.5.2 Evolving Role of IT

IT solutions have ranged from transaction control to sophisticated organized trade account planning and tracking. However, the much touted CRM software functionality has been less than effective in its configuration for the DSD world. There seems to be some white space in so far as how to conceive of imaginative solutions and options that takes elements of CRM and make them relevant and efficient for the high transaction rate world of DSD.

Furthermore, there is need for an imaginative conception and creation of a customer data base required for small store customers, which fits within the integrated world of enterprise systems. Particularly when information sources can vary by customer segment and country.

Chapter 9
Regional DSD: The Business Case for a Czech Brewer

Pavel Pucelik[1] and Alberto Zamora[2]

[1]SD&M Business Systems Manager, Plzeňský Prazdroj, a.s. U Prazdoje 7, CZ-304 97 Plzň, tel.: +420 724 617 645, e-mail: pavel.pucelik@pilsner.sabmiller.com

[2]Movilitas GmbH, Käfertalerstraße 164, D-68167, Mannheim, tel.: +49(0) 170 287 6614, e-mail: alberto.zamora@movilitas.com

Abstract

PPAS is a beverage producer in the Czech Republic. Although PPAS has implemented a standard ERP backend solution for DSD-specific IT support, the execution of the tour itself remained paper based. Struggling with the cost-intensive paper-driven DSD processes, PPAS decided to enhance to a mobile DSD solution to enable automation and to overcome the inefficiencies. In this section, PPAS shows how the respective steps of the classical DSD process are taking place today, and how this will be changed after the go-live of the mobile DSD solution which is currently in implementation.

9.1 Introduction

Plzeňský Prazdroj, a.s. (PPAS) located in the town of Plzeň (Pilsen), Czech republic, as a part of SAB Miller group is the producer of one of the world's most famous beers – Pilsner Urquell. Since 1842, its golden color gave the name to the whole beer type – Pilsner. PPAS runs three breweries in Czech republic, producing seven brands of alcoholic beers - Pilsner Urquell, Gambrinus, Radegast, Kozel, Master, Primus and Klasik and one brand of non-alcoholic beer – Radegast Birell. PPAS does not sell only their own products, but also distributes a wide portfolio of wines and spirits. The business process is based on Direct Store Delivery (DSD) for most of the customers including key store chains. The annual sales of PPAS of over 8 million hectoliters, makes PPAS the largest producer in the Czech market with almost 50% market share.

A. Otto et al., *Direct Store Delivery*,

DOI: 10.1007/978-3-540-77213-2_9,

9.2 The Role of DSD Driver at PPAS: DSD in Figures

PPAS owns 13 distribution centers across the Czech Republic and uses a fleet of 450 trucks for secondary distribution, increasing in number during the peak season. PPAS distributes 110 beer products (SKU's), handles 80 empties (most of these empties are returnable with deposit price) and 300 spirits. PPAS delivers over 7,000 deliveries per day with an average of 10 items per delivery and serves over 20,000 outlets on a daily basis. Over 80% of all deliveries are paid cash, which is fundamental to understand part of the complexity of the DSD process.

It is obvious that the role of the DSD driver is fundamental and business critical for PPAS. A delivery driver does on average seven deliveries (stops) per tour and drives between one and three tours per truck per day. PPAS delivers 5 days a week, 6 days in peak season. An employee in the delivery driver role, as it is defined today, delivers presold deliveries, handles empties and collects cash from customers.

Although the process may look simple, the figures above reveal the complexity and criticality of the distribution process.

9.3 Current State, Current Paints and Future Outlook

Given the criticality of the DSD process for PPAS, the backend DSD solution was implemented from the very beginning as a part of the SAP R/3 ERP system some years ago. The current SAP DSD backend solution supports most of the DSD business processes starting from the planning to the final settlement and supports all 7,000 daily deliveries.

However, the execution of the tour itself is still a paper based process. Today all shipments are planned in the SAP R/3 backend, then the shipment documents are printed out (containing all deliveries) and the printouts are handed over to the delivery driver, who starts the tour with "pro forma" invoices and makes his notes on the same printouts, which by the end of the day will be returned back to the back office staff, who enters the information manually in the SAP DSD backend for final settlement.

Besides the obvious duplication of efforts by entering the same data two times (on paper by the driver and in the system by the back office staff) and the error prone paper based process (misunderstanding of hand writing, lost of papers etc.), PPAS has clearly identified a business critical issue that justifies the automation of the DSD execution process via mobile devices: (1) the flexibility to modify pre-sold deliveries and (2) to create invoices ad-hoc, offline at the customer's site based on the adjusted delivery.

Today, and due to the fact that most deliveries are cash deliveries, the delivery driver has to collect the payments from the customers. To be able to collect the cash the delivery driver needs to leave the invoice printout at the customer with the details of the delivered quantities, prices and empties on it. To be able to do this, the delivery driver takes with him preprinted "kind of pro forma invoices", which he cannot change on the customer side except the returned empties quantity. Unexpected changes in the delivery quantities lead to inaccurate preprinted invoices. In these quite regular situations, the delivery driver has two options: to convince the customer to accept the delivery without adjustments or not to deliver at all and return back to the distribution center. This rigidity in the invoice and collections process is a large business problem in a company that operates 450 trucks per day, delivering more than 7,000 deliveries.

Therefore, the future outlook of the DSD process at PPAS is the implementation of the mobile DSD solution to enable automation and to eliminate the issues described above.

9.4 From a Paper Based DSD to a Mobile Supported DSD Process

PPAS shows in the description below, how the individual steps of the classical DSD process are taking place today, and how this will be changed after the SAP mobile DSD solution goes live (currently in implementation).

9.4.1 Route Planning and Truck Load

The whole sales and distribution process in PPAS starts with pre-selling activities. There are over 250 sales representatives equipped with mobile devices visiting the outlets to create sales orders. The mobile solution has been implemented based on mobile sales force automation using SAP CRM functionality in 2007.

The sales orders are replicated from the mobile application into the backend CRM and R/3 system during the day and the route planning and optimization can start. In general, PPAS operates in 24 h delivery time with some 48 h exceptions. There is a batch run to create deliveries in R/3 where one sales order results in one delivery. The route and truck planning shown in Fig. 9.1 can be done either directly in SAP R/3 using standard route planning functionality in the logistic execution module, or via an external optimization tool. PPAS uses the software "Plantour" that interfaces with SAP R/3, and calculates the best truck load split and itinerary for each delivery vehicle. The result of both approaches are shipments created in SAP R/3 with a stop sequence, a truck license plate per shipment and a planned time of each customer stop. The dispatcher at the distribution center can still adjust the shipments manually. Then the documents needed for loading the truck at the warehouse are being printed and the load is usually done over night. After the implementation of the mobile DSD solution this process will stay the same, since it is already fully automated through the SAP DSD backend functionality.

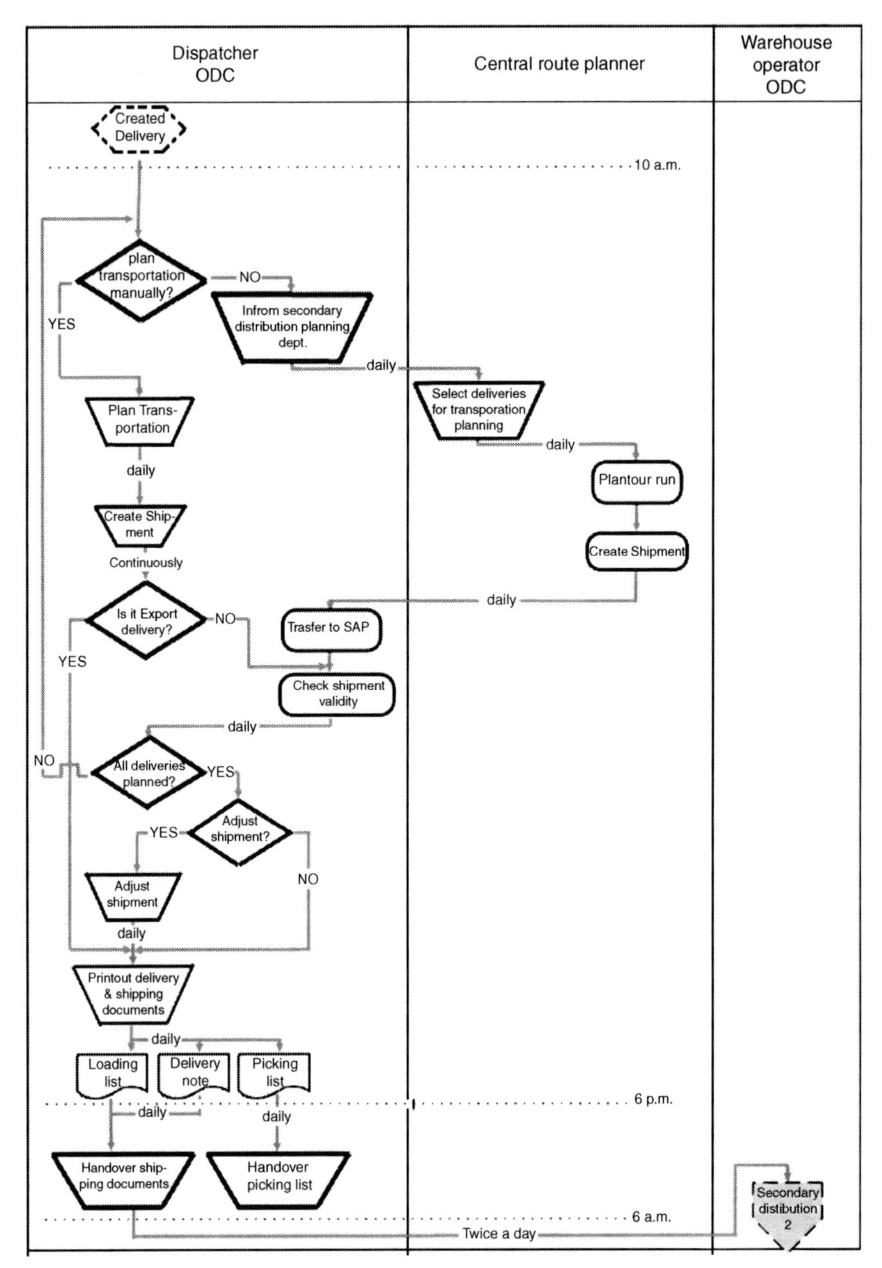

Fig 9.1 DSD process (1)

9.4.2 Check-Out

Before the shipment starts, the driver together with the warehouse operator checks the load and both sign off the loading list. Then the driver receives all other documents like itinerary, delivery notes and invoices for each customer on his route.

The check-out procedure (shown in Fig. 9.2) is done at the gate by the security staff. If the actual load corresponds with the document the gate checker confirms the check-out in the SAP R/3 system. The inventory movements are posted for all goods in the load and the truck goes on route to deliver goods and pick up empties.

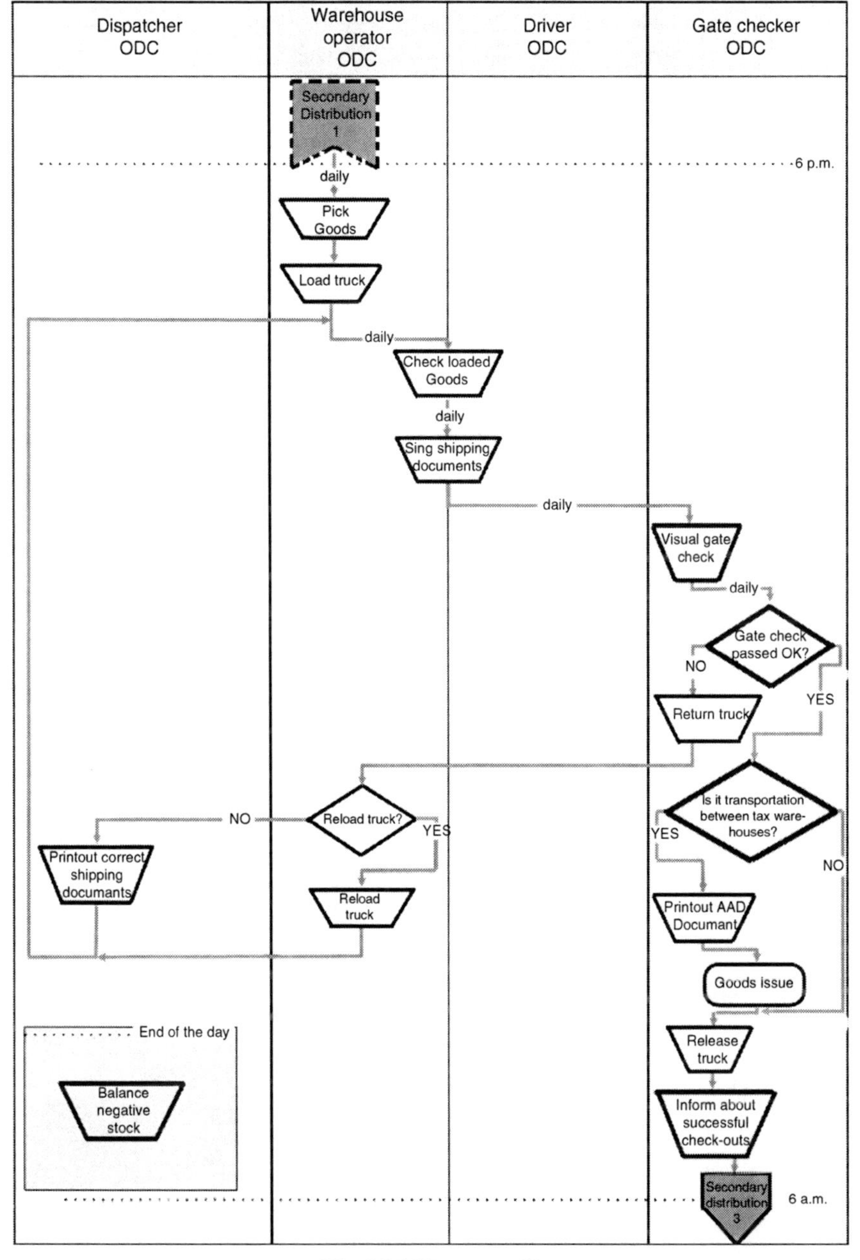

Fig. 9.2 DSD process (2)

After the mobile implementation this process will speed up, since the handover of documents to the driver will only happen within the first months as a backup solution. The driver will have all the information on the PDA at the check out. The checker will also save time, since he will not have to access the SAP R/3 floor computer to confirm the check out of the single truck. Instead, the checker will confirm the check out via a digital signature on the mobile device of the truck driver. This functionality on the PDA will be password protected, so that only the checker can confirm the check out.

9.4.3 Delivery Execution Process

There are usually agreed days and time windows for each customer for delivery. The truck scheduling has to reflect these times. Most of the customers are informed via SMS when exactly the truck will arrive and, if the delivery is paid in cash, and about the estimated amount to be paid.

After arrival the driver drops off the goods as per delivery note, picks returnable empties and collects cash. Empties and cash need to be written on the delivery note or invoice and have to be signed off by both driver and customer.

9.4.4 Empties

Since most of the products contain returnable packaging, all deliveries have to be planned including empties and also the space for returning the empties has to be allocated on the vehicles. In general, the volume of returned empties is assumed to equal the volume of deliveries, which makes the truck planning a little easier.

After the implementation of the mobile solution this process will be automated. The driver will be able to enter empties on the mobile device (today, the empties adjustments are written down manually on the delivery papers) and include the returned empties in the final customer invoice, generated ad hoc in the mobile device. It is even planned that the driver has a full empties balance for each customer on the PDA. This would give the driver and the customer 100% transparency of the empties management.

9.4.5 Cash

As it was mentioned above, 80% of the deliveries are paid cash at the customer's premises. The biggest challenge is to calculate the final amount to be paid. The driver, of course, sees the price on the invoice or valuated delivery note, respectively. However, he has to deduct the deposit from the returnable empties and returned full goods and, what is causing most of the issues, he has to calculate the correct VAT. Currently there is no automation in this process and drivers work only with pre-printed documents and pocket calculators writing the quantity of returnables and the final amount by hand. This can obviously lead to errors in the final price calculation and poor, error prone handwriting.

After the implementation of the mobile solution this will be the major release for the PPAS line of business. The driver, once all the items have been delivered and the empties are collected, will be able to automatically recalculate the final price of the delivery and to generate ad hoc a fully accurate invoice or delivery note, including taxes.

9.4.6 Check-In

Returning to the distribution center, the driver has to summarize all confirmed delivery notes and cash. Upon arrival at the gate the returned load is checked by the security staff and the actual quantity of products and empties is confirmed.

The cash is handed over to the cash desk and the goods and returnables are unloaded at the warehouse. Each operation is noted on the loading list. The delivery documents together with the loading list are then handed over to the settlement office.

After the implementation of the mobile solution this process will be accelerated, since the handover of documents to the check-in clerk will only happen within the first months (as a backup solution to the mobile solution). The checker will confirm all the reports and route summaries on the PDA of the delivery driver via a digital signature. No notes on the loading list will be needed any more.

9.4.7 Route Settlement

The settlement clerk has to re-type the actuals from the delivery documents into the SAP R/3 system. This is one of the most critical steps in the DSD process. It usually happens late in the evening and there is a large number of shipments needed to be processed in a very short time.

Using backend DSD functionality of SAP R/3 in version 4.7 PPAS faced several issues. The settlement cockpit is not a simple environment for entering the shipment and delivery actuals. It is difficult to navigate due to the large amount of information that needs to be entered, which increases the risk of losing data in the case of trivial errors.

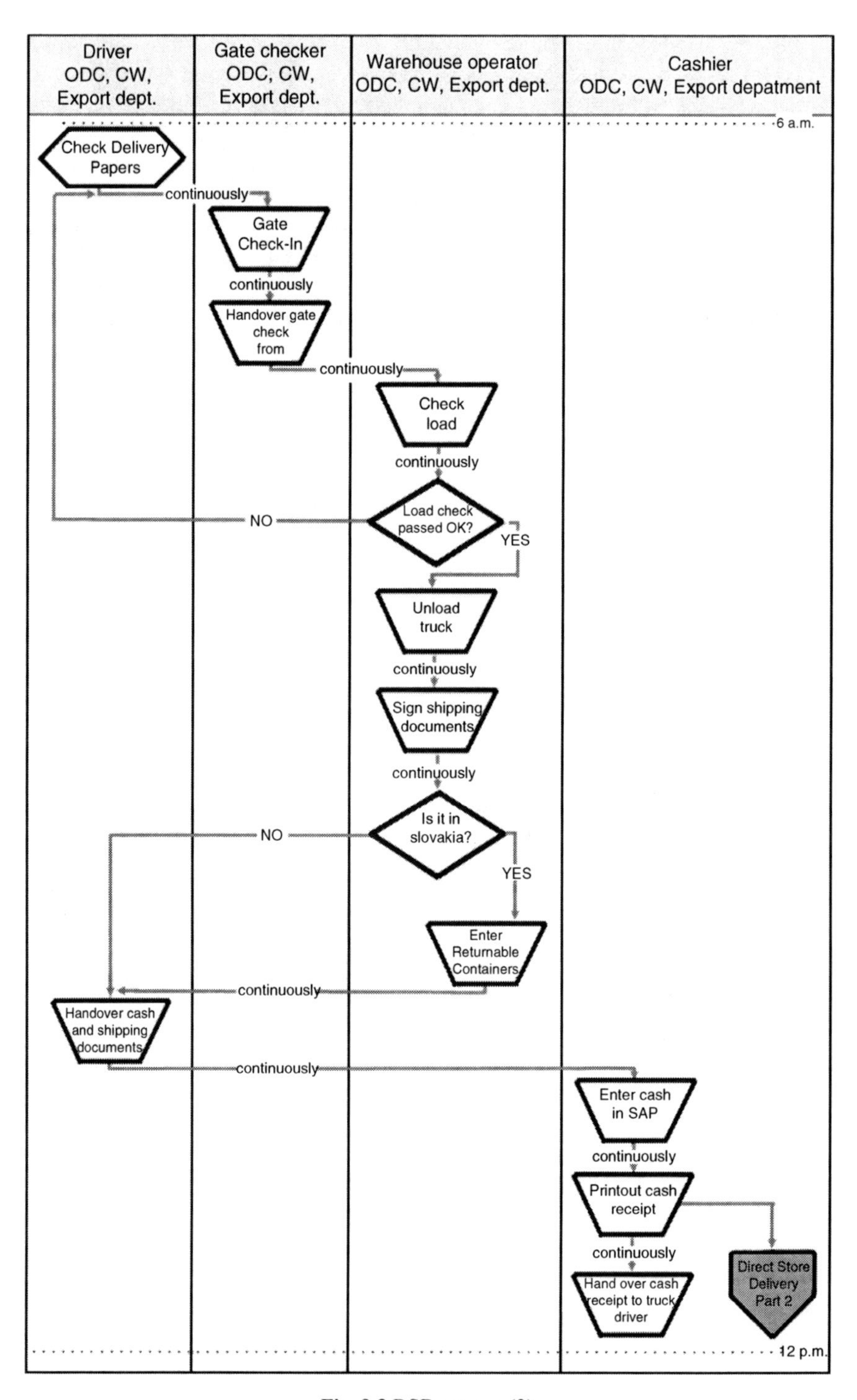

Fig. 9.3 DSD process (3)

The main problem identified during the SAP R/3 DSD implementation has been that most of the errors are discovered by the system only when the settlement posting is triggered, which is too late for additional corrections. As a part of the ramp-up partnership during the SAP R/3 implementation, PPAS together with SAP AG had to build and adjust a fast entry screen. Checks and restrictions have been built in to prevent users from making errors. Now, users can either not perform the erroneous action or there is a check to discover a solution early enough to enable a quick fix.

After the implementation of the mobile solution the settlement process will stay the same, since this process is already fully automated through the SAP DSD cockpit backend functionality. However, what will be 100% automated and will result in a significant benefit for the business, will be the automation of the data entry in the system. The delivery driver will synchronize the data captured during the tour execution to the SAP DSD cockpit and the settlement clerk will focus on checking the information coming from the trucks, rather than on reentering it again from hand written driver papers. PPAS expects a major decrease in the number of errors and efforts invested in the error handling process for the 7,000 delivered deliveries.

9.4.8 Final Settlement Posting and Invoicing

The final settlement for each shipment is then posted in the settlement cockpit. The posting triggers the background process, which posts the inventory movements and releases the order for billing of all delivered sales orders.

The actual billing run is scheduled as a sequence of background jobs. Since there are many documents being processed it has to run over night due to system resources.

After the implementation of the mobile solution the final settlement posting and invoicing processes will stay the same, since those processes are already fully automated through the SAP DSD cockpit backend functionality.

9.4.9 Sending the Invoice Versus Billing on Premise

There is a clear gap in the above described process. It has been mentioned that the cash customers receive the final tax invoice during the visit and that the invoices are created over night. Where is the truth?

The process as supported by the standard SAP R/3 system is based on an invoice creation after the final route settlement posting and on sending the invoices to the customers subsequently. This, however, is an expensive and inconvenient process for PPAS and also for most customers. Therefore PPAS had to find a solution how to be able to give the customers the final invoice during the delivery visit. This process obviously will be radically simplified after the introduction of the mobile solution.

Another requirement came from legislation stating that all tax documents must be created with sequential numbering with no gaps in the numbers and this number has to identify the tax document in both vendor's and customer's general ledgers. To fulfill this requirement PPAS developed its own functionality called "Software Cash Register". It has been certified by legal authorities and it ensures not only the sequential numbering, but also that no delivery note used as a tax document can be changed after it has been printed.

The consequence of this functionality is that no cash delivery can be changed for whatever reason. The only legal approach is to cancel the whole delivery using again the cash register for cancellation documents and create a new set of delivery notes and invoices and send it via mail. Although this is a time consuming and inconvenient process not only for PPAS, but also for the customers, this requirement needs to be met due to legal compliance reasons. The mobile solution will also support this process as it is described here.

9.5 Improving the Customer Service with Mobile DSD

Some years ago, the entire DSD process was mainly a manual task with huge efforts involved in keeping operations transparent and compliant with legislation. At that time PPAS decided to implement SAP DSD functionality as a part of the entire SAP R/3 introduction. This step yielded an enormous impact on the DSD operation. From a primarily manual process, DSD became semi automated, at least all the backend related task: from shipment preparation and tour planning to the final settlement, posting and invoicing.

Now, after several years of experience with the DSD backend process and with the confidence that the backend process is completely adopted and operational, is the time to proceed with the next step in the IT roadmap of PPAS. The objective is clear: from a semi automated DSD process to a fully automated process with zero errors.

To achieve this target, PPAS has decided to implement the mobile DSD functionality of SAP R/3. The aim of this project is to automate the DSD execution process, which means to equip all delivery drivers with handhelds and printers. This will enable the driver to record the actual drop quantities with all possible changes. Also the empties and returns picked will be recorded and the final price will be calculated in the handheld. The customer will have a chance to review the final documents, sign it off on the handheld screen and the invoice will then be printed and given to the customer. This will eliminate the first set of potential errors that PPAS is currently suffering.

After check-in the data from the handheld will be uploaded back to the SAP DSD backend system automatically, without any user interaction. The uploaded data, together with the cash entered by the cashier based on actual amount and with the empty quantities recorded at the warehouse will be the base for the final route settlement. The settlement clerk will then only confirm the data in the settlement cockpit and post the final settlement. Hence, PPAS will get rid of manual data entry and possible errors made during the re-typing.

PPAS strongly believe that the mobile solution will help the company to have the DSD process more efficient and reliable. The reliable and transparent process will improve the customer service and also the customer satisfaction. And a satisfied customer is the best partner for any business.

Chapter 10
Distributing Consumer Products in India – The DSD Context

Somjit Amrit*

General Manager and Global Head – Consumer Goods Practice, Wipro Research Cell for Consumer Packaged Goods Industry, Wipro Technologies, 475-A, Old Mahabalipuram Road, Sozhananganallur, Chennai 600041, India, tel.:+91 44 42093001,
e-mail: somjit.amrit@wipro.com

Abstract

DSD is a business process that is more prevalent in the western countries. In India, the retail industry is shifting rapidly from unorganized to organized retailing. With the rapid growth of organized retailing in India, the retail companies and the manufacturers of consumer goods are beginning to understand the value of a business process such as DSD. This article is an attempt to make the reader understand and appreciate the nuances behind the distribution processes followed in the retailing ecosystem in India and to understand the DSD relevance in this market.

10.1 Introduction

Extensive reforms such as easing of capital controls, liberalizing equity pricing, and creation of a regulatory authority (Securities and Exchange Board of India) have been instrumental in fuelling the Indian economy. Retailing is expected to be the next big thing in India after Information Technology & Outsourcing. There has been a visible shift in the Indian retail scenario. It is moving from unorganized to organized retailing. DSD is a term that is becoming increasingly popular in the retail sector, especially for large retail stores and chains because DSD is associated with providing great service.

Moving from unorganized to organized means moving from village fairs and weekly markets over neighborhood stores to supermarkets and shopping malls, offering better products (quality, assortment, availability, uniqueness), affordable prices and better service (location, in-store ambience, customer tight to customers. Supermarkets, Hypermarkets, Departmental Stores, Specialty Stores, Discount Stores and Convenience Stores are all modern day retail stores that are making inroads in India.

A. Otto et al., *Direct Store Delivery*,
DOI: 10.1007/978-3-540-77213-2_10, © Springer-Verlag Berlin Heidelberg 2009

10.2 Indian Retail Sector: Some Facts & Figures

India's growing middle class with its increasing purchasing power is indulging in conspicuous consumption. The opportunity areas are many and the scope is immense if the retailers use modern methods, or manufacturers create new distribution models.

The increasing importance of India's growing economy can broadly be summarized through the following facts and figures:

- India is predicted to be the fifth largest consuming economy by 2025 (McKinsey, 2007)
- Indian middle class is expected to grow from 50 million to 583 million in 2025 with more disposable income with them (Farrel and Beinhocker 2007)
- Currently India's population is 1.1 billion out of which 70% is less than 36 years old resulting in a huge and young consumer base. Given the increasing literacy rates, higher disposable incomes, awareness levels are high, choices have multiplied and expectations for services and quality have grown
- Indian retail industry is largely fragmented. Most of the Indian retail stores are small 'Mom & Pop' stores (floor space less than 500 ft^2) and they are located near residential neighborhoods
- Organized retailing in India is projected to grow at the rate of about 37% in 2007 and 42% in 2008 and by 2010 it would be around $45 billion (Nath, 2007)
- According to *Indian Retail Report 2007* – in the calendar year 2006 organized retail business was worth $12.4 billion which was 4.6 % of $270 billion Indian retail industry
- Food & Grocery sector with 77% of the retail business forms the largest block of the Indian retail market. Clothing & apparel sector comes next with 7%.

10.2.1 Classification of Major Indian Retail Players – Some Examples

The Indian retail market is undergoing transformation. This transformation has brought in new formats of retailing applicable to the Indian context. The following table (Table 10.1) illustrates the major Indian retailers and the formats they operate.

Table 10.1 Major Indian retail players (Nath, 2007)

Major Indian Retail Players	Apparel & Accessories	Discount Stores	Hypermarkets	Food & Grocery	Specialty Stores
Future Group	Pantaloons	Big Bazaar	Central	Food Bazaar	-
TATA's Trent Ltd.	West Side	-	Star India Bazaar	-	Time wear-Titan
Raheja Group	Shopper's Stop	-	Hypercity	-	Crossword
RPG Group's Spencer	-	-	Spencer's Hyper	Food World	Music World
Reliance Retail Ltd.	-	-	-	Fresh & Select	-

10.3 Distribution Process in India

In order to describe the importance of DSD in India it is essential to understand the different distribution processes in the country. Basically, four major distribution strategies are relevant in this context and are illustrated in the following figure (Fig. 10.1):

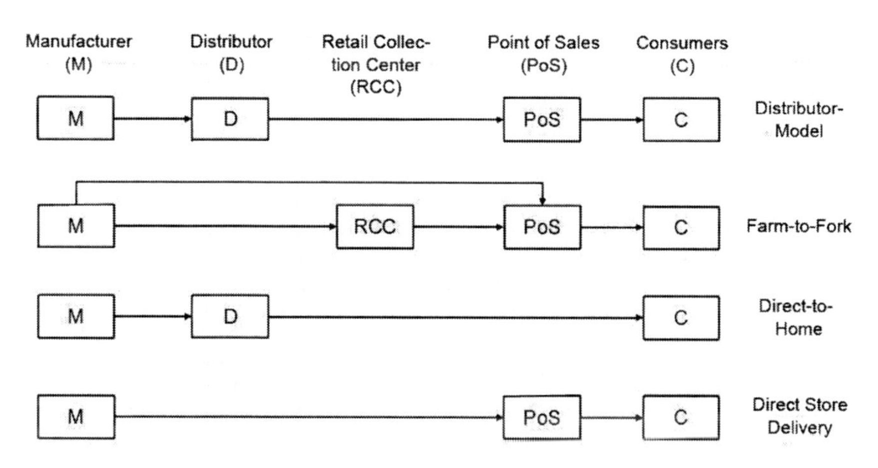

Fig. 10.1 Various distribution processes prevalent in India

Based on this, the section below describes the distribution process in some of the evolving markets in India. Beverages, Home and Personal Care (HPC) and Dairy are taken as examples.

Table 10.2 gives a brief snapshot of the size, current scenario, distribution network and future trends of the industry segments – Beverages, HPC and Dairy.

Table 10.2 Major Indian industries – present and future scenario (IBEF 2007)

Industry segments	Beverages (Carbonated Soft Drinks)	HPC	Dairy (Milk)
Size	284 million crates a year. US$1 billion Annual Growth 7–8%	US$4 billion Annual Growth 15–20%	Milk Production – 86.8 million tons Value – US$45 billion Annual growth 5%
Current Scenario	Market is highly seasonal. Market is predominantly urban with 75% market share. Rural areas contribute to 25% market share.	More emphasis on herbal and natural products. Indian cosmetic space is growing with mergers and acquisitions and entry of multinationals.	The share of organized sector is small. Private and government cooperative sector 15% Unorganized sector – 85%
Distribution Network	Non DSD – Deliveries to 'Mom and Pop' stores, super market and retail chains in the up-country market. DSD – Distribution to super markets, retail chain and 'Mom and Pop' stores in big cities. DTH (Direct To Home) – For home and institutions, deliveries are through Direct Customer/ Consumer Delivery.	Both DSD and Non DSD methods are followed.	Unorganized sector – Non-DSD process is followed; the consumer has direct and daily contact with the creamery, milkman or farmer. Organized sector: Distribution in the organized sector in India is through DSD. Organized sector comprises of both localized and national companies.
Future trends	Shift on health based drinks, so beverages companies are coming up with newer variants of health drinks.	Indian youth to dictate market trends. Service marketing, such as point-of-sale advice and counseling are future trends.	More and more dairy plants in the public, cooperative and private sectors in India. The organized sector is expected to grow at 6% per annum.

10.3.1 Distributor[1] Process

The distribution network in India is fragmented and makes the penetration of goods difficult. The distribution of products to the 'Mom and Pop' stores and retail outlets is through multiple channels based on the segment of the products, location and volume of sales. The finished goods are moved to a depot or clearing and Forwarding (C&F)[2] warehouse at different locations from the factory. From here the stocks are sold to the distributor.

The figure below (Fig. 10.2) describes the distributor process in the Beverages and HPC industry.

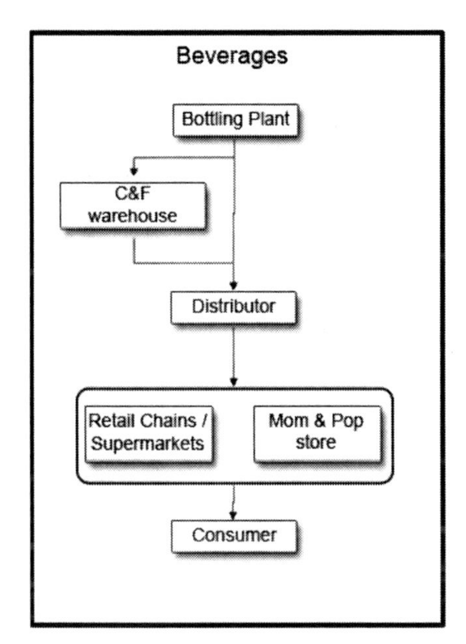

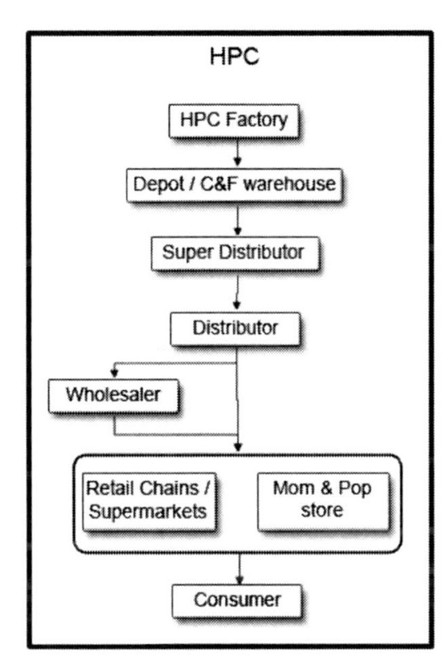

Fig. 10.2 Distributor process in beverages and HPC industry segments

The following are the activities performed by bottler/manufacturer and distributor in the cycle of distribution in Beverages and HPC industry segments:

Beverages

The bottler appoints distributors and customer executives (CE[3]) who are responsible for secondary sales of a territory. The catchments area for each distributor is demarcated and a route is chalked out for delivery of the finished goods at individual outlets. Up country market is divided either geographically or on the basis of business potential, to ensure return on investment (ROI). Both the CE and the distributor are responsible for mining new accounts and increasing sales.

The distributor raises the order through an order form and makes payment through cheque/demand draft. Finished goods are shipped from the bottling plant/ C&F warehouse[4] to the distributor warehouse on receipt of payment. The distributor appoints delivery boy's[5] who visit individual outlets, deliver the goods and service the bill. Delivery boys submit the copy of the bills and cash at the distributor warehouse. The distributor tallies the stocks and updates the data in the computer. The sales report is sent through e-mail or messaging service to the area sales manager (ASM[6]).

HPC

The distribution is classified into the categories primary (Depot or C&F to Distributor) and secondary distribution (Distributor to Retailer). The Territory Sales In-Charge (TSI[7]) and the distributor are appointed by the company and the area of operation is demarcated for each distributor. The Distributor and TSI are responsible for secondary sales of a territory.

The TSI generates a monthly forecast for the Distributor on the 10th, 20th and the 30th of every month. The Distributor raises the order on the company in a 10 days interval based on the feed back from the TSI. The finished goods are invoiced from the depot/C&F warehouse to the distributor. On receipt of the finished goods the distributor makes the payment either in cash or in the stipulated time as agreed with the company. The TSI visits the retail outlet with the salesman who is appointed by the Distributor. The TSI checks for availability of products and discusses the current promotional offers with the retailer. The salesman delivers the stock to the retailer. The retailer pays either in cash or after a given period of time as per contract with the distributor. The distributor keeps a track of the credit account and tallies the stock at the end of the day. The daily sales report is sent to the ASM.

10.3.2 DSD Process

With the current retail boom, the bottler/manufacturer directly delivers stocks to the individual retail outlets eliminating the intermediate distributors. The bottler/manufacturer and the retailer enter into a price contract for a fixed period of time. The order is raised by the retailer and the goods are shipped directly to the retailer's warehouse by the bottler/manufacturer. The distribution process to super markets and retail chain has been explained taking the example of Beverages and HPC industry segments. The distribution process to 'Mom and Pop' stores is explained using the example of Beverages.

10.3.2.1 DSD in Supermarkets and Retail Chains

The supermarkets and retail chains demand the manufacturers on various types of packaging, pricing, promotions, etc. and also expect high service levels and delivery with zero errors. The challenge for the Manufacturer is to supply different size packaging (demand generated by the retailer) and at the same time increase productivity and reduce operating cost. To meet the above challenges and time lines on delivery and in order to leverage the existing facilities the manufacturer aims to utilize the truck space and reduce the turn around time.

The figure below (Fig. 10.3) describes the DSD process in Beverages and HPC industry segments.

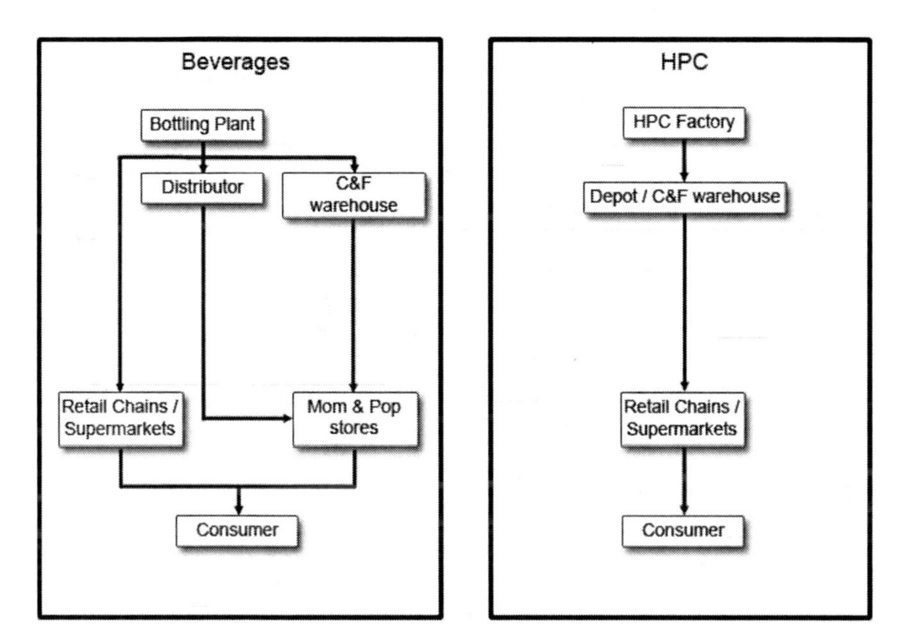

Fig. 10.3 DSD process in Beverages and HPC industry segments

The following describes the activities which are performed by the retailer and bottler/manufacturer in the cycle of distribution in Beverages and HPC industry segments:

Beverages

The indent/purchase requisition is generated by the retailer on the bottler. The bar coded stickers, supplied by the retailer are applied on the products by the bottler. Damage returnable vouchers are generated by the retailer in case of damages.

If the requisition meets the minimum requirement of the smallest full truck load, the indents are serviced within 24 h. The bottler raises the invoice against the retailer. The bottler ensures a shelf life of the product of more than 75% at the time of receipt at the retailer's warehouse. The bottler informs the retailer at least 8–9 days ahead of a promotion. The bottler gives the retailer a fixed credit limit. Once the limit is achieved, further shipments are done only on clearance of payment.

HPC

The indent/purchase requisition is generated by the retailer on the headquarters. The bar coded stickers, supplied by the retailer are applied on the products by the manufacturer. The cost on the damaged goods or shrinkage is either deducted from the same invoice or a debit note is raised on the Manufacturer.

The indents are serviced within 24 h with the minimum load meeting the contractual terms. The depot raises the invoice against the retailer. Manufacturers inform the retailer 1 week ahead of a promotion. The payment depends on the contract between the Manufacturer and retailer.

10.3.2.2 DSD in 'Mom and Pop' Stores

The distribution process of beverages to 'Mom and Pop' stores is through a presale model. In this process the route is visited by the sales executive the previous day and the order is serviced the next day. The following are the activities which are performed in the cycle of distribution.

The sales executive who is appointed by the bottler visits the stores and generates the order form after taking into account the store stock. A structured planning on pricing discounts and promotions is done keeping in mind the store sales objective. Customer sales data (SKU[8] mix) is collected from the outlet. An update on discounts and outstanding credit is taken after which confirmation of stock order is done and order form is filled. At the end of the day the sales executive returns the filled form at the distributor/C&F warehouse.

The distributor/C&F warehouse on receipt of the order form does a stock verification to ensure availability of all the stocks. The stocks are then loaded onto the vehicles for a designated route as per the requirements from the presale visit. The sales data is then entered in the system, which helps the Product Availability Manager (PAM[9]) to plan ahead on demand estimation and Supply Chain Manager for better planning.

The next day, a load check is done by the route agent at the distributor/C&F warehouse before starting on his route. Before delivering the stocks at the store a stock verification of full's/empties is performed, followed by the delivery (fulls) and pick-up tour (empties). A bill is generated and payments are received (cash/cheque) by him. He also manages the product returns.

10.3.4 DSD – A Comparative Analysis (Beverages versus HPC)

In the table below (Table 10.3), a comparison is made between Beverages and HPC industry in implementing DSD. It can be inferred that it is comparatively easier to implement DSD for Beverages as a category than for HPC.

Table 10.3 Comparison of DSD between beverages and HPC industry

Beverages	HPC
Easier implementation due to less diverse product portfolio.	Difficult to implement due to wide product portfolio.
DSD in Beverages will augment the distribution process as lesser number of hands changed in the distribution network.	Multiple layers in HPC distribution network pose a challenge for DSD acceptance.
Early replenishment is critical for beverages, so acceptance rate of DSD as a channel for distribution will be higher.	Replenishment is not as frequent as in the case of Beverages, hence the drive to implement DSD will be lower.

In both types of business some of the challenges faced in implementing DSD in the up-country markets are poor infrastructure, people capability and high attrition rates.

10.4 Prevalent and Emerging Methods of Distribution

This section discusses some of the prevalent and emerging methods of distribution process in India. These could be viewed as different variants of the DSD process from the Indian context. The example for prevalent method of distribution for products like bulk water and milk is through 'Direct-To-Home' (DTH) delivery. The emerging trend in 'Farm-To-Fork' process is through Retailer route (agricultural produce).

10.4.1 Direct to Home (DTH)

The DTH Process involves distribution of commodities to the customer's home directly from the distributor/retailer point.

In India, essential commodities like bulk water and milk are delivered at the door steps of the customers. Due to short shelf life of these commodities, it is essential to distribute these products quickly to the end consumer. For faster delivery and quick replenishment, the operating area of the distributor is localized to a small geographical region. The consumption patterns are predictable enabling the distributors to service the individual customer better.

The diagram below (Fig. 10.4) depicts the DTH Process for bulk water and milk.

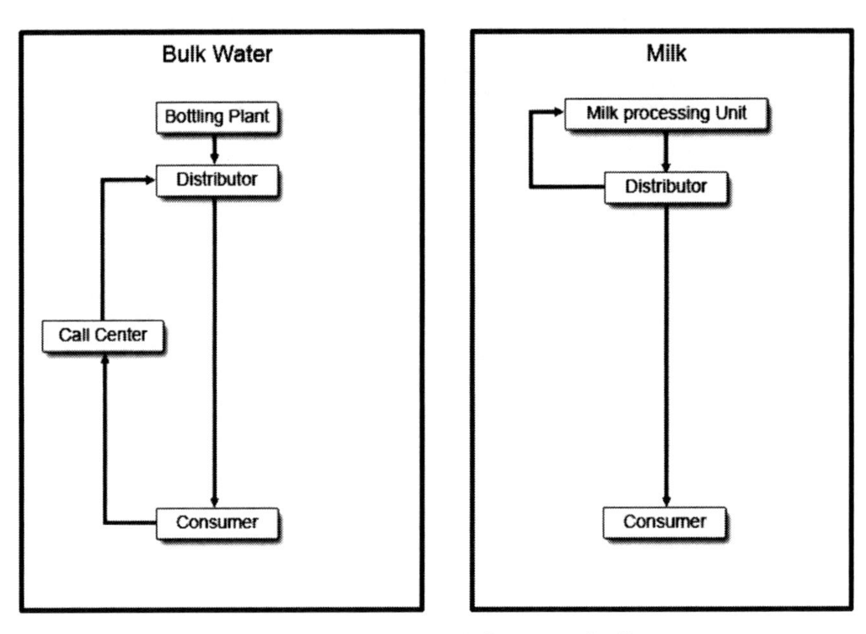

Fig. 10.4 DTH process in bulk water and milk

The DTH process of distribution of bulk water[10] and milk is explained as follows:

Bulk Water

The manufacturer appoints distributor. The area of operation of these distributors is demarcated. The distributors are equipped with hand held devices and the manufacturer enables them with call center support. The customers call the call center and place the order.

The call center executive directs the delivery boy to deliver the stock to the customer. The customer pays by cash on home deliveries and for institutions a delivery voucher is generated which is paid as per the agreement with the institution. The delivery boy with the help of the hand held device generates the bill. The data from the hand held device is uploaded into the computer at the end of the day.

Milk

The company appoints distributors and the area of these distributors are demarcated. The distributors have refrigerated storage facility. The customer contacts the distributor just once for daily delivery.

The distributor appoints delivery boys to do the delivery. The delivery boys distribute the milk based on the order. This delivery is made to individual houses. The payments are collected on a monthly basis by the distributor. The unsold milk from the Distributor is taken back by the milk processing unit where it is reprocessed into flavored milk, yogurt etc. This trend of DTH process is also emerging in the retail outlets and 'Mom & Pop' stores of India where goods purchased are delivered through "Door Delivery Service" over a minimum value purchase.

10.4.2 Farm-To-Fork (FTF)

The 'Farm-To-Fork' process aims at minimizing the steps of distribution of agriculture produce from the farmer (farm) to the end consumer (fork). The 'Farm-To-Fork' process of the Indian agricultural sector is shifting from the conventional method (*Mandi* Route) to the emerging method (Retailer Route).

In India, due to stringent policies of the *Agricultural Produce Marketing Committee (APMC)*, a farmer can sell his produce only in *Mandi*. The government has amended the policy in 11 states which has enabled the retailer to directly collaborate with the farmers by purchasing the crops grown by them, thus bypassing the middleman route.

The retailer is setting up state of the art R&D lab. With the help of these advanced methodologies they are providing the farmers with improved seeds, fertilizers and pesticides. The field scientists employed by the retailer provides technical support for multi-cropping and better irrigation methods (Drip irrigation methods). All these would raise the farmer's income by at least 30%.

In *Mandi* route about 30% of the produce is lost during transportation. Using retailer route along with government's efforts to expedite policy implementation for rapid infrastructure developments, the wastage of farm produce can come down to 5% (Fig. 10.5).

The following figure (Fig. 10.6) describes the process of selling agricultural produce (fruits and vegetables) through conventional method (*Mandi* Route) and through emerging method (Retailer Route).

The process of selling agricultural (fruits and vegetables) produce through conventional method (*Mandi* route) and through emerging method (retailer route) is explained below.

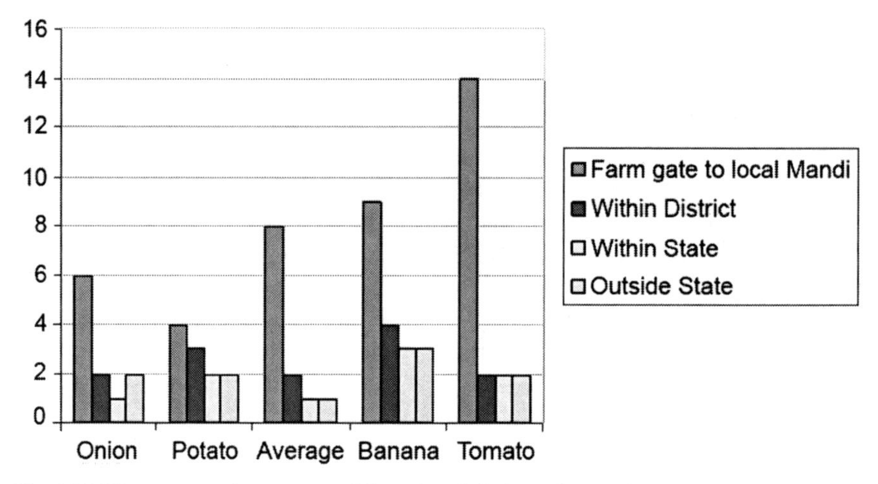

Fig. 10.5 Wastage at various stages of the value chain in India (% of total production) (Krishna et al. 2007)

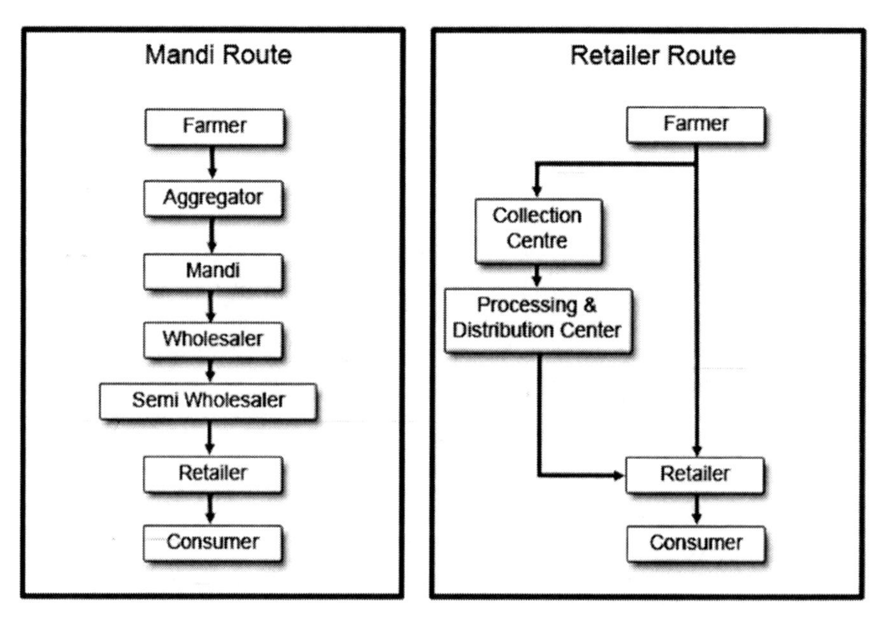

Fig. 10.6 Conventional method (mandi route) and emerging method (retailer route) (Jishnu 2007)

Conventional Method (Mandi Route)

The farmer sells his produce through the aggregator (licensed broker) at the *Mandi*. The transportation cost is borne by the farmer. The wholesaler purchases it from the *Mandi* and sells it to the semi-wholesaler in different parts of the state. The transportation cost is borne by the semi-wholesaler. The retailer purchases the produce from the semi-wholesaler in his city and the customer buys it from the retailer.

Emerging Method (Retailer Route)

The farmer sells his produce directly to the retailer. The expenses of transportation are borne by the retailer. With distant locations the retailer has a collection/processing center where all the fruits and vegetable is processed before dispatching to the retail outlet.

10.5 Case Study: DSD – Low ROI Despite a Promising Future for the Indian Market

The following chapter gives insight into the feasibility of implementing DSD in the Indian context. A pilot trial was conducted by a global company selling pet food in India to compare and study the nuances and the benefits of traditional distribution processes vis-à-vis a DSD process. The goal of the study was to suggest an appropriate method of distribution for the considered context.

The study was conducted to assess the distribution efficiencies for the pet food *before* the implementation of the DSD (=traditional method) and *after* the implementation of DSD (=DSD method). The collected data were analyzed and the two scenarios were compared. The efficiency of the DSD method was computed using the ROI. All data presented in the case study result from real world observations made in context with the DSD implementation. The financial data are presented in USD (1USD = 40 INR as on July 2007).

Given the similarity of markets in the Indian subcontinent, the study results hold largely true for the countries around the Indian subcontinent.

10.5.1 Challenges Faced by the Company in the Traditional Model

The challenges faced by the company while distributing to organized retail chains in the traditional model of distribution are listed below:

- Retail chains operated on a hub & spoke model with purchase and deliveries taking place at the hubs. Stock out is a commonly faced issue at the stores. This was mainly due to inaccurate demand forecasting and inventory management. These problems mainly arise as these retail chains did not have proper systems in place to do real time inventory management and demand planning
- These stores were characterized by poor visual merchandising and poorly maintained stock. The primary reason for this was the poor warehouse management by the retail chains. The considered product, pet food, attracted rodents. This led to a high shrinkage. Shrinkage and pilferage could be as high as 10% of the stocks.

The objective of running a pilot of the DSD model was to understand and address these problems. A DSD model brings in direct control of the stocks by the manufacturer thereby avoiding the need to store in poorly maintained retailer warehouses.

10.5.2 Case Study Data

Table 10.4 Location – A city in western India

Number of outlets served (60 of the 400 outlets belong to two retail chains)	400
Sales volume (kg/month)	7,000
No. of working days per month	26
Average sales (kg/day)	269
Average cost per kg ($)	1.75
Average total sales per day ($)	470.75

Table 10.5 Distributor's investment

Value of stock ($)	4,492
Value of credit of 7 days ($)	2,858
Average investment in claims from manufacturers ($)	1,500
Total distributor's investment ($)	8,850

Table 10.6 Distributor's expenditure per day

Fuel cost per day ($)	6.25
Driver's salary per day ($)	2.50
Delivery boy's salary per day ($)	1.88
Computer operator's salary per day ($)	1.25
Stationary cost per day ($)	0.50
Sales man's salary per day ($)	5.00
Other administration costs per day ($)	1.25
Gross distributor's expenditure ($)	18.63

10.5.3 Methodology Used for the Study

In the traditional model a typical three tier distribution system is followed. In a three tier distribution, the manufacturer supplies to the distributor who in turn supplies to the retailer hub warehouse (Table 10.8). In the DSD model the distribution pattern remains the same, except that the orders are collected from and deliveries are made directly to the retail stores.

The distributor's delivery process is characterized by (Table 10.7):

- The delivery man delivers the material by next day ('presale' model)
- The distributor delivers pet food along with another company's goods (non competing category) for optimizing capacity utilization of the delivery van. The van has the carrying capacity of 400 kg (100 ft^3)
- Typically the distributor services a couple of non-competing category manufacturers
- Space utilization on an average would be at 90%, followed by route optimization.

Table 10.7 Distributor's delivery process

Frequency of outlet coverage (in no. of days)	14
Average time spent/month/outlet by salesman for booking orders at hub of retail chains	0.5
Average delivery time at hub (in no. of hrs)	1
Sales volume of the two retail chains taken together (kg/month)	1,500
Total no. of hours a person works per day	8

Table 10.8 Facts observed in the DSD operations

Facts Observed in the DSD Operations	Impact on ROI: (↑), (↓) or No change
(a) Increase in no. of outlets brought under coverage = 58 (these were not being covered directly earlier)	(↑)
(b) Increase in sales through the retail chain sales only: 450 kg/month (considering all outlets for the month)	
(i) Depth of distribution was ensured (expected sales increment of 20%, i.e. additional sales of 300 kg)	(↑)
(ii) Visual merchandising was better (expected additional sales of10%, i.e. 150 kg).	
(iii) Total additional sales generated = 450 kg (i + ii), i.e. a per day increase in gross earnings of $1.68	
(c) Increase in salaries and wages on account of overtime payments to salesman, delivery boy and the driver	(↓)
(d) Increase in order booking time taken at each newly added outlet = 0.5 h/outlet	(↓)

(Continued)

(e) Increase in delivery time at each newly added outlet = 1 h/outlet	(↓)
(f) Increase in expenditure on account of exclusive vehicle deployed for delivery plus increase in idle time due more number of stoppages.	(↓)
(g) Productivity of generating orders (productive visits/total visits) = 25%	No change
(h) Route coverage done fortnightly	No change

10.5.4 Calculation of ROI for Traditional and DSD Model

Step 1: Calculation of Gross Earnings per Day

Table 10.9 Calculation of gross earnings per day

	Traditional method	DSD method	% Change
(a) Average quantity sold (kg)/day	269	286	6.32%
(b) Price/kg ($)	1.75	1.75	0%
(c) Revenue (inclusive of gross margin) ($) (a × b)	470.75	500.50	6.32%
(d) Cost of goods sold ($)	444.10	472.17	6.32%
(e) Gross margin mark-up (%) [(c – d) / d] × 100	6	6	0%
(f) Gross earning ($) (d × e)	26.65	28.33	6.30%

Step 2: Calculation of Gross Expenditure per Day

Table 10.10 Distributor's expenditure per day

	Traditional method	DSD method	% Change
(a) Fuel cost ($)	6.25	8.37 [1]	34%
(b) Salesman salary ($)	5.00	6.40 [2]	28%
(c) Drivers salary ($)	2.50	3.34 [3]	34%
(d) Delivery boy salary ($)	1.88	2.51 [3]	34%
(e) Computer operator salary ($)	1.25	1.25	Nil
(f) Stationary cost ($)	0.50	0.50	Nil
(g) Administration cost ($)	1.25	1.25	Nil
(h) Gross expenditure ($) (a + b + c + d + e + f + g)	18.63	23.62	27%

Workings for Increased Expenditure in Implementing DSD

[1] The carrying capacity of the vehicle is 400 kg. At 90% utilization rate the distributor was able to send around 360 kg of stock for delivery. After the implementation of DSD, the bundling of deliveries was not possible as the delivery boy had to spend more time at each outlet and routes were also reshuffled slightly. Hence the entire cost of running that vehicle has to be borne by the company, i.e. 360/269 × 6.25 = 8.37.

[2] Determination of the additional salesman man-hours needed in the DSD process for booking:

- 58 Outlets × 2 calls per month × 0.5 h/call = 58 h/month
- Additional salesman man-hours per day: 58/26 = 2.23 h/day (assuming 26 working days with 8 h).
- Therefore, the additional costs for booking amount are:
  Salesman salary per hour × Additional man-hours per day = 1.40 USD per day.

[3] Same logic as [1] above.

Step 3: Return on Investment (ROI)

ROI = [(Gross Earnings − Gross Expenditure) × 100]/Investment

For ease of comparison of the two scenarios, ROI will be calculated on a per month basis. An ROI of 2.0 % per month will be a healthy ROI for the distributor.

ROI in the Traditional Method

ROI/Day = [(26.65 – 18.63) × 100]/8,850
ROI/Day = 0.09%
ROI/Month = 2.34%.

ROI in the DSD Method

ROI/Day = [(28.33 – 23.62) × 100]/8,850
ROI/Day = 0.053%
ROI/Month = 1.38%.

Step 4: Observations and Comparative Analysis

The table below (Table 10.11) gives a comparative analysis of the impact on ROI of implementing DSD vis-à-vis the traditional method of distribution.

Table 10.11 Comparative analysis of the traditional and the DSD method

Traditional method		DSD Method	
Quantitative			
No. of outlets covered	342	No. of outlets covered	400
Total calls made	684	Total calls made	800
Total sales call hours	208	Total sales call hours	266
Gross expenditure ($)	18.63	Gross expenditure ($)	23.62
Gross earnings ($)	26.65	Gross earnings ($)	28.33
ROI (%) per month	2.34	ROI (%) per month	1.38
Qualitative			
Inefficient shelf management of products		Improved shelf management of products	
Poor visual merchandising		Better visual merchandising	
Poor brand image		Enhanced brand image	
Inaccurate data/documentation		Accurate data/documentation	

10.5.5 Recommendations from the Case Study

Based on the above case study, for an implementation of DSD to be financially feasible in the Indian context, the following could be inferred:

1. The percentage increase in gross earnings should be more than the percentage increase in expenditure. In the above case study increase in the gross earnings is only 6.3% as against expenditure which increases by 27% on implementation of DSD. Hence DSD implementation is not profitable in for the volume considered. However with increase in volume as mentioned in the case study, DSD would be beneficial in the long term. DSD will also result in other benefits like improved shelf management of products, better visual merchandizing, enhanced brand image and better market intelligence
2. The volume per outlet on implementation of DSD should increase significantly to ensure the ROI. In the above case study, it was observed that the DSD process will be effective if the minimum sales go up to 330 kg from the current 269 kg
3. Capacity utilization of the vehicle plays a very important role. The recommended level for DSD to be profitable in the case as above is 75%
4. Route optimization and accessibility to retail store backrooms would play a significant role in turnaround times and hence ROI.

To summarize, due to the fragmentation of retailing landscape in the Indian scenario DSD is more expensive to implement as volume per outlet in the present context is low. Further, due to overcrowding in cities, availability of retail space to cater to the extra demands of storage and retrieval of goods is a challenge.

The additional expenditure incurred in employing DSD should ideally be budgeted and considered as marketing expenditure towards building of brands at the place where it matters the most, i.e. "the shelf".

10.6 The Way Forward for DSD in India

Some of the factors which will support DSD or inhibit DSD implementation from the Indian perspective are discussed in the following sections. The concluding section explains the role of technology in augmenting DSD.

Factors Supporting DSD

Cost Advantage: Unlike the western market, the Indian market consists of large number of small and big producers. The small producers thrive where product complexity is low and manufacturing costs are less, for example snack foods. They offer high margins to the retailers but have little control over distribution practices. Thus a competitive environment of low prices is created. Using DSD, big producers can offer higher margins to the retailers directly without going through other intermediaries and thus can beat the competition. Big producers also have the advantage of high volumes of sale and therefore can use DSD as a profitable method of distribution.

Distinct shopping patterns: Shopping for some families is a social or an entertainment-driven event. The whole family or the extended family shops together, so retailers need much wider aisles. Effectively it means that a retailer needs more space in front, so to maximize space efficiency he needs to focus at improving the front end. To do this, he has to streamline operations. So for this, both the manufacturer and the retailer can use DSD as a medium for goods delivery.

Burgeoning Malls: With growing number of shopping malls in India, DSD is gaining importance as these malls have very few storage space. Stocks are replenished in these malls by manufacturers/distributors as and when required by using delivery vans.

10.6.2 Factors Inhibiting DSD

For effective implementation of DSD, companies need to understand and tackle various challenges. Some are industry specific challenges whereas some are macro level challenges. But both impact distribution processes in certain ways as mentioned below:

Industry Specific Challenges

Unorganized Retail Sector: (1) DSD is a process that will predominantly benefit the organized retail outlets. In India, with close to 95.4% of the total retail sector being unorganized, the successful implementation of DSD is an uphill task. The regional variance in consumption patterns of commodities is high. For example, in North India the consumption of wheat is high whereas in South India rice is the primary consumed commodity. In Indian 'Mom & Pop' stores the volume of goods sold is small. For example: in beverages, for buying a crate of 24 bottles, the store could buy 8 bottles of 3 different flavors. Furthermore, the number of SKU's is large and the stock levels are not monitored. Finally, the purchase from manufacturer/wholesaler/distributor and sale to customer is not documented in Indian 'Mom & Pop' stores. In other developing countries like Venezuela, there is a degree of documentation that is followed which would enable DSD. (2) There are no DSD-employing companies for the unorganized retail sector as this market is too fragmented for any manufacturer to reach the critical volume per outlet to make DSD feasible. The case study in section above aptly illustrated this. (3) However, organized Indian retail sector is growing at a rapid rate and this would embrace DSD in future.

Physical distribution & channel management in rural India: (1) The problems of physical distribution and channel management adversely affect the service as well as the cost. The existent market structure consists of primary rural market and retail sales outlet. It involves stock points in feeder towns to service these retail outlets at the village levels. Furthermore, it becomes difficult to maintain the required service level in the delivery of the product at retail level.

Macro (Country) Level Challenges

Infrastructure – logistics and transportation: (1) India is a vast country with diverse household patterns such as villages, panchayats and towns. Presence of such a large and heterogeneous geographical spread with uneven population density poses a problem of connecting various regions. (2) Last mile connectivity in terms of roads and rail is still a big bottleneck. There are no proper routes to connect rural parts of India and suburbs. Regulatory Challenges: Taxation barriers between states hinder efficient inter-regional distribution. The implementation of DSD in India may be promoted by the case of proper technology. These are technologies that already exist in western countries, but are only slowly being introduced in India.

RFID

RFID is going to come to India in a big way in the next 10 years. Although it might be implemented only on a pallet level, but to align operations with the technology, DSD especially for the large retailers is going to provide the effective channel for optimizing work flows at the back room. Benefits will include at least that stock monitoring and replenishment will become easier for the manufacturers with the combination of RFID and DSD.

Handheld Devices

Mobile terminals deliver the power of advanced handheld technology with a customized, comprehensive solution for system integration that delivers the tool one needs to manage the complete supply. This device will come in handy for DSD as with this stocks and sales will become real time.

10.7 Concluding Notes

With the evolution of organized retailing in India, the manufacturers and retailers are increasingly adopting different distribution methods like the DSD process. The paper discusses the DSD process followed in India in different retailing formats like 'Mom & Pop' stores, Supermarkets and Retail chains with examples of some industry segments such as Beverages, HPC, Dairy and Pet Foods. Through a comparative analysis in these industry segments, issues such as diverse product portfolio, replenishment and multiple layers of distribution were noted as important criteria for acceptance of DSD. Using the case study in Pet Food, a recommendation was made on how volume of business is critical for profitable operation of DSD. The report also highlights certain existing trends like DTH and new emerging trends in Farm-To-Fork which are unique to India. Finally, the article lists the challenges & opportunities in adopting DSD and also how technology will play a pivotal role for DSD in future.

References

Farrel, D. and Beinhocker, E. (2007): Next Big Spenders: India's Middle Class, Business Week, May 19.
IBEF (2007): Indian Brand Equity Foundation, in: The Great Indian Bazar.
Jishnu, L. (2007): The New Middle Man, Farm Retail, Business World, Issue: 9 July.
Krishna, V. et al. (2007): Krishna, V.; Natti, S.; Abhyankar, J.: Greenhouse Effect, Farm Retail, Business World, 9 July.
McKinsey (2007): Mc Kinsey Report: The 'Bird of Gold': The Rise of India's Consumer Market.
Nath, K., Commerce and Industry Minister, Government of India: (2007): Indian retail report, 9 Jan.

Endnotes

[*] Contributors: Ajay Chaudhary, Wilson Dhanaraj, Gaurav Tiwari and Aviral Gupta (Wipro Research Cell for Consumer Packaged Goods Industry).

[1] Agent appointed by the Manufacturer responsible for getting the products to retailers.

[2] C&F – Clearing and Forwarding Agent – Third party agent possible for getting the goods from one place and transport to other location.

[3] Customer Executive – Operates in a smaller area (depending on the volumes). Responsible for the volumes, promotions and credit levels in his history.

[4] C&F – Warehouse – Warehouse owned by the C&F agent for collection and distribution of goods. (C&F Warehouses in different Indian states are meant for saving Central Sales Tax levied by the Govt. of India, prevailing rate being 4%). He also takes care of all the petty expenses such as toll charges.

[5] Delivery Boy is employed by the Distributor for delivering and collecting payments from the Mom and Pop stores.

[6] AREA Sales Manager – Is responsible for a larger geographical area with 4–5 CE's reporting to him. Responsible for operating costs and sales volumes.

[7] Territory Sales In-Charge – Involves in forecasting, planning and sale fort he territory. He is responsible for managing high value accounts. His area of operation covers few cities/towns.

[8] Stock Keeping Unit.

[9] Product Availability Manager.

[10] Drinking water supplied in 20, 25 L jars to home and institution.

Chapter 11
Operations – How to Run DSD Efficiently

Direct store delivery is an expensive mode of distribution. The previous chapters sought to explain why companies nevertheless do DSD. Once the decision has been made in favour of DSD, the focus will have to shift on how to perform DSD operations efficiently. This chapter addresses execution related issues.

A major cost element in DSD operations is the transportation cost. As **Müller of Offenburg Polytechnical School** and **Klaus of University of Nürnberg** explain, a viable start to managing these costs is to calculate and benchmark them properly. Based on a recent European-wide project, they presented a robust calculation schema and country based cost benchmarks which may help to position one self in terms of delivery efficiency.

Technology and especially information technology (IT) offer opportunities to improve DSD operations. As **Becker, Winkelmann, and Fuchs of University of Münster** argue in their technology overview, supply chain event management, radio frequency identification, master data management, and service oriented architectures (SOA) are among the most promising technology bits the DSD community will develop and apply over the next years.

Schoppengerd of SAP focuses on SOA. Considering the fact that no single software vendor currently offers a complete DSD package and considering that DSD processes and in turn also the DSD related software requirements change over time and vary by region and product portfolio, he suggests understanding SOA as a strategic investment for a future proof DSD software environment. Furthermore, there will be a need for multiple software vendors to collaborate on DSD.

Daily DSD operations heavily depend on robust and reliable hardware. **Rasmussen of Intermec** presents an overview of state of the art DSD hardware technology, covering handheld computers, data capture tools, peripherals, and communication devices.

Finally, as **Mukai and Natchetoi of SAP Research** and **Dagtas of University of Arkansas at Little Rock** stress, mobility and mobile solutions will penetrate and affect DSD operations to a much higher degree than seen today. The rise of the mobile web and the availability of powerful mobile phones will allow for mobile solutions. Some business cases are already available in the long run ending up with a "live DSD supply chain".

A. Otto et al., *Direct Store Delivery*,

DOI: 10.1007/978-3-540-77213-2_11, © Springer-Verlag Berlin Heidelberg 2009

Chapter 12
More Expensive or Too Expensive? Calculating Delivery Costs in Europe

Stefanie Müller[1] and Peter Klaus[2]

[1]Hochschule Offenburg, Campus Gengenbach, Professur für Speditions-, Transport- und Verkehrslogistik, Klosterstraße 14, D-77723, Gengenbach, tel.:+49 7803 9698-78, e-mail: stefanie.mueller@fh-offenburg.de

[2]Friedrich-Alexander Universität Erlangen-Nürnberg, Rechts- und Wirtschaftswissenschaftliche Fakultät, Lehrstuhl für Betriebswirtschaftslehre, insbesondere Logistik, Schlossplatz 4, D-91054, Erlangen, tel.: +49 911 5302-444, e-mail: klaus@logistik.uni-erlangen.de

Abstract

By analysing driver wages, vehicle costs, and administrative costs the article examines how expensive deliveries are in different European countries. By doing a comparison with LTL (less than truck load) business it is considered whether DSD is more expensive. In a search for process benchmarks (also in comparison with LTL) the authors finally approach an answer to the question whether DSD is potentially too expensive.

12.1 Direct Store Delivery: The Attractions and Challenges of Delivering Consumer Goods Directly to Retail Outlets

The Coca Cola truck has become an essential component of the Coca Cola brand. It is often to be seen in TV and movie ads (just think of the annual "x-mas truck" campaigns). Even more often it is seen in everyday life – parking in front of a shop, a kiosk, or a restaurant where the Coca Cola driver is just doing deliveries.

This red truck, however, is not only a means of promotion, enhancement of the image of the Coca Cola brand, and supporting an intimate direct relationship between a consumer goods supplier and the retail customers. Maybe more importantly, it represents a specific logistical system that has been employed successfully by Coca Cola (and many other consumer goods suppliers) already for many years. The merchandise is moved directly from a supplier's plant or distribution center to the retail outlet (retail shops, kiosks, vending machines, restaurants, cafeterias, takeaways, and others) avoiding handling and change of ownership at intermediary levels of wholesale or retailer-operated cross-docking facilities (GMA 2002, p. 2). Today, the concept is an established practice under the name of Direct Store Delivery (DSD).

A. Otto et al., *Direct Store Delivery*,
DOI: 10.1007/978-3-540-77213-2_12, © Springer-Verlag Berlin Heidelberg 2009

From the manufacturers' point of view DSD means that their logistical responsibilities are significantly expanded. DSD increases their systems' complexity. It is a massive expense factor: There are large fleets of trucks to be operated; dispatching and route planning are to be organized. The typical geographical structure of the system is demanding: The delivery points are many, often at difficult to reach locations, and the size of shipments being "dropped off" at each location is small (GMA 2005, p. 5). From logistical perspective this structure there are several problems:

- Vehicle sizes, road access, and parking are restricted at many typical outlet delivery addresses
- Time slots for delivery are narrow in order to avoid deliveries disturbing vending processes
- Owners/staff are not always present at their premises
- There is no dedicated staff for receiving goods, but sales and other service personnel at the outlet has to be asked for help
- There is no truck-docking and unloading equipment.

The resulting logistical challenges – relative to consumer goods distributions systems that employ indirect methods through intermediate wholesaler, retailer, or logistics service provider cross-docking and consolidation facilities – are:

- A larger number of outlet stops required for the delivery of a given volume of goods
- Enhanced, more complex planning demands due to multiple restrictions for deliveries at outlets
- Reduced efficiency of delivery truck operations due to smaller truck sizes, relatively longer times spent at the outlet stops
- Additional time needed for the performance of value-added services at the consignees' locations
- Idle times accumulating for drivers when they need the consignees' signatures or other proof of delivery while staff is just serving customers.

Direct Store Delivery as a logistical system offers many attractions and many challenges.

This article is based on the assumption that the cost and benefits of DSD – hence the decision about whether, when, and how to employ the concept – should be informed by assessing the relative cost as rationally and efficiently as possible. The following discussion focuses on one of two possible types of implementing DSD: "route sales" and "pre-sales". In *route sales* on the one hand the sale of a product is accomplished in the moment when being delivered. In this type the route driver is at the same time sales person replenishing a store based on immediate needs. On the other hand there is the *pre-sales* approach to DSD where the order placements occur prior to planning and doing delivery operations. In this version of DSD orders are placed in advance by telephone, fax, or internet communication between the customer and the consumer goods supplier/distributor

(GMA 2002, p. 21). To avoid the difficulties of having to assess trade-offs between the cost and benefits of alternative selling and marketing concepts in this discussion, it will focus on pre-sell approach to DSD only.

The discussion of delivery costs will proceed in three main steps (sections 12.2–12.4): In section 12.2 the question how "expensive?" is DSD is answered by showing a basic cost calculation for deliveries (on a daily basis). In section 12.3 the question of how much "more expensive?" is DSD relative to indirect delivery logistics is examined by evaluating the relevant cost and productivity drivers and comparing the efficiency of a Direct Store Delivery with deliveries in other logistic systems (on the level of one individual delivery). In section 12.4, finally, an attempt is made to answer the question whether and when DSD may be "too expensive?" by discussing the cost-efficiency and possible cost saving potentials in Direct Store Delivery. Some conclusions in section 12.5 finish the article.

12.2 Expensive? – Calculating a Delivery Vehicle

In this chapter the cost calculation for Direct Store Delivery is discussed by examining typical current costs of the delivery vehicle and of the driver as the basic production resources in a DSD system (section 12.2.1). Cost differences between various European countries will be shown by comparing the cost situation in selected countries (section 12.2.2).

12.2.1 How to Calculate a Delivery Vehicle

A delivery activity may be compared to the activities taking place at an industrial production work station. The cost for the delivery may be assessed by calculating the cost of providing the production resources for the time needed to perform a certain production activity (a month, a day, a minute). In this discussion the question about the cost of providing a truck and a driver for a full working day is raised first. The focus is on direct costs on a daily and on a "per job" basis and to relate indirect costs to this calculation basis where this is adequate.

Depending on the quantity and the kind of goods to be delivered, the vehicle is either a truck (up to three axles, max. 7.5 t overall weight), or a bus, or an estate car, sometimes equipped with refrigerating facilities. The delivery vehicle is normally manned with one driver (holding a particular driving license for trucks).

In total the delivery costs are composed of three different cost groups:

- Personnel cost (driver's wages plus employer's contribution to social insurance)
- Vehicle cost (fuel, depreciation, tax, insurance, etc.)
- Administrative cost (overhead for fleet management, tour planning, etc.).[1]

An overview of the three cost groups and the different cost elements of a delivery is shown in Fig. 12.1 The following delivery cost calculation assumes a delivery by truck without special equipment and presents a calculation of the German cost level.[2]

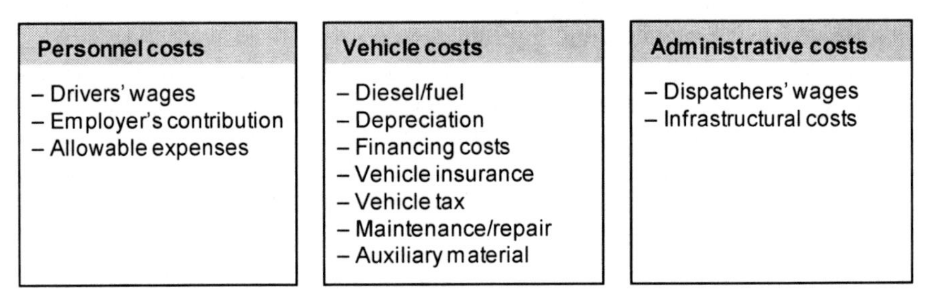

Fig. 12.1 Cost elements of a delivery

The following cost information is drawn from data in Germany, status 2006/2007 and data collected at the Nuernberg Fraunhofer institute by the authors: *Personnel cost* represent the dominant cost factor within the calculation of delivery costs. A driver's basic gross wage per month – varying according to age and professional experience – is at 1,706€. (Ver.di 2005, p. 3). Calculating with 18 working days per month on average the gross wage costs amount to 95€ per day. Adding average overtime payments and expense allowances, which are a regular element of drivers' pay, the total personnel costs come to approx. 110–120€ per day. Employer's contribution is to be considered by a surcharge of approx. 25% (BDF 2005, Reg. 7, 6) thus adding up to 27.50–30.00€ per day. In total the driver wage is to be calculated with 137.50–150.00€ per day.

Purchasing and operating a truck causes several kinds of *vehicle cost.* The largest cost items here are fuel (diesel) and depreciation. Other cost elements are financing costs, vehicle insurance, motor vehicle tax, maintenance/repair, and auxiliary materials.[3] Altogether the daily costs for vehicle operation of a delivery truck (7.5 t) sum up to 87.50€. An overview of the vehicle-related costs and their calculation is shown in Table 12.1.[4]

The first cost element, *diesel costs* can be calculated by the diesel price (per liter; figures from Shell online (2007)). Average diesel consumption per 100 km is approx. 18 l for a typical delivery truck and the number of kilometers the vehicle runs on a tour is approx. 150 km (urban area). The result is 25.00€ per day.

For the calculation of *depreciation costs* the purchase of a typical delivery truck (7.5 t gross weight category) with a purchasing price of 45,000€ (o.V. 2005, p. 99) is assumed. The terminal value is 10%, the depreciation period is 6 years, with a linear depreciation.[5] These figures lead to daily costs of 27.00€. Besides depreciation costs the purchase and operation of a vehicle also causes *financing costs,* since the purchase either requires a bank credit thus causing interest costs; in case of own financial means available the amount invested in the vehicle could

Table 12.1 Calculation and level of vehicle costs

Cost element	Calculation	Costs (approx.)
Diesel	$0.92 \frac{€}{ltr.} \cdot 18 \frac{ltr.}{100\,km} \cdot 150\,km$	$25.00 \frac{€}{day}$
Depreciation	$(45{,}000\,€ - 4{,}500\,€)\,/\,6\,years\,/\,250 \frac{days}{year}$	$27.00 \frac{€}{day}$
Financing costs	$40{,}500\,€ \cdot 58.3\% \cdot 5.5\%\,/\,250 \frac{days}{year}$	$5.20 \frac{€}{day}$
Vehicle insurance	$3{,}125\,€\,/\,250 \frac{days}{year}$	$12.50 \frac{€}{day}$
Vehicle tax	$600\,€\,/\,250 \frac{days}{year}$	$2.50 \frac{€}{day}$
Maintenance/repair	$2{,}500\,€\,/\,250 \frac{days}{year}$	$10.00 \frac{€}{day}$
Auxiliary material	$1{,}325\,€\,/\,250 \frac{days}{year}$	$5{,}30 \frac{€}{day}$
TOTAL		**$87.50 \frac{€}{day}$**

have been used alternatively thus having yielded interest revenue. Our calculation of annual/daily interest costs assumes a consistent paying off: At the end of the first period of usage 1/6 of the credit amount (i.e. the truck's purchasing price minus the residual value) is paid to the bank (total period of usage = 6 years, see above discussion). Consequently, in the second period there remains a share of 5/6 of the original credit amount to be paid interest on; in the third period 4/6, and so on. On average this means that in each period 58.3% of the original credit value to be paid interest on.[6] Considering an interest-bearing annual amount of 23,625€ (on average), an interest rate of 5.5% (data provided by the carriers interviewed; official interest rates to be found in Eurostat (2007b), and 250 employment days per year, the daily financing costs amount to 5.20€.

Insurance costs are paid on a yearly basis in order to cover risks like traffic accident, theft, fire, etc. The yearly amount payable (depending on the type of vehicle, the no-claims bonus, and the contract/conditions the insured company gets with the insurers) of a comprehensive insurance amounts to approx. 3,000–3,500€ per year, i.e. approx. 12.50€ per working day.[7] Moreover for every registered vehicle tax has to be paid. *Vehicle tax* has to be paid to the fiscal authorities also on a yearly basis. In Germany the yearly tax obligation amounts to approx. 600€ for a truck of 7.5 t (BMF online 2007). Per day this leads to costs of 2.50€.

The last two cost elements of vehicle costs are directly related to vehicle operations. The first of these cost elements is related to necessary maintenance activities in order to avoid damage or defect and repair activities in order to remove occurred damages. These *maintenance/repair costs* can be assumed with 2,500€ per year, resp. 10.00€ per day. The second cost element is related to all costs occurring for *auxiliary materials,* like replacement tire, lubricants, cooling water, etc. These auxiliary materials cause costs of (estimated) 1,325€ per year and 5.30€ per day.[8]

The third cost group, the *administrative costs,* is only to be estimated on a rough basis. The administration and dispatching of delivery trucks comprehends costs like wages of fleet manager, fleet controllers, or tour planners, furthermore costs for workspaces, IT, and office equipment required by this staff (Mielentz 1994, p. 12; Czenskowsky et al. 2002, p. 85). If the monthly wages (of a combined planning/steering/controlling function) are assumed to be approx. 3,400€ (including ancillary labor costs), each of these clerks cares for 10 vehicles and works 18 days per month on average, the resulting daily wage costs amount to 19.00€. Adding a lump-sum for rooms and infrastructure the total daily administrative costs can be estimated to be approx. 25€.

Overall, a delivery truck in Germany costs approx. 250€ per day, with personnel costs constituting 55% of the total costs; vehicle costs are at 35%, and administrative costs at 10%.

12.2.2 Delivery Vehicle Costs in European Countries: A Comparison

The cost data presented so far apply to Germany and the central and northern European countries who have similar cost structures and levels of economic development. There are significant differences in cost levels and structures, however, in southern and eastern European countries, mainly due to extremely different wage levels. According to annually published EUROSTAT data the wages per hour (2004) are 24.70€ in Germany, 32.40€ in Switzerland, 6.30€ in Czech Republic, and 2.10€ in Bulgaria – there is a factor of 16 between the highest and the lowest wage level in Europe (Eurostat online 2007a).[9]

Purely vehicle-related costs, like depreciation, financing costs, insurance, diesel, or auxiliary materials are, however, relatively similar between European countries. This can be partly explained with arbitrage or with centralized purchasing strategies which are possible especially for large, multinational companies.

For other costs elements there are also differences between European countries, although they are not that grave as with driver wages. This applies to all cost elements including a (major or minor) percentage of wages, e.g. maintenance/repair (consisting of material costs and of human labor), or administrative costs (consisting of infrastructure costs and of human labor).

A comparison of several European countries shows the dominance of driver personnel costs, being stronger the higher the wage level in a country is. On the other hand the vehicle-related costs are dominant in countries with low wages. This effect is shown in Fig. 12.2 with a comparison of delivery cost composition in several European countries.

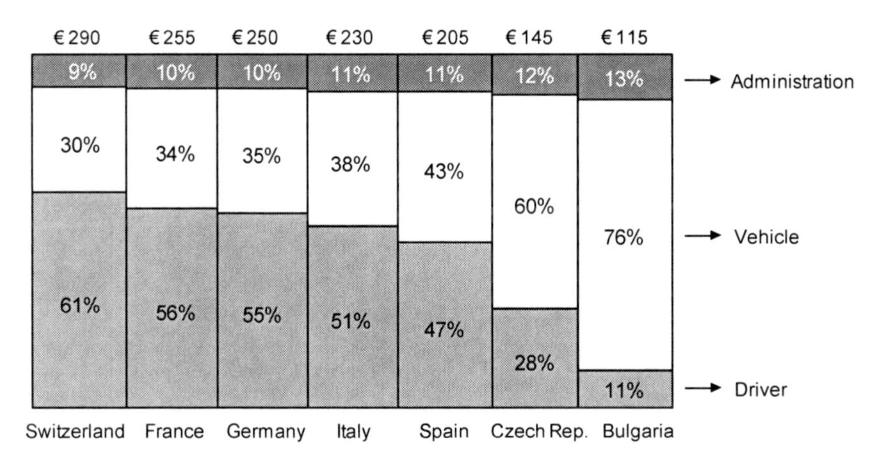

Fig. 12.2 Percental composition of delivery costs in European countries

12.3 More Expensive? – Calculating the Cost of a Typical Direct Delivery to a Retail Outlet

Section 12.2 of this article provided a current assessment of the cost of providing a day's capacity of a typical delivery truck. Now, the cost of an individual delivery to an outlet shall be assessed.

This part of the discussion is based on data collected at the authors' Nuernberg Fraunhofer institute from analyses of pick-up and delivery operations – done with several LTL system operators.[10] The assumption is that LTL delivery operations have very similar characteristics to DSD operations; so these data may be helpful to analyze also the DSD cost situation. However, what can be expected to be different between LTL and DSD is the productivity, i.e. the number of deliveries that can be done per day.

In order to approach a comparison of productivity between LTL and DSD, section 12.3.1 will define a base for comparison from the LTL delivery data. A comparison of LTL and DSD will be discussed in section 12.3.2.

12.3.1 Cost per Stop

The productivity of a delivery process is measured by the time used and by the quantity of goods delivered on as single delivery. The time factor means that delivery productivity is restricted by the available time per day (and is dependent on the driver's maximum shift time). Since each stop consumes a certain amount of time the typical daily number of stops (in the logistics service provider industry it is called "stop factor") is between 15 and 20 per day in LTL operations (Müller 2007, p. 38).[11] The weight factor implies that in case of large shipments the stop factor will be lower than 15–20, because the vehicle load capacity will be reached already with few deliveries. This load capacity (approx. 2.8–3.2 t for a truck with 7.5 t overall weight) allows for about 15 stops of 0.2 t each (Müller 2007, p. 40).

The following considerations will concentrate on the time restriction as the most relevant one in typical LTL (and DSD) operations.

Given an allowable driver shift time of maximum 9 h per day (EC 2006, Art. 6 (1)), the above stop number results in 27–36 min per stop. Dividing the total daily costs (250€) by 20 respectively 15 stops results in an average cost of 12.50–16.70€ per stop. For delivery routes with lower stop numbers, the costs per stop increase correspondingly.

On the level of the individual delivery it is still necessary to distinguish between the delivery stop on the one hand and the delivery of one order on the other hand. In case of one order being delivered in one stop both are identical. If, however, two or more orders are delivered within the same stop, the above stop costs are allocated to several orders and the delivery costs for each individual order decrease to ½, ⅓, ¼, etc. of the stop costs.

12.3.2 Delivery Costs in LTL and DSD: A Comparison

So far, a "baseline" assessment of the cost of a typical delivery has been done, using data from LTL operations. There are several differences between LTL and DSD operations which need to be considered next: How far "more expensive" is DSD?

To find answers to this question, a closer look on both operations – on the delivery process, its individual activities, and the time drivers need for each activity – is required. This will not be done by a numeric comparison with alternative stop cost calculations in LTL and in DSD. Since there is no empirical evidence about daily stop numbers and truck productivities in DSD yet, the article focuses on comparing both delivery processes in order to identify "best practices" thus detecting process benchmarks.

Figure 12.3 shows an overview of this process and the relevant performance drivers. For each activity the factors determining the time needed and the differences between LTL and DSD will be discussed. Summing up we will approach the stop costs in Direct Store Delivery.

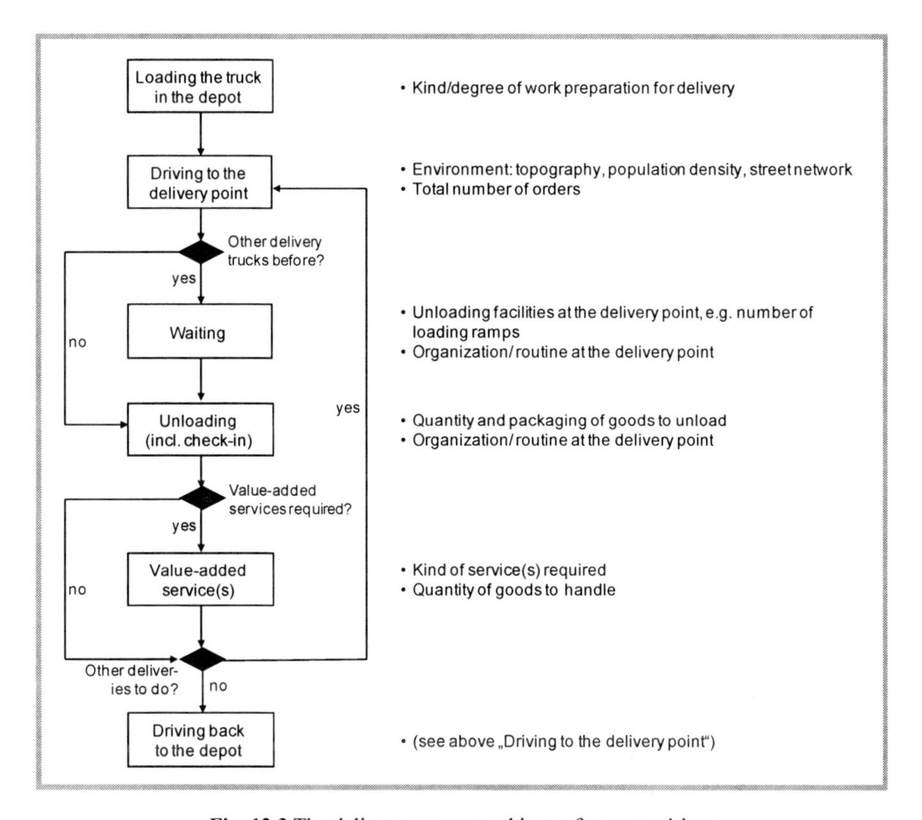

Fig. 12.3 The delivery process and its performance drivers

A delivery tour starts with *loading the delivery vehicle.* This happens either on the day of delivery (early in the morning) or on the day before (in the evening). Regarding this activity there is an important difference between LTL delivery and DSD: In LTL business the drivers of the delivery trucks (who are often owner-operator sub-contractors) take their trucks to the LTL depot in the morning, loading the trucks from a hustling LTL-depot platform (normally without help from depot personnel) and get the delivery documents from the dispatch department. Even under favorable conditions this takes approx. 1 h before the driver can start for his delivery tour. The driver's shift hours, however, have started even earlier, when the truck had been moved for the first time and the tachograph had started recording the driving activity of the day. As a result this means that typical LTL drivers loose one "unproductive" hour or more of their daily driving time by going to the depot, loading, and waiting for paperwork. In DSD this is partly done in the same way. Partly, however, picking of goods, preparing for loading, and the actual loading activity is performed by the suppliers' shipping dock staff. The "unproductive" time used for pre-trip activities is less in this case. In this procedure of pre-loading trucks by supplier's staff a best practice can be identified, since the driver's working time can be utilized in a more effective way. Especially the latest amendments in European social regulations concerning drivers' hours (EC 2006) are accelerating restrictions regarding drivers' "shift times" and necessary interruptions. Thus, pressure for an optimal planning and utilization of these driving times is increasing.

The next activity in the delivery process is *driving to the (next) delivery point*. The driving time "on the road" depends on distance and speed.[12] There are two groups of factors influencing driving time: (1) Geographical respectively infrastructural factors such as the topography of the delivery region (e.g. regions with many high mountains, fjords, bays or lakes), the population density (compare a large urban and a rural area), and the density of the street network (compare Northern areas in Scandinavia and Central Europe) (Müller 2007, p. 41f.). (2) The second factor is the number of orders to be delivered within a distribution region: If the number is high, there will be less distances between two deliveries and the stop factor will be higher (Müller 2007, p. 43). This applies to LTL delivery as well as to DSD.

Next, there are various effects on the "stop time", the actual presence of the truck and driver at the consignee's premises. There may be *waiting* times prior to unloading due to simultaneous arrivals of several trucks. Stop time is also affected by the availability and suitability of manoeuvring/parking space and unloading equipment (such as forklifts, leveling unloading docks, etc.). Another factor besides unloading facilities and equipment is the organization and routine at the delivery point. Waiting times might occur if the responsible person is not permanently present in the goods receipt area or if the necessary equipment, paperwork, data, etc. have to be organized before unloading can start. In inner city areas it could furthermore become necessary to wait for a parking lot. Such waiting times can occur in LTL delivery as well as in DSD. In DSD, however, the driver can typically develop more routine in the delivery process than in LTL, since there is a high degree of repetitivity in the stops and on-site activities to be performed.

Unloading a shipment and bringing it into the premises of the consignee can vary substantially. In case of parcel deliveries this takes only very few minutes since the driver just takes out the parcel by hand and carries it into the rooms of the consignee. In LTL the on-site delivery efficiency depends very much on the situation: If the consignee is equipped with unloading ramps and the driver just has to drop the rear plank and take out e.g. one pallet, the unloading can be done rather quickly. If, however, a tail-lift has to be lowered and a pallet has to be pulled by pallet-truck over a ground which is not quite plane, the unloading activity is more time-consuming. Unloading time is also extended, if the cargo to unload is not palletized but consists of loose packages. Finally, the time need for unloading is determined by organization and routine at the delivery point including the handling of incoming goods and creating the proof of delivery. Comparing the unloading activities of LTL and DSD the latter in many cases profits from routine effects and drivers being familiar with delivery points and the logistics situation there. They know where to go, where to put down the goods, and whom to turn to. In LTL business companies tend to employ bar codes, scanners, and electronic signature devices to simplify and accelerate the delivery process. However it can be assumed that both processes – LTL delivery and DSD – can vary very much; hence it cannot be stated in general whether one process is more efficient than the other.

Sometimes there are also *value-added services* to be performed by drivers upon delivery. This could be unpacking the shipment delivered, sorting of the goods into the shelves, disposal of packing material, and others. For the time need of this activity the question is what kind of service is to be done: Does the consignee just require unpacking goods and taking away the empty pallet or does the driver have to unpack and sort many small articles of several kinds into shelves? Furthermore the time need depends on the quantity delivered: Is the content of only one carton or the content of three pallets to be put into shelves? Such value-added services are rather unusual in standard LTL business, but they are an important part of Direct Store Delivery. As a result it can be stated that the necessity to deliver such services tends to extend the time need for an individual stop in Direct Store Delivery and consequently reduces the daily number of stops possible.

For most of the activities, especially for value-added services, it is hard to generalize their impact on the stop costs, since they can differ very much. The following consideration could, however, be an approach to a quantification: 10 min spent for value-added services would represent the 54th part of a full daily shift (9 h) thus equaling 1/54 of the total daily costs of 250€ and amounting to approx. 4.60€. It can be resumed that value-added services themselves often are not very expensive since they are not very time-consuming. However, it needs to be pointed out that with their time consumption they influence the daily stop numbers. If for example each stop includes 10 min for value-added services the time need for a stop increases to 37–46 min and the daily number of stops possible decreases to 12–15 (see section 12.3.1).

Apart from the delivery process and the time need of each of its activities the delivery costs for each order are also influenced by the number of orders per stop. In LTL delivery this factor approximates 1 (Müller 2007, p. 38). In Direct Store Delivery this factor tends to be 1.5–2.0.

Figure 12.4 compares the performance of LTL and DSD deliveries. Some of the above factors influencing productivity, like traffic infrastructure, stop density, or goods specifics are not considered in this comparison: These are environmental conditions which cannot be influenced in the short run and should therefore not be considered in a best practice examination.

Figure 12.4 shows that there is no generalizable answer to the question whether DSD deliveries are more expensive than LTL deliveries. DSD locations are often less equipped with docks and other "professional" unloading facilities. In many cases value-added services are to be performed within DSD – which tend to reduce the delivery truck's daily performance in terms of number of stops. On the other hand DSD clearly profits from other circumstances: pre-loading of trucks, familiarity of drivers with customers and locations, and a higher number of orders delivered on each stop.

Performance driver	LTL	DSD
Loading preparation	○ (Less advantageous)	● (Advantageous)
Unloading facilities	◐ (Medium)	◐ (Medium)
Routine at delivery point	◐ (Medium)	● (Advantageous)
Value-added services	● (Advantageous)	◐ (Medium)
Delivery orders per stop	○ (Less advantageous)	● (Advantageous)

● Advantageous
◐ Medium
○ Less advantageous

Fig. 12.4 Delivery performance in LTL and DSD – overview of the results

There is some weak empirical evidence that DSD tours, overall, are not less efficient than LTL tours: Three consumer goods providers report stop numbers of 17–20 per day – figures that are similar, if not slightly higher than the stop numbers of systemized LTL forwarders (see section 12.3.1). Of course, this sample is too small to be representative, but the inquired companies prove that it is *possible* to do Direct Store Delivery in an efficient way.

12.4 Too Expensive? – Cost Saving Potentials

The discussion of sections 12.2 and 12.3 showed that the efficiency of DSD is broadly comparable to the efficiencies of comparable LTL operations carried by the large and highly professional European LTL transport networks. But – are they too expensive, nevertheless?

In order to try and answer the "too expensive" question, some qualitative considerations shall be added in this section of the paper.

Three possible reasons can be identified why DSD costs might possibly be too high:

- There is cost saving potential of the current system that has not been exhausted yet
- The costs are not covered by adequate revenue or benefits
- There are cheaper alternatives.

In a general consideration it was pointed out that DSD is a process in which best practices can be identified (see Fig. 12.4). *Unexhausted cost saving potentials* could possibly be found in the "upstream" consolidation of Direct Store Deliveries through cooperation between suppliers serving the same category of outlets. More consolidation would increase the number of orders per stop thus reducing the costs per order. In this context it could make sense to question the frequency of delivery. However, such a decision has to be made by the individual company regarding their individual situation and their customers' demands: Do the customers' demands allow a reduction of delivery frequency? Does this make sense according to the individual tour planning?

Regarding the question whether DSD costs encounter *adequate revenues or benefits* two considerations can be made: Firstly the relationship between stop costs and value of goods, secondly the comparison of Direct Store Delivery costs and logistics costs in "traditional" consumer goods distribution.

Referring to the cost-value-relationship it can be said that stop costs of 12.50–16.70€ (see section 12.3.1) will surely be too expensive if only a very small value of goods (in the Coca Cola example, maybe one handling unit) is being delivered. Also in order to achieve a better relationship between goods value and delivery costs a consolidation of deliveries as suggested above (e.g. by adjusting delivery frequencies) would be advantageous, since the delivery costs (which are rather fix per stop) would be allocated to more orders.

Referring to the comparison between DSD and "traditional distribution" there is the obvious benefit of the elimination of intermediate goods handling facilities and operations at wholesaler and retailer distributions and cross-docking centers in favor DSD. One whole supply chain level (grocery, central/regional warehouse or cross-docking point) and the related transports are avoided. These cost savings compensate the extra costs for Direct Store Delivery to a certain extent.

However, if those intermediate echelons in the consumer goods supply chain structure are necessary anyway – for example to handle high volume "very fast moving" goods efficiently, or to divert large numbers of DSD stops from retail outlets, then only some "incremental cost" for indirect deliveries may be counted against the DSD cost. The question whether DSD costs are too expensive compared with indirect distribution costs can be answered only dependent from the individual company and the situation: In peak seasons with truck fleets being utilized intensively DSD costs tend to be less expensive whereas in low seasons with trucks running half empty this cost advantage might disappear.

In some cases, third alternatives may apply. From the suppliers' perspective such an alternative might be outsourcing Direct Store Delivery to one or several logistics service provider(s) who can realize consolidation economies. Such an outsourcing solution would refer to the last of the above mentioned "Too expensive reasons" – the existence of *cheaper alternatives*. For logistics service providers such a distribution service would be a promising market segment. Suppliers could shift the utilization risk by charging a logistics service provider with the distribution.

A "counter-trend" to DSD, increasing concerns against delivery operations in inner city and environmentally sensitive areas provides a further strong argument for reducing the number of direct deliveries to store and for consolidation, be it within and between the consumer goods suppliers' own logistics systems or within logistics service providers' network.

12.5 Conclusions

Direct Store Delivery is an important alternative approach to consumer goods distribution logistics. Its systematic development was pioneered by US consumer goods producers, such as Coca Cola. It is increasingly considered and implemented also by European suppliers. Despite this wide acceptance in consumer goods industry the question we tried to answer in this article was: Is DSD really a cost-efficient and powerful tool or maybe only a costly instrument within a company's distribution policy in order to get closer to the customer?

Since factor costs (for delivery vehicles and drivers) are rather fixed and relatively equal for all companies operating delivery systems cost-efficiency mainly depends on the daily performance of the production resources, i.e. the number of delivery stops and the number of delivery shipments the vehicles accomplish per day. By comparing delivery processes in LTL and DSD "best practices" on both sides can be identified: In (systemized) LTL delivery process standardization and automation could be such best practices. In DSD superior practices are pre-loading of trucks, drivers' intimacy with consignees and their habits, and a high consolidation of orders per stop.

Basically the answer to the efficiency question is that Direct Store Delivery is not necessarily inefficient and therefore *too expensive*; in fact this depends on the process organization in the individual company. There are already consumer goods suppliers who are operating Direct Store Delivery systems in a cost-efficient way. The comparison of LTL and DSD reveals, however, that both sides can still learn from each other and thus improve their process efficiencies.

References

Ansahl online (2007): Ansahl Consulting GmbH: Tarifvergleich Kfz. In: www.ansahl.com/Haftung-und-Recht/Autoversicherung/Kfz-Haftpflicht.html, 03.02.2007.

BDF (2005): Bundesverband des Deutschen Güterfernverkehrs (BDF): e.V.: Kosten-Informations-System für die leistungsorientierte Kalkulation von Straßengütertransporten. 22. Ergänzungslieferung. Frankfurt/M.: BDF.

BMF online (2007): Bundesfinanzministerium: Übersicht zur Kraftfahrzeugsteuer für Nutzfahrzeuge. In: www.bundesfinanzministerium. de/cln_01/nn_312/DE/Service/Downloads/Abt_ IV/024, 17.09.2007.

Czenskowsky, T.; Poussa, J.; Segelken, U. (2002): Prozessorientierte Kostenrechnung in der Logistik. In: KRP – Kostenrechnungspraxis, 46. Jg., 2002, Heft 2, S. 75–86.

EC (2006): Regulation (EC) No 561/2006 of the European Parliament and of the Council of 15 March 2006 on the harmonisation of certain social legislation relating to road transport and amending Council Regulations (EEC) No 3821/85 and (EC) No 2135/98 and repealing Council Regulation (EEC) No 3820/85.

Eurostat online (2007a): Statistisches Amt der Europäischen Gemeinschaften (Eurostat): Arbeitskosten pro Stunde, Daten für die Verkehrs- und Nachrichtenübermittlung. In: www.epp.eurostat.ec.europa.eu, 20.01.2007.

Eurostat online (2007b): Statistisches Amt der Europäischen Gemeinschaften (Eurostat): Langfristige Zinssätze, Renditen auf 10-jährige Staatsanleihen, Sekundärmarkt, Jahresdurchschnitt (%). In: epp.eurostat.ec.europa.eu, 17.09.2007.

Grocery Manufacturers Association (GMA) (2002): E-Commerce Opportunities in Direct Store Delivery: A White Paper. Washington, D.C.: GMA.

Grocery Manufacturers Association (GMA) (2005): Unleash the Power of DSD: Driving DSD Supply Chain Efficiencies and Profitability. Washington, D.C.: GMA.

Hassa, E. (2007): In der Kostenfalle. In: VerkehrsRundschau, Jg. 2007, Heft 35, S. 22–24.

Kerler, S. W. (2001): Fit für den Preiskampf: Fahrzeug-Kostenrechnung für den Güterkraftverkehr. 2. Auflage. München: Heinrich Vogel.

Mielentz , H. (1994): Preisgestaltung im Güterkraftverkehr. Trainingsbuch für Unterricht und Selbststudium. Nürnberg: Mielentz.

Mielentz H.; Trump, E. (2004): Der richtige Preis: Ein Kalkulationsleitfaden für Güterkraftverkehr und Spedition. Nürnberg: Mielentz.

Müller S. (2007): "Pick-up and Delivery" als zentrales Element des Wertschöpfungsprozesses in der Stückgutspedition: Betriebswirtschaftliche Bewertung und Angleichungstendenzen in Europa. In: Logistik Management, 9. Jg., 2007, Heft 1, S. 34–49.

o.V. (2005): Nutzfahrzeugkatalog 2005/2006: Das Jahrbuch für den Transportprofi. München: Heinrich Vogel.

Shell online (2007): Kraftstoffpreise in Deutschland, Jahresstatistik. In: www.shell.com, 16.02.2007.

Ver.di (2005): Vereinte Dienstleistungsgewerkschaft (Ver.di) e.V., Landesbezirk Bayern: Lohn- und Gehalts-Tarifvertrag, für die gewerblichen Arbeitnehmer und Angestellten des Speditions-, Transport- und Logistikgewerbes in Bayern (Lohntarifvertrag Nr. 27), gültig ab 1. Oktober 2004. München: Ver.di, 2005.

Endnotes

[1] A similar classification can be found in Mielentz/Trump (2004): 38.

[2] The vehicle cost data is based on eight in-depth interviews conducted with German short-haul carriers in December 2006 and January 2007. As far as possible these costs were verified by data from official sources like authorities, associations, and unions.

[3] Toll is not considered in this calculation since toll roads are of minor importance in distribution business.

[4] Similar calculations are to be found in Kerler (2001): p. 30.

[5] Assuming linear depreciation is justified since the fleet of a logistics service provider or an other company doing deliveries normally consists of trucks of different ages. A declining depreciation would possibly be realistic for one particular truck but distort the calculation of an average yearly depreciation.

[6] For simplicity reasons interest on interest is not considered in this calculation.

[7] The approximation of the annual insurance premium results from a comparison of the premium quotations by four German insurers (VHV – Vereinigte Hannoversche Versicherungen, D.A.S. Versicherungen, Zürich Versicherung, and Aachenmünchener Versicherung). This comparison was done using an online tool by Ansahl Consulting (Ansahl online 2007).

[8] Both cost informations (maintenance/repair costs and auxiliary materials) are based on data supplied by the interviewed carriers. If the costing was done absolutely exact, these cost elements should be calculated per kilometre, similar to the calculation of diesel costs. However, since maintenance/repair and auxiliary material are costs of minor importance, we consider it justified to do a simplified calculation on a daily basis.

[9] These figures per hour are higher than the driver wages discussed in section 12.2.1. The Eurostat figures, however, comprise the sector "traffic and communication". In communication and news transmission the wages tend to be higher than in transport industry. Moreover, in the Eurostat figures, white-collar employees are considered as well as blue-collar workers whereas the calculation of driver wages would only require the (lower) blue-collar workers' wages.

[10] LTL = "less than truck load" (shipments between approx. 30 and 2,500 kg).

[11] A study regarding driving personnel which was recently executed by Fraunhofer ATL Nuremberg on behalf of the German forwarders' association DSLV brought similar results: On average short-haul trucks are doing 14 stops per tour (Hassa 2007, p. 24).

[12] It needs to be pointed out that both factors are dependent from each other: In case of long distances the speed tends to be higher than with short distances. If, for example, two delivery points are only a few hundred meters distant from each other, the vehicle will hardly speed up to more than 30–40 km/h, especially if both delivery points are within the same borough with speed limits to be obeyed. If, however, there is a long distance of 10 or more kilometers, there will be less speed limits on the one hand and autobahn or motorway connections allowing higher speeds on the other hand.

Chapter 13
DSD Infrastructure: IT in the Consumer Products Industry

Value-Add and Future Trends from the Scientific Perspective

Jörg Becker, Axel Winkelmann, and Philippe Fuchs

Westfälische Wilhelms-Universität Münster, European Research Center for Information Systems (ERCIS), Leonardo-Campus 3, D-48149, Münster, tel.: +49 251 83 38 100, e-mails: becker@ercis.de; axel.winkelmann@ercis.de; philippe.fuchs@ercis.de

Abstract

Technological and social changes lead to transformations of the Consumer Products Industry and to an increase in DSD. Its importance within a supply chain grows together with the increase in data availability, information retrieval and flexibility. Modern information systems play a key role for DSD because they assure the necessary supply and exchange of information and data. The success of the consumer products industry is determined by current state and quality of ERP implementations. Furthermore, the flexibility of modern information technology has an impact on strategic and organisational potentials. The article discusses the impact of modern technologies on DSD and gives recommendations on flexible IT architectures.

13.1 Transformation of the Consumer Products Industry Driven by Technological and Social Change

In the consumer products industry, every quarter of a century since the year 1800 a wave of innovation has been initiated by changing political or technological realities as well as the transformation of the type of business. This amends the long-term economical observations by Kondratjew und Nefiodow. Whilst the beginning of the 18th century merchant shipping dominated trade from its centres in trading towns such as Amsterdam, London and Hamburg, the focus shifted to domestic trade in Europe with the omission of monopolistic barriers to trade. In the following of the Congress of Vienna the state of Prussia created a tariff regime for its own territory that was joined by more and more smaller states. At the end of that century the first larger department stores evolved and cooperative federations followed. Starting around the year 1925 mail-order trade emerged. Growing

A. Otto et al., *Direct Store Delivery*,

DOI: 10.1007/978-3-540-77213-2_13,

individual mobility paced the way for the development of large out-of-town retail parks. Since the 1980s the development of business models in trade is driven by technological advances – especially information technology enables further specialisation and multi-channel strategies (see Table 13.1).

Table 13.1 Trade innovations and long economic cycles (Adapted and Translated from Hallier 2001, p. 64)

Long economic cycles and most important fields of innovation								
England		England Germany USA		England Germany USA		Germany Japan USA		
Steam Engine Cotton Wool Clothing		Steel Trains Transport		Electrotechnology Chemistry Mass Consumption		Petrochemistry Automobile Individual Mobility	Psychosocial Health Information Technology Health	
1800	1825	1850	1875	1900	1925	1950	1975	2000
Maritime and imperial wholesale and foreign trade	German Tariff Union (Deutscher Zollverein) Start of domestic trade	Employees' self-help associations Local consumer co-operative societies	Start of warehouses and department stores	First national buying association	Start of first mail-order businesses	Introduction of self-service Supermarkets	Self-service department stores Shopping-center Specialist retailers	Internet B2B B2C

The importance of DSD within a supply chain grows together with the increase in data availability, information retrieval and flexibility. The aim is the further reduction of the out-of-stock-quota and inventory expressed by costs of capital lockup. Besides fast and direct replenishment by the supplier, direct delivery to retail locations offers the possibility to supervise the handling of goods until they are sold. Flexible IT architectures and Ubiquitous Technologies like radio frequency identification (RFID) could technologically support and improve this process. In a survey conducted during the EHI Technology Days in November 2007, around 80% of the surveyed trade technology experts predicted a rising importance of DSD business compared to warehousing business in the future (Fig. 13.1; own survey).

Modern information systems play a key role for DSD because they assure the necessary supply and exchange of information and data. The success of the consumer products industry is determined by current state and quality of ERP implementations. Furthermore, the flexibility of modern information technology has an impact on strategic and organisational potentials.

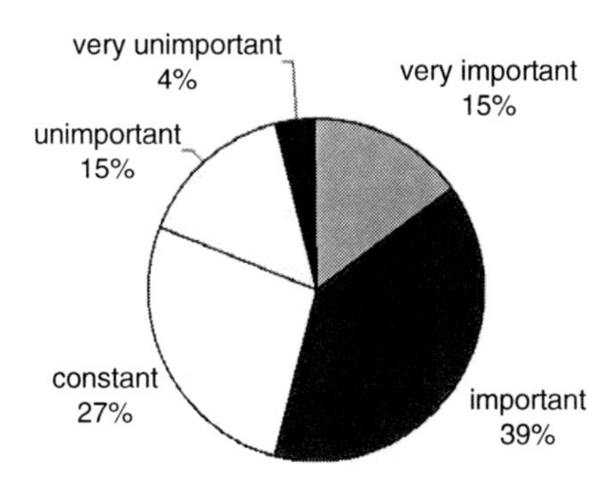

Fig. 13.1 Impact of DSD in contrast to warehousing business in the future

ERP systems today support all processes of production, procurement, logistics and sales. Especially the inter-organisational data exchange between different ERP systems is becoming increasingly relevant. Therefore, the majority of ERP systems offer modern software architectures. A recent survey of the European Research Center for Information Systems (ERCIS) indicates that over 50% of all ERP architectures have been developed since the year 2000 (Winkelmann et al. 2007). Furthermore, numerous technological innovations will drive changes in the Consumer Goods Industry in the coming years. Gartner identified several technologies in its Hype-Cycle-Retail-Study that have already left the experimental stage and are on the way to become industry standard in retail (see Fig. 13.2). Besides optimization technologies, like self-checkout and touch less payment, several of these technologies will have a direct impact on DSD and the Supply Chain.

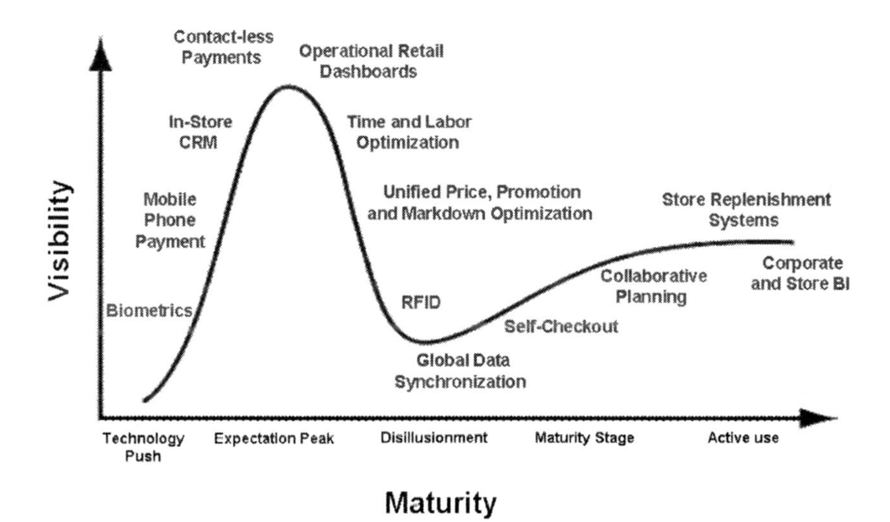

Fig. 13.2 Hype cycle for retail technologies (http://www.gartner.com)

13.2 Supply Chain Event Management (SCEM) in Inter-Organizational Processes

The term SCEM sums up telematic services that are used to manage the logistic chain. Whilst the objective of procurement and manufacturing is cost reduction by constantly improving processes, the objective of distribution and sales is to operate just-in-time sales to the full customer satisfaction. Technical approaches and methods such as tracking and tracing – online-based monitoring and planning of goods, loading equipment and vehicles – are bundled and enhanced with additional functionality (example: automated alerts) for an improved decision support and steering along the supply chain. A stronger involvement of external partners and service providers into logistics, information management and even production processes make the quality management more fragile. Usually each supply chain partner uses its own units for information and goods; therefore it can only provide its own company-specific status information. But supply chain management requires the cooperative availability of information to eliminate warehousing as much as possible and to transform fixed costs from capital lockup into variable costs in the context of DSD. Especially online retailing reflects the tight integration of customer, supplier and others partners, when goods are just requested or even supplied in the moment the order has been placed (Fig. 13.3).

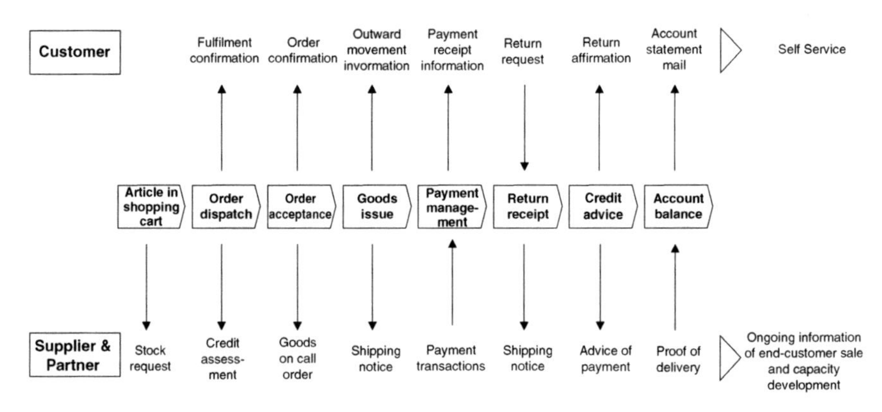

Fig. 13.3 Supply-chain-operations in online retailing (Becker and Winkelmann 2008, p. 408)

Ideally, companies organize their supply chain on the base of shared business objectives and processes (Merrilees and Miller 1996, pp. 86–99). They arrange their IT-systems in a way to enable collaborative planning, execution and decision making in real-time, targeted on pro-active interaction directly out of the process chain. Predefined rules, in suitable SCEM software, define the reaction to deviations from the ideal process. Ideally hereunto, real-time data is available to react flexible to changes in the supply chain. That real-time data is increasingly registered by RFID systems.

13.3 RFID Technologies as Foundation for the Digitalisation of the Flow of Goods

The application of the RFID technology has become mature. Although first experimental applications of the new technology already took place in the mid-1990s, serious applications in the domain of logistics have been available since 2003. Since last year, RFID tags have been used operational in the daily business of stores, for example in back-tracing deliveries in the context of DSD. It could be assumed that within the next 10 years the application will be expanded to consumer packing units (see Fig. 13.4).

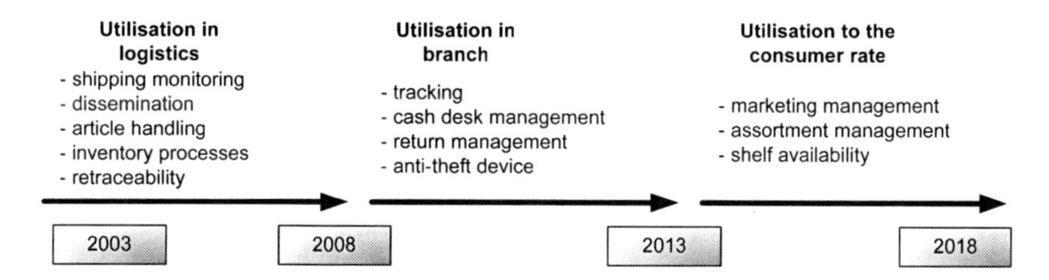

Fig. 13.4 Changes of the RFID-landscape in retailing (Pretzel, 2007)

RFID – understood as supply chain standard – has several layers. The Electronic Product Code (EPC) is used to identify each specific RFID tag. Each EPC is a worldwide unique number to identify any kind of object. The EPC Tag Data Standard defines a data head with control data, an EPC manager to identify the issuer, an article reference to relate to groups of objects and finally a serialised numerical part to identify a single object.

Additionally, the Gen 2 Air Interface Protocols define physical and logical requirements for RFID systems. The core EPC Infrastructure standards are Reader Management, Reader Protocol, mechanisms to detect single RFID tags within batches (filter & collection) and especially the EPC Information System Protocol (EPCIS). EPCIS is used to precisely track all movements of goods or logistical units along the supply chain. In order to do so, manufacturers need to make databases available. Those contain further information for each product type or even a single good identified by its EPC. Further information could include product specifications, licenses, and best before dates. Within EPCIS it is possible to trace who saved which information where and why. The "Object Name Service" (EPC ONS) translates the EPC vendor identifier into the web-address of the corresponding database. Authorised persons (via Subscriber Authentification) can use a Discovery Interface to search for information within such a database (Fig. 13.5).

From the perspective of DSD especially the growing application of RFID in stores and logistics offers huge advantages over the conventional handling of goods. Fast registration of goods on the level of whole pallets as well as single items

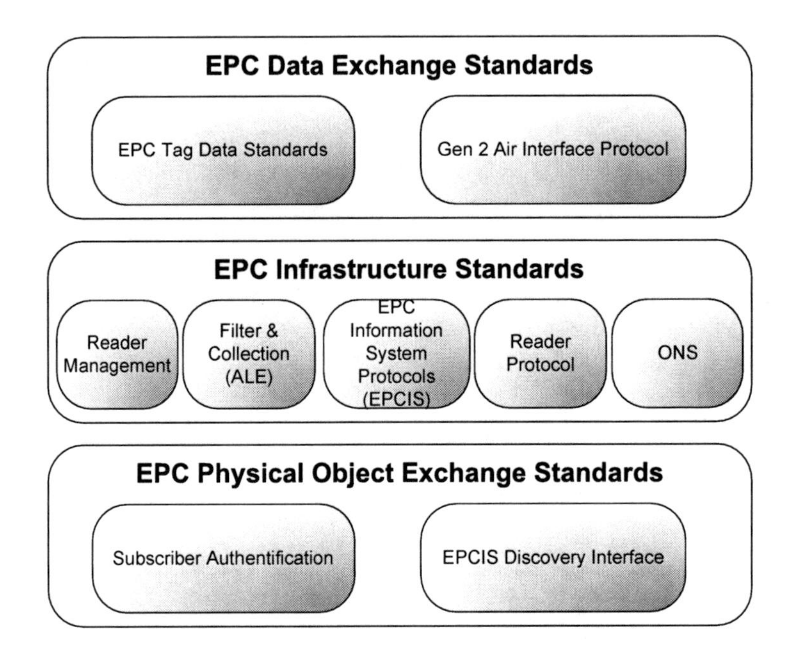

Fig. 13.5 EPC global Standards for RFID-based identification

enables an efficient control of the flow of goods. In the future, sales persons will be able to compile replenishment orders on the spot at the customer's location, because the required numbers can be recorded touch less with RFID technology. In a second step even the number of calls could be reduced. Real-time in-store article coverage creates the chance to let merchants collect information and just send it over to the supplier (see Fig. 13.6; Alexander et al. 2002).

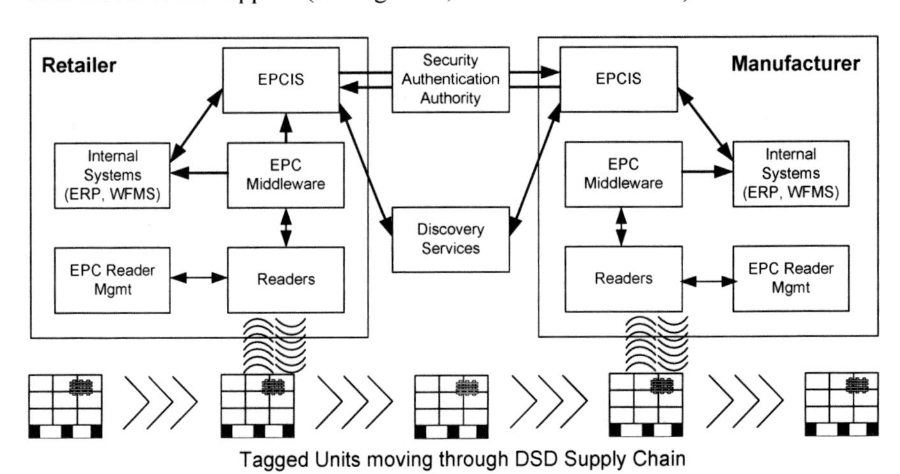

Fig. 13.6 RFID units moving through the DSD supply chain

Procter&Gamble showed one possible line of development with the introduction of the "Gilette Fusion Power" shaver. Each packaging had been tagged with a RFID chip to allow tracking of the use of promotional displays and sales in store. Stores and transit stations in the Supply Chain were equipped with reading devices to control availability and sales of the shavers. In doing so, Procter&Gamble found out that only 45 out of 100 displays had been used as such and only two-thirds of those as shelf separators. In nearly every third store the status "out of stock" indicated further demand for displays.

Table 13.2 outlines benefits and costs for producers and retailers for RFID usage from the perspective of the Consumer Products Industry. The potential of RFID in the Consumer Products Industry will apparently become useful for DSD as it offers real-time data about availability and sales that can be used for more targeted replenishment.

Table 13.2 Benefits and costs of RFID usage in the consumer products industry

Benefits	Costs (hardware/software)
• Reduction of efforts for goods is-suing in the suppliers' warehouses through automated identification of RFID tagged items • Thus, better truck fleet efficiency because every quantity unit is individually controllable (Saygin et al. 2007, p. 9). • Reduction of wrong loading • Reduction of effort in each store's goods arrival by automated adjustment of order and shipping notice (Sotriffer 2004, p. 16). • Reduced effort for detailed controls (best before, number, weight, etc.) Lee and Wolfe 2003, p. 12). • Automated identification and protocol of containers	• RFID gates for reading points (especially arrival of goods) • RFID handheld devices • RFID printer to produce EPC tags • Adjustment/extension of legacy systems, especially software

13.4 Need for Data Management Improvement

The consumer products industry has been actively discussing collaboration, RFID and global data synchronisation for a more efficient information flow. Nevertheless, in order to efficiently manage products digitally, basic product data quality has to be reliable (Mason and Burns 1998, pp. 122–127.) For example, self check-out and a stronger store digitalisation enforce the need for reliable article data. New sales promotion instruments such as couponing have to rely on high data quality at the POS in order to automatically match redeemed coupons and purchased products.

Entering and editing master data such as price, weight or storage conditions is necessary for the sensible automated product handling. Automatic disposition in DSD is another demanding application for correct master data. So far, accuracy and consistency of product data are lacking at both ends of the supply chain. Even worse, bad data quality on one end will affect other companies once the data is exchanged in a collaboration effort.

At the ECR Europe Conference 2004, Nestlé stated that half of their data entries are either redundant or false. The standard EAN*UCC global data dictionary (GDD) has more than 150 attributes such as weight, number of products in pack, product dimensions, sub-brands, etc. Even more, the number of attributes tends to increase. Therefore, a proper data quality management is very difficult for retailers and manufacturers.

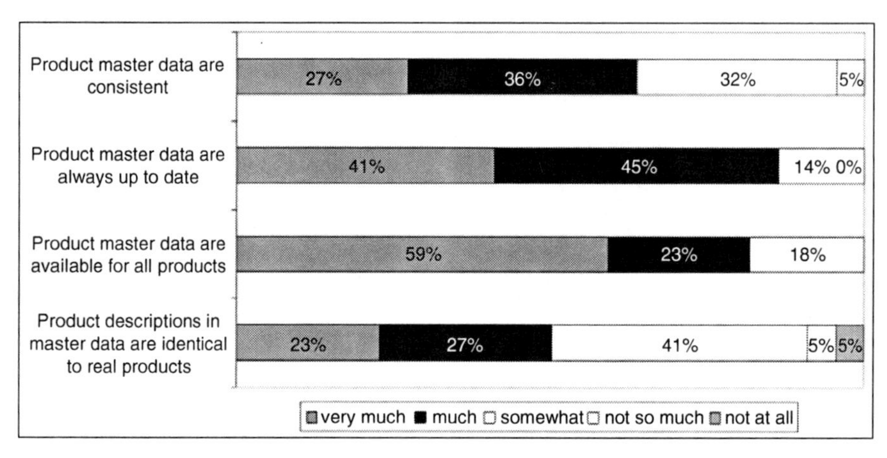

Fig. 13.7 Survey about recent master data quality within the companies of 22 retail experts in 2007 (Own Survey)

The synchronisation of data between retail and industry is one of the most important topics regarding information technology, because aligned master data is the basic requirement for electronic business relations. Multiple entries within a supply chain lead to unnecessary failures and costs. This in mind, trade and industry exchange business-relevant data either bilateral or over so-called master data pools. The creation of centralised article master data is a large complex constant task that is especially necessary for the acceptance of scanner cash registers. The advantage for trade companies lies in the reduction of master data entering as well as the avoidance of errors and the effort to fix them especially in the areas of arrival and audit. Data is checked multiple times within a master data pool for consistency; therefore merchants can easily pick the required data from the pool and realise cost savings that way. This also drives the growing demand for such services, but there is also the problem of fragmentation into regional or industry-specific master data pools (see Fig. 13.7).

The Global Data Synchronization Network (GDSN) concept, developed by the standardisation organisations GS1, UCC and CGI, tries to solve the fragmentation problem virtually in real-time. The concept is based on exchanging master data over additional standards between different pools and a global directory. Each manufacturer uploads data to its master data pool; then they are automatically recorded in the Global Registry and can be identified by other master data pool. The retailer can request this data from its master data pool that then synchronises with the one of the manufacturer.

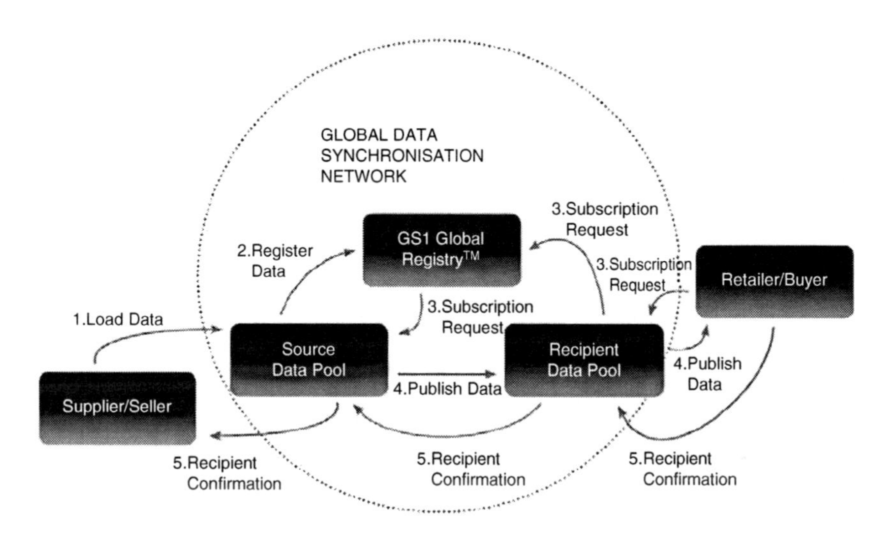

Fig. 13.8 Exchange of master data (http://www.gs1.org)

There are also initiatives towards data exchange in the area of the electronic product code that is required for the use of RFID technology in order to identify a single item (Fig. 13.8). The GS1 EPCglobal Network enables trading partners to engage in the capture, sharing and discovery of Electronic Product Code (EPC)-related data through the use of standards-based hardware and software components. The GDSN and EPCglobal Network are complementary solutions. The GDSN and data synchronisation ensure that trade item information about a product (e.g. dimensions, descriptions, price) is accurate across trading partner systems at any time. The EPCglobal network tracks the whereabouts of products in the supply chain.

The GDSN improves business processes based on dispatching processes in the fields of data registration, compliance to standards and data synchronisation; leading to lower data management costs within the supply chain. The EPC global network improves dispatching processes with regard to status information by enabling partner of a supply chain to collect and share EPC data. This reduces costs for loss, products recall and order fulfilment and enables the improvement of warehouse management as well as tracking and tracing.

Table 13.3 Differences between GDSN and EPCglobal network (http://www.gs1.org)

	GDSN	EPCglobal Network
Business Use	Collaborative e-commerce	Supply chain visibility
Mission	Ensure **information quality** between trading partners	**Track and trace** The physical movement of items
Primary Functions	**Data synchronisation and GS1 System compliance validation**, as a foundation for collaborative transaction management (B2B electronic commerce)	**Records supply chain history** with events and states changes, enabling real-time supply visibility over the internet
Type of Information	**WHAT and WHO:** Item, price and party master data GTIN (what) and GLN (who)	**WHEN and WHERE:** Instance-specific information, the unique identification of individual items using serialised EPCs

13.5 Building Flexible IT Architectures with SOA

A fundamental aspect to enable data exchange and shared functions within the Consumer Products Industry is building IT architectures that are appropriate to inter-organisational co-operation. The managerial concept strives for an architecture aligned to the desired business processes. Furthermore, the IT should be built in a way that allows for quick changes in the case of changes in the business environment. The system concept underlines the provision of services that represent atomic steps in a process.

Service-oriented architectures (SOA) describe system architectures in which functionality is implemented in reusable, technical independent and functional loosely linked services. Each service is a small software building block that can be used over its interfaces. Instead of changing large parts of a system for every new or changed business process, the idea of SOA is to line up service calls to achieve maximum reusability.

In the case of Harrods, the address validation and revision is implemented as reusable service for different applications. This makes it much easier to analyse specific parts of a transaction throughout different channels of distribution and different software applications. In this case the implementation was much easier, with fewer costs and a faster development (Loderhose 2006).

Important aspects of service-oriented architectures are simplification, lower TCO, shorter development cycle and faster rollout of software. Additionally, the effort needed for integration is lower. The ability to analyse certain parts of a business over different channels and software applications in a fast and flexible manner is an essential requirement for operational cooperation of trade and industry in the DSD business.

An important part of trendsetting inter-organisational software systems is the connection of mobile data input devices. In DSD business they are currently used to record data at all parts of a store. However, in the moment not all ERP systems support mobile data access. Numerous ERP companies have reacted to market demands regarding mobile access to company data. About two third of ERP systems offer some sort of mobile access (mostly via Windows PDA) (see Fig. 13.9).

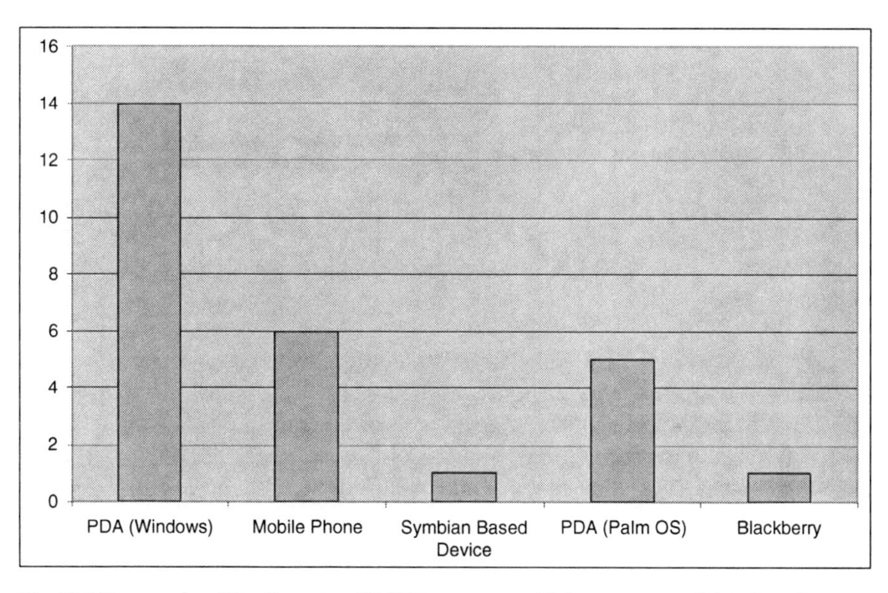

Fig. 13.9 Supported mobile clients (n = 26 ERP systems, multiple answers possible) (Own Survey)

13.6 Inter-organisational Reporting

The phrase “information beats value” coined by Tietz is becoming increasingly true for the relation between supplier and retailer. For nearly half of all trade experts that have been surveyed in autumn 2007 improving their reporting system is important or even very important. Problems in harmonising terms, performance figures and reference objects are the most often mentioned aspects of the existing business intelligence systems. Thiry-two percent consider improving reports in general as very important and 46% consider it to be important (Fig. 13.10).

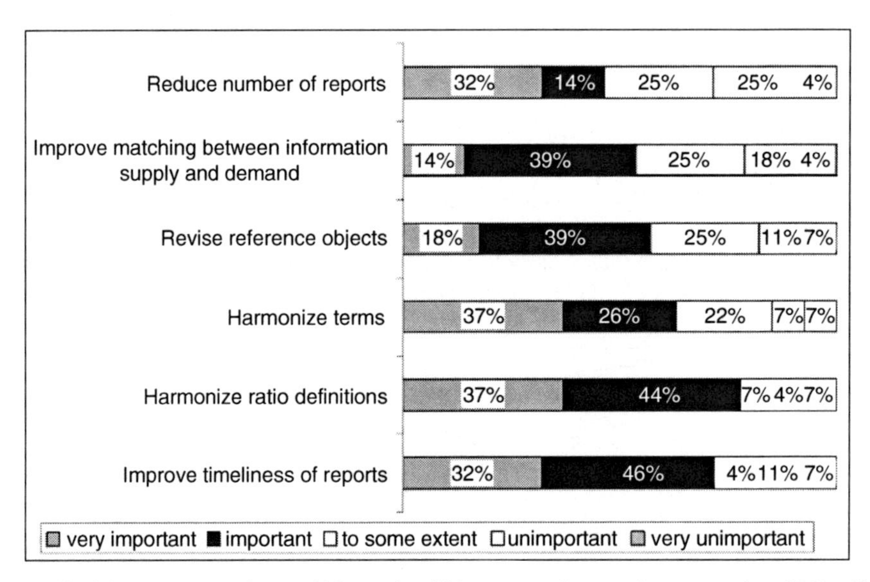

Fig. 13.10 Improvements that could be made within company's reporting system (n = 28 Retail experts) (Own Survey)

Supplier portals as part of a business intelligence strategy in retail become increasingly important even in midsized commercial enterprises. These portals offer current sales to the supplier and enable thereby timely replenishment. The aim is to detect quality defects in the supply chain and on the other hand to provide data suitable for DSD. For example the Metro Group uses different scorecards to measure the relation to their consumer product suppliers in different selling channels. The main topics are promotions, sales, delivery reliability and ECR implementation. In total, 60 key performance indicators are used to rate up to one thousand suppliers in the business units Cash+Carry, Real und Extra (Becker and Winkelmann 2008, p. 462). Over the extranet platform a supplier can access multiple scorecards reflecting its performance in the sense of benchmarking. Market research data like scanner data can also be considered for these scorecards. Suppliers can also track their sales increases for promotions and the accuracy of forecasts.

13.7 Conclusion

From the IT point of view, flexible ready to integrate IT architectures combined with the coordinated adjustment of high-profile data are essential value-drivers. There are no specific revolutionary technologies driving DSD in particular but there are several evolutionary technologies that will help to simplify and develop DSD further. The way towards an integrated supply chain is not revolutionary but evolutionary. Technologies such as RFID and service-oriented architectures create new opportunities for merging business processes among the supply chain and hence reducing warehouse stocks in favour of DSD. An increase of reliable and high quality master data will lead to ongoing changes in supply chain business processes. Hence, the importance of DSD for the consumer products industry will increase.

References

Alexander, K.; Birkhofer, G.; Gramling, K.; Kleinberger, H.; Leng, S.; Moogimane, D.; Woods, M. (2002): Focus on Retail: Applying Auto-ID to Improve Product Availability at the Retail Shelf. White Paper, www.autoidcenter.com, 2002.

Becker, J .; Winkelmann, A. (2008): Handelscontrolling. 2nd Edition. Berlin.

Hallier, B. (2001): Praxisorientierte Handelsforschung. Köln.

Lee, H. L.; Wolfe, M. (2003): Supply Chain Security Without Tears. In: Supply Chain Management Review 1, pp. 12–20.

Loderhose, B. (2006): Harrods hebt mit neuer IT ab. In: Lebensmittelzeitung vom 10.11.2006.

Mason, J.B.; Burns, D.J. (1998): Retailing. Houston, TX.

Merrilees, B.; Miller, D. (1996): Retailing Management. A Best Practice Approach. Victoria, Australia.

Pretzel, J.; RFID (2007): Standortbestimmung und praktische Erfahrung. Vortrag auf den EHI-Technologie-Tagen, 13./14.11.2007, Köln.

Saygin, C.; Sarangapani, J.; Grasman, S.E. (2007): A Systems Approach to Viable RFID Implementation in the Suppy Chain. In: Jung, H.; Chen, F. F.; Jeong, B. (Eds.): Trends in supply chain design and management: technologies and methodologies. Berlin et al. 2007, pp. 3–28.

Sotriffer, I. (2004): RFID und Rückverfolgbarkeit : Neue Perspektiven für die Logistik. 1. RFID Kongress, Bad Homburg.

Winkelmann, A.; Knackstedt, R.; Vering, O. (2007): Anpassung und Entwicklung von Warenwirtschaftssystemen – eine explorative Untersuchung. In: Becker, J. (Ed.): Handelsstudien 2007.

Chapter 14
Adaptable DSD Business Solutions

Franz Josef Schoppengerd

Vice President Emerging Solutions & Architecture, Industry Solution Management – Consumer Products & Life Sciences, Product Technology Unit Industries, SAP AG, Dietmar-Hopp-Allee 16, D-69190, Walldorf, tel.: +49 6227 748820,
e-mail: franz.josef.schoppengerd@sap.com

Abstract

Efficiency and operational excellence in the DSD business depend heavily on the adequate IT support of the DSD business processes. There are a variety of IT vendors delivering solutions for all kinds of business processes; we can also find a lot of home-grown applications and even today many companies still perform their visit execution with paper-based processes. This chapter discusses today's IT coverage of the DSD business processes and how future trends and challenges can be met. The collaboration of different IT vendors on a commonly agreed architecture will be a prerequisite for higher flexibility and adaptability, and a lower total cost of ownership.

14.1 Is There a One-Size-Fits-All IT Solution for DSD Business Processes?

Dimas Rodrigues is a store owner in Cusco, Peru. His store is located in a residential area about 1 mile from the historical center of the ancient Inca capital. He mainly serves the households of the neighborhood and tourists staying in near-by hotels. His store has a size of about 300 ft^2 and his main products are food & beverages and home & personal care articles. Dimas opens his store at 7 am and closes at around 10 pm.

Charles Miller has recently been promoted to store manager for a huge retail store in Toledo, Ohio, US. His store is located outside the city close to other department stores. Charles's customers typically come in via car and carry out the shopping for the week. Charles' store has a size of 80,000 ft^2; the store carries about 40,000 different products. Charles is responsible for about 250 employees running the store 24 h 7 days a week.

How Dimas and Charles run their store operations is significantly different, but from the point of view of the manufacturer and his interest to serve the consumer we see common targets.

A. Otto et al., *Direct Store Delivery*,
DOI: 10.1007/978-3-540-77213-2_14, © Springer-Verlag Berlin Heidelberg 2009

What are the most relevant common targets for the IT support of the DSD business process?

- The consumer is boss: having the goods ready in the store when the consumer stands at the shelf and chooses a brand to purchase is the so-called first moment of truth (Arlqueeuw 2008)
- IT solutions have to be effective from a logistics point of view (e.g. minimizing out-of-stock situations) and at the same time deliver excellent support for the customer relation management (e.g. account and promotion management)
- Increased customer loyalty (here the loyalty of the store manager) is a critical success factor
- IT solutions must efficiently support at the point of sales. Relevant information should be provided to the store manager to enable better decisions for purchasing and merchandising (GMA 2005)
- Information gathering at the point of sales for improved demand visibility: while DSD is often viewed from the logistics aspect only, information gathering is entering into the focus of the DSD operations (Otto and Shariatmadari, 2008). The various IT components (mobile application, middleware and back-end application) need to enable the seamless flow of information
- Sales and logistics efficiency as a foundation for growth in a cost competitive environment:
  the DSD-process is strongly dependent on human resources. Thus, growth can be reached either by expanding the human workforce or by increasing the efficiency of the human workforce. IT applications, mainly in the mobile area, play a significant role for this target
- The goals of the CP manufacturers show many similarities independent of which type of store they serve. In contrast, the execution at the store level is significantly diverse. The challenge for an IT solution is to deliver those components that allow scalability and reliability for the common goals and at the same time to enable the specific differentiation in a cost-effective way.

14.2 Today's IT Support for DSD Business Processes

The focus for DSD lies often on the visit execution. Therefore, "***mobile*** DSD applications" is used synonymously with DSD applications. However, DSD operations require excellent back office support and the seamless functioning of all IT components.

Most companies base their back-end-operations and visit planning on standardized ERP-systems. In many cases visit execution is performed with the help of offline mobile applications that are synchronized at the beginning and the end of each route. The number of companies using paper-based operations is still huge, whereas pure online scenarios are still the exception.

In the following, we will discuss how a typical IT support for the route sales scenario[1] looks like, which IT solutions are used, how companies evaluate the importance of the various process steps and how users evaluate their current IT support for DSD.

14.2.1 How do IT Systems Support Route Sales Today?

The number of DSD process variants is huge and the ways companies operate DSD show significant differences. Some companies operate DSD on separate and independent instances; they synchronize their systems regularly with their ERP-systems. Other companies operate DSD completely within their ERP systems and connect mobile devices to the ERP system. More sales & marketing oriented approaches use both the company's CRM and ERP systems to support DSD.

Independent of the scenario used, the daily operation for route sales can be described using a simple process flow model.[2] The model shown does not claim completeness nor can it consider specifics such as different distribution models via interim storage locations. It is meant to describe the general principle.

Order Management: Companies typically support order entry via different channels. Orders are received by EDI, fax or other means and entered directly into the company's back-end system. Often call centers for inbound or outbound tele-sales manage order-taking via phone, entering data online into the ERP-system. Or, thirdly, the mobile sales force takes orders on mobile devices with subsequent synchronization with the back-end system.

Within the ERP's order management system the prices are calculated and at least some preliminary delivery routes are assigned. Sometimes the availability of products is already checked at this stage; some companies, however, assume full availability of their products or execute the availability check after the receipt of all orders. Most companies have service level agreements in place and have a defined cut-off time to accept orders for delivery on the following day.

Tour Preparation: The typical tour is defined by the customer visits scheduled for one truck on 1 day. In urban areas one truck may have multiple tours per day, whereas in remote areas a tour can span multiple days. In the route sales process the load quantities have to be forecasted. In addition to the already known sales orders, the system estimates the quantity for those customers who will be visited but had not placed an order.[3]

The tour preparation differentiates between static and dynamic routes. Static routes have a predefined customer visit sequence for each day of the week. In this case, the assignment of an order to a route is relatively simple and the tour preparation uses criteria such as the day of the week or the customer number. Additional necessary checks such as vehicle capacity are performed during tour preparation to alert and support the planner.

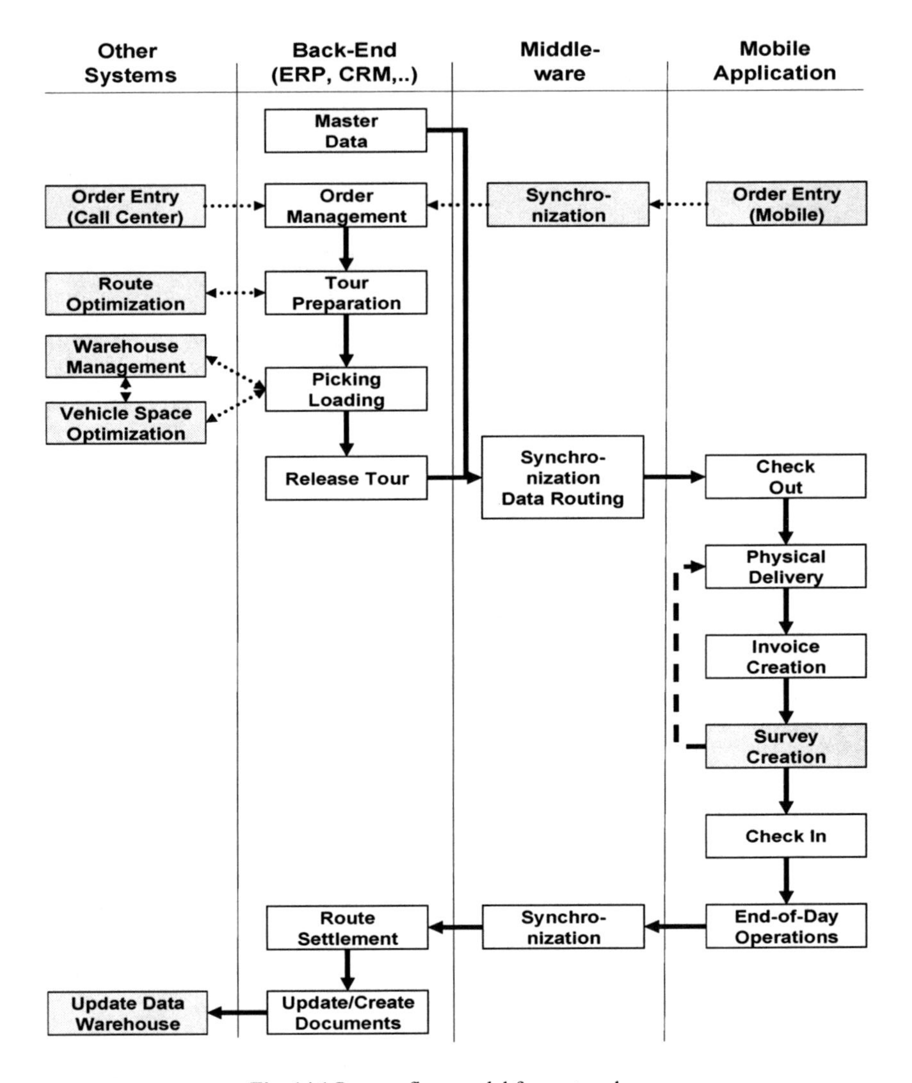

Fig. 14.1 Process flow model for route sales

In the dynamic case, routes are newly defined for each tour. Dynamic routes can be created by using heuristics such as the capacity of the vehicle, the maximum distance per day or the maximum working time per driver. Scenarios that are more sophisticated work with route optimization applications to determine the optimal delivery sequence (Fig. 14.1). Optimization applications connect to the ERP system via standard interfaces.

The support for **picking and loading** is similar to non-DSD distribution processes. The sequence of customer visits generally determines how the truck is loaded. Some companies operate with vehicle space optimization software – either interfaced to the ERP System or to the warehouse management system – to determine the packing of mixed pallets and the loading sequence on a truck.

Synchronization is carried out by the mobile middleware. The middleware collects from the back-end systems all relevant data for a tour, including the relevant master data. This is the customer and product master data as well as pricing information. The main task of the mobile middleware is to map the back-end data to the mobile data structure and to route the correct information to the correct mobile device.

During **check-out** the inventory on the truck is finally counted and discrepancies are recorded. Check-out is often executed on the device of the delivery driver. The advantage is that the inventory on the mobile device can be adjusted without additional synchronization with the back-end system.

The delivery driver performs the **tour execution** solely using the mobile device. Depending on the mobile connectivity of the mobile device, information between the back-end system and the mobile device can be exchanged during tour execution. Sales orders received from customers and entered in the mobile device can be transmitted to the back-end system. This allows early preparation for the next tour. In the same way, tour information or tour changes can be communicated to the delivery driver.

At the end of a tour the driver executes the **check-in** and the **end-of-day-operation.** All information such as the remaining inventory on the truck or cash collected is prepared by the delivery driver for final **synchronization** with the back-end-system.

The **route settlement** checks the consistency of the tour results and technically initiates the update of the relevant information to the back-end system. Delivery quantities are updated and invoicing and payment information is stored in the back-end system. Sales orders taken along the route are entered in the back-end system. The **data warehouse** is not directly updated by the route settlement but via the documents created through the route settlement. This standard update process ensures consistency between DSD and non-DSD operations.

The above model for the route sales process shows that synchronization between the back-end system and the mobile device is the most critical operation. Specifically, if the back-end and mobile application is supplied by different vendors, the maintenance effort to keep both applications in synch is very high. Consequentially, process changes have to be planned carefully in advance.

14.2.2 Which DSD Solutions are Used Today?

When looking at the DSD operations, it is interesting to discuss which back-end and which mobile applications are used. As we can see from the following diagram, the mobile application market is very fragmented and the use of home-grown solutions at 14% is relatively high. For the back-end applications the study shows a

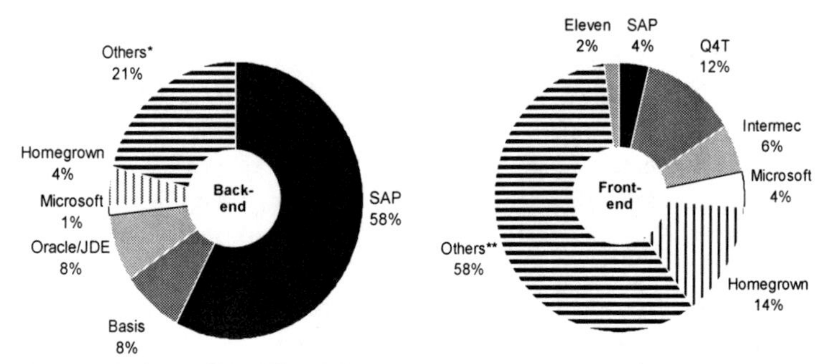

Fig. 14.2 The DSD software market (Otto and Shariatmadari 2008)

different picture; one vendor – with a market share of 58% – serves the majority of customers. The share of home-grown applications is only at 4% (Fig. 14.2).

These figures clearly point towards the diversity of requirements for the visit execution using mobile devices. This market fragmentation is caused by the fact that in the past companies and vendors developed tailor-made mobile applications, and thus far no consolidation has occurred. In addition, the variety of technical mobile platforms does not support the porting of applications from one mobile platform to the other. Moreover, the device performance and the needed efficiency can often only be reached by providing mobile device-specific applications.

The above study also found that currently no vendor fulfills more than 65% of all important DSD business requirements (Otto and Shariatmadari 2008).

14.2.3 How do Companies Assess the Importance of DSD Process Components?

DSD allows the manufacturer direct access to the point of sales, and thus to the product-consumer-interface, on a regular basis. Consequently, the manufacturer can perform various activities which generate a value-add to the consumer products companies as well as to their trading partners. This value-add clearly goes beyond the logistics operations towards marketing support. Hence, DSD companies request IT support from both areas – logistics, and the sales & marketing area.

Excellent IT support in both areas becomes a critical success factor during physical distribution. However, not all functionalities are of equal importance. The study of Otto and Shariatmadari broke down the DSD requirements by functional area, and found significant differences in the rated average importance per area. It has been observed that overall requirements in the area of logistics are viewed as most important, with execution of deliveries, management of goods returned and stock management occupying the top positions.

In the area of sales & marketing, capturing of orders, sales analysis (e.g. sales history and customer profitability) and information gathering are ranked highest. While some requirements have special relevancy in certain regions or segments, this conclusion remains valid for the majority of requirements across all boundaries.

The following figure (Fig. 14.3) illustrates the different levels of importance of selected DSD requirements during the customer visit.

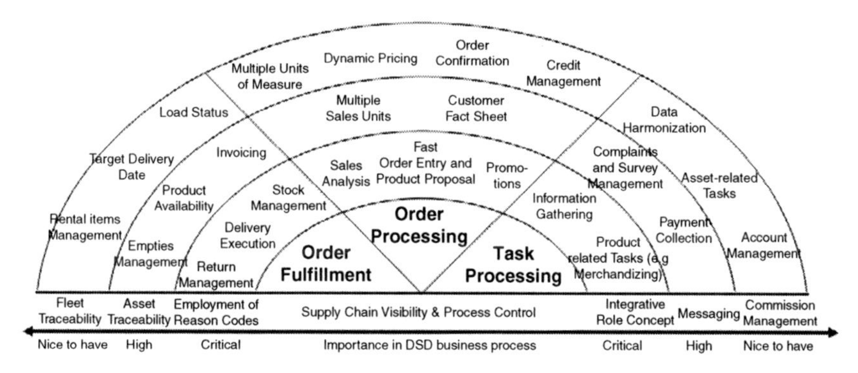

Fig. 14.3 Relative importance of the IT support for DSD (Otto and Shariatmadari 2008)

14.2.4 How do Companies Assess Today's IT Support for DSD?

When looking at the challenges for future IT support, it is important to highlight how companies view their current IT solutions. Today, most solutions focus on either logistics or on sales & marketing operations. The starting point for logistics applications was traditionally the pure delivery process, for sales & marketing applications, order-taking support came first. Although the assessments of the two types of applications show unlike results, most companies view their IT support as sufficient.

In **order management**, the basic needs are largely supported by IT solutions. Order entry by various channels (Call Center, EDI, Presellers) is regarded as one of the most important requirements. Planning aspects in order management, such as demand management or estimation, are also considered as important but lack IT support. For the planning tasks, most companies still rely on the expertise of their sales personnel and desire increased support from IT solutions.

With **tour preparation** many companies historically use fixed routes to execute the delivery process. Therefore IT solutions support this type of route management in a stable way. Dynamic route processing is considered to be important as well, but satisfaction with the current IT solutions is significant lower as for the fixed route processing.

Accuracy of truck inventory and minimizing shrinkage are the main reasons for executing a **check-out** before the truck leaves the company premises. The check-out is time-consuming and companies have introduced various methods to speed up the process. The support from IT solutions is viewed as satisfactory except for some minor requirements in the area of sealed vehicles or vehicle security checks.

In the **physical distribution** process the truck drivers execute typical logistics and sales-related activities. The evaluation of IT solutions for the physical distribution process shows significant differences between solutions that are viewed as "logistics-oriented offerings" and those that are viewed as "sales & marketing-oriented offerings".

In order processing, sales & marketing-oriented solutions show a much better coverage of DSD process requirements. While pure order capturing can be performed by most front-end solutions, the ability to capture instructions for orders as well as the capability to identify products by a broad range of options (e.g. barcode, RFID) act as the major differentiating factors. Sales & marketing-oriented solutions seem to have a significant advantage for the execution of customer-specific order proposals. In addition, the on-site exploration of cross selling and up selling potential is well supported.

The biggest differences between the two types of solutions are found in the gathering of information at point of sales and the execution of product-related tasks (such as direct product merchandizing and working on product's placement & positioning).

When the trucks return to the distribution center, in most cases a **check-in** is executed. Similar to the check-out, the IT support in this area is quite good.

After the check-in, the **route settlement** synchronizes the information of the mobile device with the back-end application. Although route settlement fulfills most critical requirements, certain features, such as driver-specific reporting and the daily collection report are not well supported.

The evaluation shows that the fundamental processes in the logistics area are favorably covered. In contrast, the support of information gathering and its subsequent analysis are often not covered to match the needs of the company. Beyond the pure data capturing results, the integration into the various transactional and analytical applications is lacking.

With regard to comparing the results to the vendor category (logistics vs. sales and marketing), it will be difficult to find a vendor who can support the logistics process equally as well as the sales & marketing activities. Looking at the need for a "best of class" DSD process is an important challenge to IT vendors.

14.3 Which Trends will Influence IT Support for DSD Business Processes?

The DSD processes are designed to efficiently fulfill the consumer demand at the point of sales. The change of consumer demand is increasingly difficult to predict. Product offerings and placement in the store will change more often, new products or new product categories will require additional merchandising activities and the DSD processes must adapt to these changes. In contrast to this need for flexibility, many companies invest tremendous effort in process harmonization; they implement integrated ERP-solutions on a global scale. How can this trend for single harmonized platforms and the need for flexible process adaptation be managed? On top of this increased complexity, technical innovations – specifically for mobile devices – will continue to influence the business processes. These three trends are discussed below.

14.3.1 Flexible Process Adaption: The Evolution of Standard Roles

The store execution will focus on more value-generating tasks and on better and more efficient data-gathering activities (GMA 2005). The traditional roles – pre-seller, van-seller, delivery driver, merchandiser – only carry out set tasks in the store. Hence, up until now, IT solutions have only focused on these specific activities.

In the future, IT solutions will have to follow the transformation of traditional roles into hybrid roles. As an example, a pre-seller will additionally execute merchandising tasks or capture competitive information. The example below of a European DSD company shows how diverse the activities can be depending on the country where the process will be operated and which role is assigned to the workforce (Table 14.1).

This example shows that even the same role executes different tasks during the visit execution depending on the country. As an example, the role "A2" performs opportunity management only partially in country 1 and not at all in countries 2 and 3. The activity management in the different countries illustrates even bigger differences. The tasks per roles will not stay stable, however; business needs – as discussed above – will change and therefore the roles will frequently be modified in the future. The challenge for IT solutions will be to manage this change in a seamless way for the mobile workforce. An easy-to-use application with clear instructions must be provided in order to ensure efficient task execution despite the increased complexity. As a consequence of the expansion of roles, the exchange of information and data between mobile devices and back-end applications will

Table 14.1 Example of a diverse task assignment in various countries

Process	Country 1								Country 2				Country 3					
Roles ->	A1	A2	A3	A4	A5	A6	A7	A8	A2	B3	B4	B5	A2	C5	A6	A7	C6	B5
Opportunity Management																		
Link between Opportunity/ Activities	d	d	d	d	d	d	d	d	n	n	n	n	n	n	n	n	n	n
Opportunity Search	d	d	d	d	d	d	d	d	n	n	n	n	n	n	n	n	n	n
Delegating Opportunities	y	y	n	n	n	y	n	n	n	n	n	n	n	n	n	n	n	n
Activity Management																		
Surveys	y	y	y	y	y	d	d	d	y	y	d	d	y	y	y		d	d
Visit summary Survey	n	n	n	n	n	n	n	n	y	y	d	d						
Survey Template Sync	y	y	y	y	y	d	d	d	y	y	d	d	y	y	y		d	d
Sales Cycle Brief	y	y	y	y	y	y	y	y	y	y	y	y	y	y	y	y	y	y
Field Sales Academy Card	y	y	y	y	y	y	y	y	y	y	y	y	y	y	y	y	y	y
Last Visit Info	d	d	d	d	d	d	d	d	d	d	d	d	d	d	d	d	d	d
Automatic objective generation & allocation	y	y	y	y	y	d	d	d	n	n	n	n	n	n	n		n	n
Next Visit Objective	y	y	y	y	y	d	d	d	y	y	y	y	y	y	y		n	n
Selection of visit period from/ till	y	y	y	y	y	y	y	y	y	y	y	y	y	y	y		d	d
Activity creation in the past	y	y	y	y	y	y	y	y	y	y	y	y	y	y	y		n	n
Visit planning absences	y	y	y	y	y	y	y	y	y	y	y	y	y	y	y		n	n
Route Planning	y	y	y	y	y	y	y	y	y	y	d	d	y	y	y		n	n
Controlling & Monitoring	n	n	n	n	n	n	n	n	n	n	y	y	n	n	n	n	n	n
Sales Order Management																		
Copying orders	y	y	y	y	n	n	n	n	y	y	n	n	y	y	n	n	n	n
Different text fields in orders on HH	y	y	y	y	n	n	n	n	y	y	n	n	n	n	n	n	n	n
Payment and Delivery Terms	n	n	n	n	n	n	n	n	n	n	n	n	y	y	n	n	n	n
Rejected Orders	d	d	d	d	d	d	d	d	d	d	d	d	d	d	d	d	d	d

y – required today; n – not required; d – delayed

require easy adaption as well. The synchronization process for a role will no longer work with fixed data sets; for hybrid roles more data will be exchanged and the rules for data selection will become more sophisticated.

14.3.2 The Need for Flexible Process Configuration

The market for mobile DSD solutions is very fragmented. Many companies operate on home grown applications.[4] Based on the history of these IT solutions the IT support for the business processes varies from company to company. Only in cases where the process is defined by a standard – such as DEX – do the processes show identical or similar behavior. As there are little common processes, implementation of new features or process changes is costly. In most cases, changes have to be made on a company-specific level. The integration of standard IT applications into the existing landscape is often very difficult and combined with a huge risk and effort.

The question is whether there could be a higher degree of harmonization of processes and therefore a better ROI by implementing preconfigured and predefined IT solutions. Will mobile DSD applications follow the process harmonization that we find in other areas such as Enterprise Resource Planning (ERP)? How different are the business processes between companies delivering to the same stores?

Recently the author's company conducted several workshops with a group of multinational companies to define the communalities in the DSD business process and hence the requirements for the related IT support. The companies found many common business components such as activity management, surveys, planograms, and order management with product and quantity proposals.

When trying to define a common process the group could not agree on a completely identical process. Even straightforward processes such as backdoor delivery provided so many variants that it was impossible to define a common process.

What were the difficulties in defining common processes? It is obvious that companies have optimized their DSD business processes over time. They focused on both process efficiency and customer service; but in fact, they historically put emphasis on different areas. Even though all companies agreed upon the same general structure for execution of a delivery tour from start of day to end of day tasks, it is almost impossible to get agreement on the **exact sequence** of steps to be executed during a single customer visit. For example, should the delivery driver first start with goods delivery, collection of money for open items or a check of the backroom situation? And this is only one example; it will become even more difficult when regional differences come into play, when requirements from different outlet types have to be considered, and, last but not least, when different product categories have to be supported.

The future challenge for IT support for DSD processes will be in defining and delivering the right and reusable process components. This is necessary to allow companies to model individual business process based on standard components. If, in addition, preconfigured templates are provided, companies can reduce the modeling effort significantly by switching template components on and off. These templates would also provide excellent implementation support when switching from paper-based to a mobile device supported DSD process (Fig. 14.4).

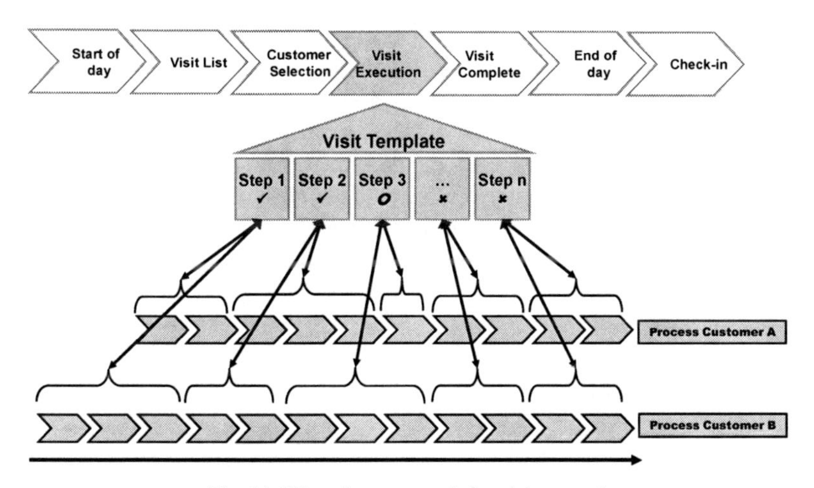

Fig. 14.4 Template approach for visit execution

14.3.3 How will Technology Affect IT Support for DSD?

The fast development of new mobile technology and the rapid growth of a reliable mobile infrastructure will open up many opportunities for the manufacturer. In the last chapter of this book, we will discuss how technology will influence the tasks of the mobile workforce. In this chapter, we concentrate on the process support for the technology enabled scenarios.

Let us take the scenario of a sales representative during a customer visit. He needs comprehensive information such as the sales history, the store profitability for certain brands or planned promotions. In an offline mobile scenario, the needed data would have to be synchronized with his mobile device at the start of the tour. The information level has to be selected carefully and the mobile user is limited by the synchronized data. In an online or online-on-demand scenario, however, the sales representative could access any available information or reports at any time during his visit. The sales representative is no longer limited by the data on his device. Furthermore, for important topics, such as the availability of products, the sales representative would be able to work with up-to-date information. Another advantage in this scenario is the ability to immediately provide the company's back-office with sales order information. As a result, the reservation of products for the next day can be initiated online.

From a process definition point of view, it becomes obvious that the needed services (e.g. provisioning of a report or a business transaction) have to be aligned between the back-end and the mobile application. In most back-end systems these services already exist, but often they are only defined for consumption by other back-end systems. For consumption by mobile applications, the services have to be much simpler and the amount of transferred data has to be minimized. If this is not taken into consideration, the adaption of new mobile technology will often become costly and possibly not feasible.

The consequence for the design of a back-end application is to provide the services tailored to the needs of the mobile user.

The above trends demonstrate that the flexible composition of process components is needed to meet future business requirements. Taking into account that no vendor today covers more than 65% of the required functionality in DSD (Otto and Shariatmadari 2008), IT vendors will have to collaborate more closely in order to support the companies' growing needs for adaptation to the fast changes in business and technology.

14.4 An Architectural View of the DSD Business Processes

In a perfect world, a company could use preconfigured process components and predefined templates to model the company's individual DSD processes. The process components and template would be provided for both the back-end and the mobile application. If we added the right technology components, we could talk about business process platforms for the back-end and for the mobile world. Such platforms would be the foundation for the development and modeling of DSD business processes. These two platforms would guarantee stability and reliability for the main processes leading to a fast implementation and a lower TCO. An open platform would also ease the reuse of IT components from different vendors and the porting of applications would be simplified as the platform takes care of the technical infrastructure.

How does such a platform approach look? What is the right architecture for such an approach? Moreover, how could the regional and product specifics for DSD be implemented on such a platform? How can different IT vendors collaborate on such a platform without losing their own competitive advantage?

A service-oriented architecture (SOA) for DSD processes seems to be the best answer to all of the above questions. All leading IT vendors already communicated their SOA strategy. They are building new solutions according to their SOA strategy and service-enabling the existing applications. For DSD, a technical SOA approach decoupled from the business framework cannot deliver the needed agility. The semantics of the services together with the business content are the prerequisite for successful modeling of DSD operations and rapid innovation. When different IT vendors collaborate in value networks they can jointly define the business process content and thus expand the availability of their solutions to a broader audience. The advantage for the companies using DSD IT solutions is obvious, as they can pick and choose from a wider set of application offerings.

14.4.1 A Service-Oriented Architecture for DSD

Service-oriented architecture allows the use of business processes without knowing how and where the services are implemented. If the services for order-taking and store surveys exist, it should be easy to create a new business process such as "Customer visit with order entry and competitive product survey". It is only necessary to create or compose a new user interface and execute the relevant services. In principal, there is no difference whether this is done in a typical back-end application or in a mobile application. In an offline mobile DSD scenario the challenge is to synchronize the mobile business process and mobile data with the back-end application. How does the synchronization work if the services on the back-end and front-end platforms have different granularities? For example, in the above mentioned new business process "Customer visit with order entry and competitive product survey", the back-end process could consist of more process steps (services) than the related process on the mobile application. In today's implementations, a mapping algorithm will typically be implemented in the middleware layer to harmonize back-end and mobile application. From experience, the middleware application is the most expensive to implement, the most difficult to maintain and the most inflexible to change.

A service-oriented architecture could minimize this effort when the business objects and the services in the mobile and back-end platform have the same semantics, an identical structure and a similar granularity. In that case, the middleware would focus on its original tasks, such as routing the data and executing the device administration.

Another advantage of an SOA approach would be the reusability of already existing services. Many services – such as order entry or customer maintenance – already exist in many back-end systems. They could either be used one to one or could be simplified for mobile usage without the necessity to change the underlying architecture. The same is true for the mobile platform; there are already many services in mobile sales applications that could easily be adapted to DSD needs. In some cases only an adjustment of the user interface for the process sequence would be required. DSD vendors could make use of these services and focus on the DSD specifics such as tour management and cash collection.

The following figure (Fig. 14.5) illustrates such an approach. The DSD specific services have a gray background.

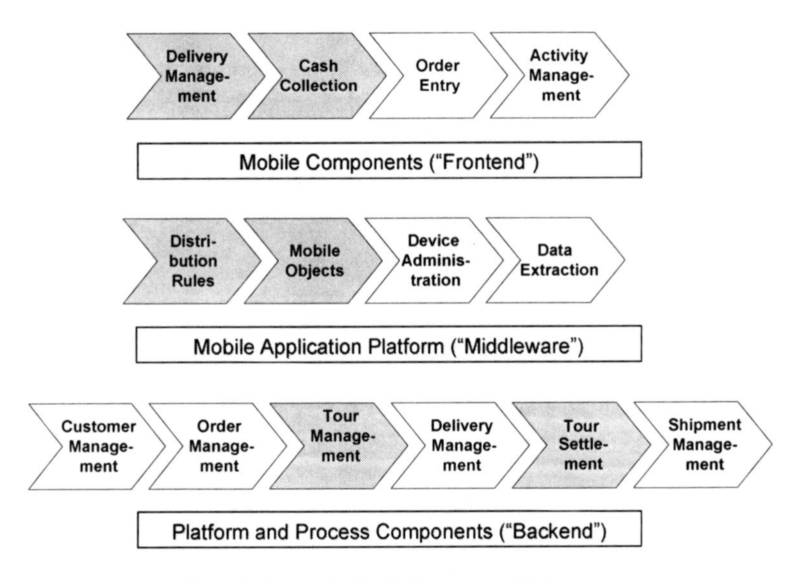

Fig. 14.5 Example for DSD and non-DSD services

All of the above count for offline mobile applications. SOA will also deliver significant advantages when the mobile worker is connected online. The author assumes that in the near future we will not find many pure online scenarios, as the risk of losing connectivity might be regarded as too high. Low risk operations, such as getting the latest sales report from the back-end system is easy to implement in service-oriented architecture. Once the service for such information is implemented it could be used by the mobile work force. It is also not important for the mobile application whether the data for this report resides in the ERP application back-end or in a data warehouse.

A SOA approach for DSD will deliver many benefits. The critical success factors for this approach will be that the semantics of the business objects can be used on both mobile and back-end applications. On the other hand, not all services in the back-end might be ready for consumption by mobile applications. Here again, good collaboration between application providers is necessary.

14.4.2 Collaboration and Co-Innovation of IT Vendors

IT vendors view the service-oriented architecture as an excellent foundation for their development activities. In addition, and of even more importance, SOA provides the right platform for open IT systems. Customers and IT vendors are able to compose new business processes on top of existing application platforms or connect existing solutions based on open, published web services. This way of implementing new processes or solutions shows significantly lower costs and reduced implementation time. The overall TCO over a longer period depends on the constancy of the service definition; changes in the service definition should be the avoided or at least communicated early in a proactive way.

We have discussed earlier that for DSD no IT vendor provides more than 65% of the needed functionality. Furthermore, the business trends require more flexible business process modeling and better support for regional or product-specific needs. The collaboration in an open (service) community could encourage IT vendors for back-end, middleware and front-end applications to deliver better IT support and foster co-innovation. Such a service community for DSD would bring together leaders from customers and IT vendors to jointly identify and define high-value services. In addition, the community could be the forum for best practice sharing of key business challenges. Needless to say that such a community requires a solid legal foundation to protect the individual member's rights. If the members can agree on a feasible governance model, this community could be the umbrella for the various and diverse interests in DSD.

14.5 Conclusion

Consumer product manufacturers operating DSD will follow the general industry trend to put the consumer and the consumer demand even more into focus. The proximity to the point of sales and thus to the consumer, and the direct interaction with the store owner, will be important assets for the manufacturer. IT solutions are crucial to manage these assets. The efficiency of the workforce and reliable logistic services will continue to be key performance indicators for the quality of IT support.

The mandate for increased flexibility and process adaptability will lead to a rethinking of the current IT approaches. The move to service-oriented architecture will most probably not be a revolution, but it looks like the way to go for the majority of IT vendors.

It can be disputed whether manufactures could use identical DSD IT solutions to serve the stores of our friends Dimaz and Charles, presented in the introduction. But it is without question that a collaboration of IT vendors on a common platform can lead to IT components which are independent of the individual business processes.

It is widespread knowledge that aligning on common principles is difficult and time consuming. Nevertheless, it has often resulted in significant benefits to all parties involved.

References

Arlqueeuw, P. Extended Retail Solutions (2008): http://www.extendedretail.com/pastissue/article.asp?art=268540&issue=177, 2008, p. 1.

Grocery Manufacturers Association (GMA) (2005): Unleash the Power of DSD, Washington DC, p. 18.

Otto, A.; Shariatmadari, R. (2008): Direct Store Delivery: Understanding DSD in Sales and Logistics, Results of the "Global DSD Analysis", Regensburg.

Endnotes

[1] See section 1.4.1.1 in this book.

[2] See Fig. 14.1 in this chapter.

[3] See section 14.4.1.2 in this book.

[4] See "Which DSD Solutions are used today?" in this chapter.

Chapter 15
DSD Technology: More Efficiency in Daily Business

Jon Rasmussen

Director, Consumer Goods, Industry Marketing, Intermec Technologies Corporation, 550 Second Street S.E., Cedar Rapids, IA 52401, USA , tel.: +1 319 369-3508, e-mail: jon.rasmussen@intermec.com

Abstract

DSD operations heavily rely on robust technology since it takes place "in the field" beyond the borders of protected production and DSD logistics facilities. This paper attempts to pursuit state of the art technology with a focus on hardware covering handheld computers, data capture, peripherals and communications.

15.1 Introduction

Direct store delivery (DSD) managers have been automating orders and deliveries since 1979. Technology has come a long way in the last 30 years, when only proprietary solutions were available, including hardware design, programming languages, and communications. Personal computers, and more importantly, laptop computers have brought greater research and standards, which have advanced mobile computing tremendously. However the DSD job has not really changed, DSD personnel still have to order, deliver, and invoice products. Their job is not to be a computer operator, so each technology has to have a practical application or it simply gets in the way of selling product.

This chapter begins by presenting several solutions and the motivations behind them, followed by an in-depth study of present day standards and technologies that are the most meaningful for DSD. More importantly, the impact they are having as integral components woven together for a highly productive work force today and in the future will be discussed.

To give a good visual on the computer (the heart of DSD) and the peripherals, the following presents a series of pictures with feature notes (Figs. 15.1–15.3).

A. Otto et al., *Direct Store Delivery*,

DOI: 10.1007/978-3-540-77213-2_15,

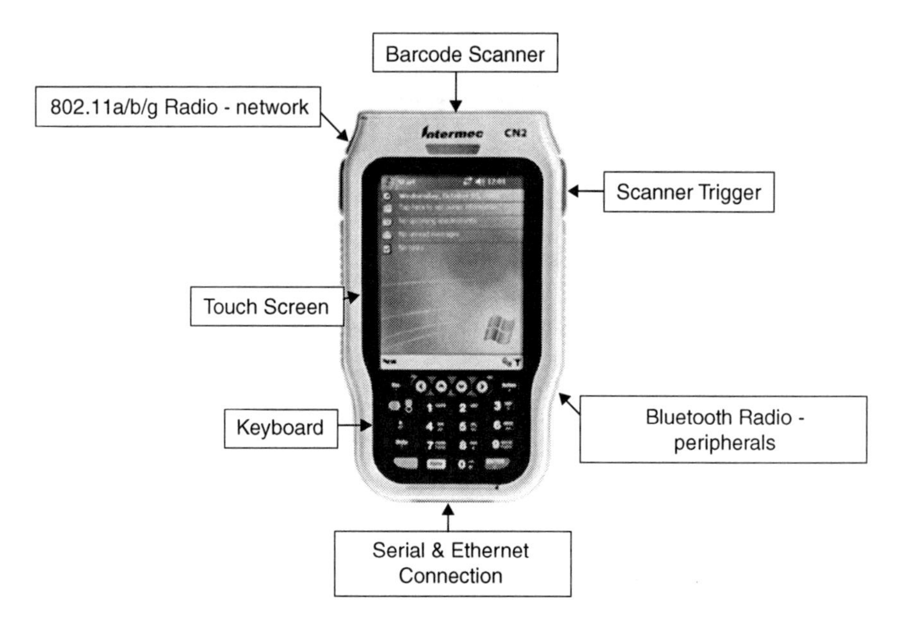

Fig. 15.1 A basic DSD handheld computer

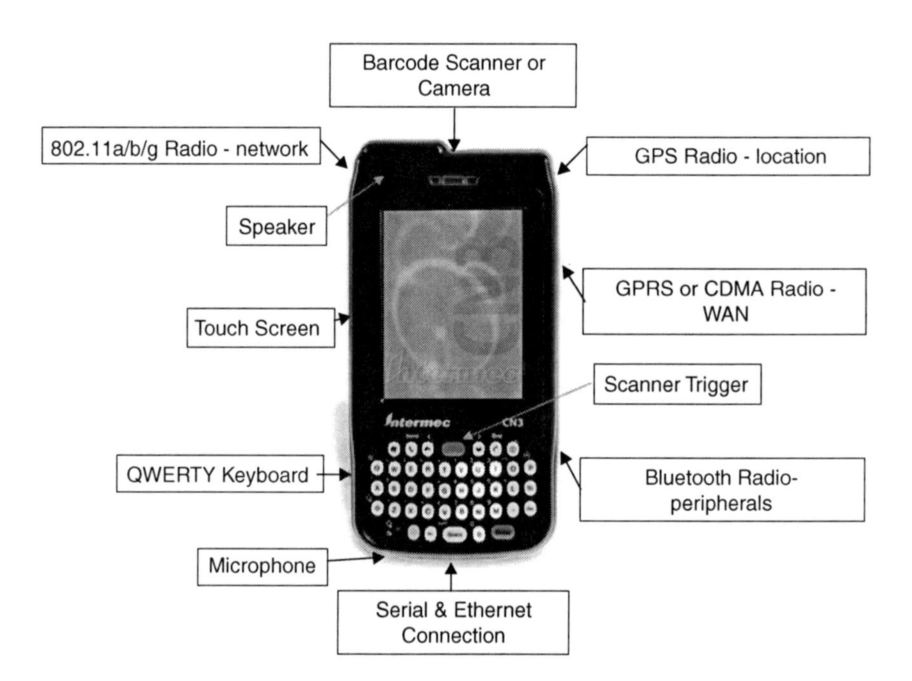

Fig. 15.2 An advanced DSD handheld computer

Fig. 15.3 Peripherals to fit specific job and company profiles

There are different types of computers in use in DSD operations today. The Table 15.1 charts the jobs, requirements, segments, costs, maintenance, and other features that are important selection criteria to determine the best fit for the job.

Table 15.1 provides a rough outline, but by no means gives the full picture. List pricing is for an order of a quantity of 1. Discounting is typically volume based starting with small quantities and ranging up to 40% on deals of over 10,000 units.

Standard is a 1 year warranty, and most vendors offer a range of service programs up to and including "no fault" coverage. Experienced DSD companies (third to fourth generation) will opt for more rugged products and "no fault" coverage to reduce down time and to expand the life span (7–10 years). Recent research conducted by the Venture Development Corporation (2007) comparing the total cost of ownership (TCO) of consumer grade, durable, semi-rugged and rugged devices over 750 companies showed that though the durable and consumer grade devices are less expensive up front lower failure rates, longer replacement cycles, and productivity impacts over a 5 year time span reduce the TCO of fully rugged devices down to 35–50% of consumer grade or durable devices.

Table 15.1 Comparing types of DSD handheld computers

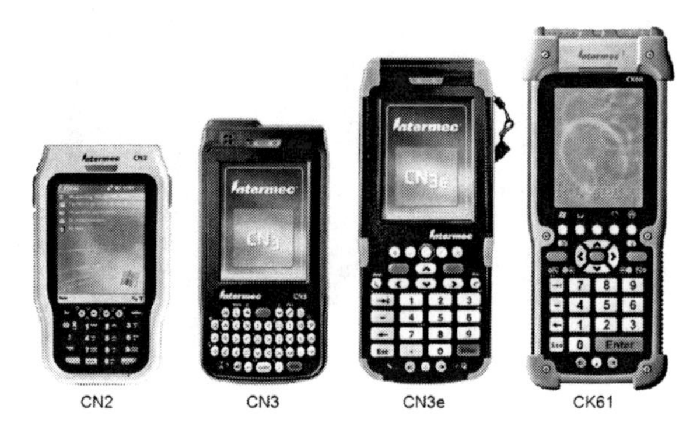

Item	CN2	CN3	CN3e	CK61
Segment Preference	Soft Goods	Beverage, Soft Goods	All DSD	All DSD
Jobs	Merchandising	Merchandising, Pre-Sales and Route Sales	Route Sales and Delivery	Route Sales and Delivery
Primary Input	Scanning	Scanning	Keying in Quantity	Keying in Quantity
Ruggedness	Durable (indoor)	Semi-rugged	Fully Rugged	Extremely Rugged
Communications	Once a day	Each stop	Each stop	Once a day
Directions	Not needed	Necessary	Necessary	Occasional
Replacement	3 years	4–5 years	5+ years	6+ years
Install base monthly failure rate	3%	1.5%	1.3%	1.0%
List Price (in USD, 2007)	$1395	$2395	$2895	$3795

The need for ruggedness differs between the job styles.

1. DSD personnel have to unload trucks, move products to the receiving room and stock them at the shelves. Constantly moving products with the computer on the top of the cases, the units often "go diving" from 4 to 5 ft. DSD personnel also make between 20–50 deliveries per day, while a merchandiser/presales person typically works only one or two superstores per day
2. DSD personnel, especially on perishables, have to key in returns/stales, inventory, and then make order adjustments, typically on a suggested order based on sales history and promotions due to sales initiatives and incremental selling to the store manager. This adds up to more key entry requirements (mainly quantities) and large keys become helpful, especially when the users become proficient at "blind entry", no longer looking at the keyboard while keying. Dairy

and bakery products, due to the product's short shelf life, typically have more quantity entry
3. Beverage and snack companies, due to their higher number of products (flavors, sizes, packaging), tend to do more scanning and have pre-sales personnel to provide better merchandising and create more selling opportunities (additional locations within the store, promotional displays, coolers, snack racks, etc.) especially in large format stores, where it should be noted that pre-sales/merchandising is expanding to smaller formats as well
4. Most DSD companies try to make sure they have a "suggested order", for a future delivery, before they leave the retailer. This enables better production and delivery planning. They will then adjust the order to the actual amount during the next delivery. Bulk deliveries to superstores and hypermarkets are typically generated by the pre-sales personnel and the deliveries are shrink wrapped on one or more pallets for delivery to a specific store. In this case, advance shipment notices (ASN) and serialized shipping container codes (SSCC) are used to accelerate deliveries.

15.2 The Foundation: Handheld Computers and Their Key Elements

Microsoft Windows Mobile (WM) is the preferred operating system for DSD oprations because it natively enables several other key technologies like touch screens for input and signature capture (eliminates the need for multi-part forms), BlueTooth radios for peripherals, Ethernet for docked communications, and wide area network radios for in-transit communications. WM also provides one of the most widely used development platforms, opening up a choice of vendors for application solutions. Though WM supports a lot of functionality (like push email), additional software from device manufacturers is usually critical to making a solution perform all the functions needed from the device, while lasting for a full day's operation.

Application development is made easier in the WM realm with third and fourth generation tools and a wide range of solution providers and developers have extensive experience developing in the WM environment. GUI (graphical user interface) development and "forms" are fairly easy to accomplish, allowing the software provider to focus on the complexities of DSD promotions, pricing, taxes, DEX/UCS (Direct EXchange, Uniform Communication Standard) and other sales related items.

There is a wide range of RISC (reduced instruction set computer) processors available today that will run WM. They are achieving higher levels of integration all the time, which lowers costs and drives down power requirements, while supporting newer features. Still, the key is to keep the balance of speed and capability as to not slow down DSD personnel. Unlike processors and operating systems in personal computers, the mobile computing processors and operating systems do not necessarily perform faster with more memory and hence require smarter programming approaches.[1]

Intel having sold their RISC based mobile processor line, called StrongARM or Xscale, to Marvell in June 2006 has opened up the market to consider other processors from companies like Texas Instruments and should increase competition and feature set offerings. Advances in smart phone designs and integrating communications will also provide some twists in processors and chipset offerings that should provide lower power and more flexible network options that will better utilize existing coverage. These designs will also find their way into ruggedized computers.

Batteries have come a long way since alkaline chemistry. Rechargeable chemistries like NiCd (nickel cadmium) developed a bad reputation for "memory" effect. Fortunately, Li-Ion (lithium-ion) does not exhibit "memory" effect and has a very predictable discharge pattern giving the user good, timely information to manage battery swapping or charging. Real usage of these batteries often exceeds 2 years, depending on the hardware provider's design before they will not make it through a full shift. The technology is still on the steep ramp side of the curve providing capacity improvements every 6–12 months reducing the need down to two battery packs during a 5 year life. This is important because most computer depreciation schedules are only 3–5 years.

The DSD job often includes the wide area network radio communications for each transaction adding to the power consumption of the device and the need for a transparent power management.

Memory densities have exponentially increased and prices have dropped to enable cost effective storage of over a year's worth of sales history and promotions. You can even purchase memory cards that provide over a gigabyte of removable storage to enable recovery from even crushed hand-held computers, and to support ever increasing amounts of data. This allows to put more information into the hands of the DSD personnel so they can present more product selection, placement and pricing, as well as, achieve better forecasting. You could even store promotional videos. All of which will help to spur sales.

DSD origins pre-date wide spread bar code usage so route personnel would memorize the SKU (stock keeping unit) numbers (typically only three or four digits) and using the large keys on the device would "blind key" enter item numbers and quantities very fast. As a matter of fact, most can "blind key" an item number and quantity faster than aligning a barcode and scanning the product then moving to quantity entry. Though the technology keeps getting smaller and smaller, many DSD companies still want computers that support large keys. Many companies have also tried to facilitate entry speed by presenting the products in a plan-o-gram sequence (marketing usually creates and the route person alters based on their familiarity with the store's demographics). This helps with merchandising, getting route personnel to display the product in marketing's preferred location, and data entry, by sequencing the product so all the user has to do is type the quantity and hit enter for each item in the sequence.

15.3 The Improvements: Adding Accuracy and Efficiency

Once these basics have been mastered there are a multitude of other technologies that bring accuracy and efficiency. These technologies fall into three main categories: Data capture (input), peripherals, and communications.

15.3.1 Data Capture

As consolidation has occurred and new products have been introduced, in the last 5 years the average number of items manufactured and distributed by consumer goods companies have increased by more than 30%. Add to that number temporary promotional packaging and you have a significant contribution to the complexity of operating a route. This increase has caused some companies to scan bar codes to properly identify the products. This is especially crucial in the absence of software that handles plan-o-gram functionality. For a long time, laser scanners offered good functionality and performance, but today two dimensional (2D) imaging technology offers similar or better reading distances, faster collection, and better performance. The biggest factor in why 2D is better than laser scanner or linear imager solutions is that the user does not have to align the beam (illumination) to go perpendicular with the bar code. Now all they have to do is make sure the bar code is illuminated. The 2D imager will capture the bar code as a picture and the decode software will pick out the bar code in that image and decode it much faster than a user could align a scanner (saves 30–60% of the overall time to identify and scan). This is critical because the barcodes will be on shelves and packaging at all levels and orientations. Imagers also handle shrink wrapped product, wrinkled packaging, and highly reflective surfaces much better than a laser.

2D imaging can also be used to capture black and white images, which many companies have added special functionality to handle the capture, association and storage of these images. Just think, you now can gather promotional compliance information, store stamp invoice images, point of purchase asset damage, competitive information and the like, allowing to save time and to provide clarity to other departments like field service and marketing. If color would help, you can also get hand-held computers with an integrated color camera to get photo quality images. It is worth noting that imaging technology is advancing rapidly, even offering solutions that can read bar codes beyond 50 ft (15 m), which is applicable in a warehouse, but not really meaningful for use on a route (Figs. 15.4–15.6).

Fig. 15.4 Color picture – Competitive

Fig. 15.5 Auto-ranging – Read to the ceiling

1234567890123456789012345678901234567890123456789012345678
2
3
4
Ref:12345678901234567890123456789012345678901234567890123456

CORREOS
AVISO DE RECIBO ELECTRÓNICO

1° INTENTO | ENTREGA DOMICILIARIA

IDENTIFICACIÓN

FIRMA EMPLEADO*

1. Entregado a Domicilio
2. Dirección Incorrecta
3. Ausente Reparto
4. Desconocido
5. Fallecido
6. Rehusado
7. No se hace cargo

NOTIFICACIÓN INFORMATIZADA

SELLO DE LA OFICINA DE ENTREGA O DEVOLUCIÓN

Fecha y Hora

Nº En

NOMBRE Y APELLIDOS DEL RECEPTOR: DNI

FECHA

RELACIÓN CON EL DESTINATARIO

FIRMA DEL RECEPTOR

Entregado
Rehusado

1234567890123456789012345678901234567890123456789012345678901234
2
3
4
5

Fig. 15.6 Black and white document image

GS1, the governing body for UPC/EAN, in 2007 announced the expectation for 100% support of DataBar (sample below) by data collection equipment vendors by the year 2010. This is to facilitate the migration to DataBar from UPC/EAN because there is a big need for more companies and products, additional information like weight and serial numbers, and the need to support this incremental data on smaller packages (Fig. 15.7).

RFID (radio frequency identification) is another technology that offers unique, serialized tracking. Economically at this time RFID in DSD is only feasible at the case/tray/crate level and primarily on re-useable containers or promotional displays and other point of purchase assets. RFID can provide true asset tracking and utilization so that you can know exactly which assets have been deployed at which customer locations and should eventually be returned from there. It has been stated that plastic tray and crate theft is a billion dollar problem for the DSD industry.

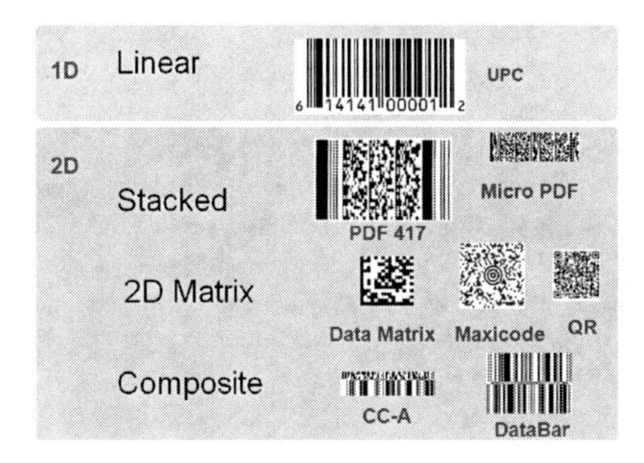

Fig. 15.7 2D Barcodes

So by adding RFID and hand-held readers you can now identify the problem locations and can begin taking corrective action with those retailers. Innovative customers are also using RFID to determine proper delivery and availability of promotional items, which is especially critical if your products have backroom storage location at the store.

Speech recognition is viable on today's hand-held computers, however its use is primarily found in warehouse picking which is a "directed" application (step by step, item by item activity). DSD is typically more dynamic and fast paced and so speech would actually slow down a route person.

Cordless scanning (Fig. 15.8) is also available, though like speech, it is not typically a productivity enhancer on the route (the exception is merchandisers for greeting cards, hosiery, and other products that have stock location cards). It is being used by companies that have their route personnel pick their own product in the warehouse and have the warehouse personnel inspect and verify their activity. Typically, a route person would return to the warehouse at the end of the day, using previously generated orders and the current status of their truck inventory, they would pick up a cordless scanner with a wrist band and would associate it with their hand-held computer. Executing their pick function, they would be directed around the warehouse to pick the necessary products, scanning the location and item numbers. At the conclusion of their picking, they would find

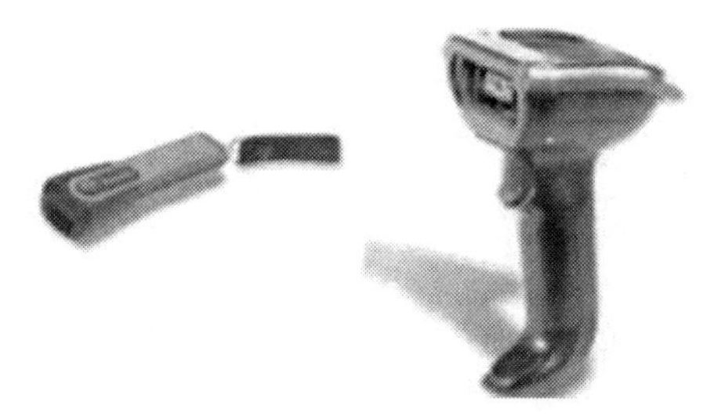

Fig. 15.8 "Flashlight" and auto-ranging cordless scanners

the warehouse supervisor and print out their picked "order" and then check out. Most typical operations have separate personnel for routes and warehousing to prevent theft and collusion.

GPS (global positioning system) radios carry a common misconception that they can communicate the computer's whereabouts to corporate headquarters. A GPS radio is actually a one way radio that simply receives signals from GPS satellites and then triangulates the radio's current position. There is no outward communication unless you add a WWAN (wireless wide area network) radio into the handheld, this will be referred to when we talk about communications technologies. GPS is very useful in three ways. Number one is use in combination with driving direction software. It can help new or substitute route personnel find the location of the store for the delivery (Fig. 15.9). Number two is they can be used to add location and time "stamps" to the route personnel's transactions. This way you can confirm that the user was at the proper location and not just entering data or skipping stops without ever going to the location. The third use is to essentially "bread crumb" the route and then analyze the data from multiple routes to determine if route re-alignment can make your operation more efficient. Coupled with a WWAN radio, you could even identify the location of a stolen device, provided your software is still intact and the computer has power.

Fig. 15.9 DSD handheld computer with GPS and direction software

15.3.2 Peripherals

The second category of technology is peripherals. Historically, route personnel have used a dot matrix printer (for multi-part forms) with a hand-held dock mounted in their vehicle and a DEX/UCS cable as their only peripherals. These options have expanded greatly in recent years.

BlueTooth radios for personal area networking (PAN) have brought great flexibility to DSD operations. At first there was IrDA (infrared data association) which used infrared technology to eliminate cables to portable printers, however it had problems. With this technology you needed line of sight to make a connection, transmissions could be impacted by direct sunlight and certain kinds of fluorescent lighting would flood the infrared spectrum, so it was not reliable. With the advent of Bluetooth and its broad adoption in a wide variety of peripherals, cables could be eliminated (the highest failure item in any mobile system) and provide true portability for multiple devices and their simultaneous usage. Typical range is 30ft (9 m), however many vendors use the higher powered version that has a range of 100 ft (30 m) and up to 300 ft (100 m) so that communications can take place with devices in vehicles while the user is outside the vehicle doing work.

Printers have seen the most dramatic changes. The technology has moved from dot matrix (dating from the 1980s for personal computer printers) that printed full page (8.5" × 11" or A4) multi-part forms that were a continuous feed to 4" belt mounted thermal printers that can print the same amount of data, only faster and less expensively. Depending on the country you are operating in, they might have regulations that preclude thermal printing, but the technology today can be used over a much wider range of temperatures −20°C (−4°F) to 50°C (122°F). Thermal printers also handle graphics much faster and more efficient than the older printers, so you can quickly print signatures, logos, 2D barcodes and other images. Some operations can even drop down to 2" wide paper versions. These printers also use Li-Ion batteries in the same form factor as used in some hand-held computers, so you can leverage spare batteries and chargers (Figs. 15.10 and 15.11).

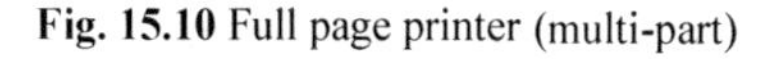

Fig. 15.10 Full page printer (multi-part)

Fig. 15.11 Belt mounted printer

Workboard versions of thermal printers have a docking slot for a hand-held computer. These were very popular upon their introduction and still are selling well, however most companies are migrating to the belt mounted version (Fig. 15.12).

Improvements in battery technology have resulted in the ability to use the same battery pack for over 2 years. However, running out of power while on the route must be avoided, so most operators have charging capability in the vehicle. Fixed mount printers historically had wires running to the vehicle's firewall where a

Fig. 15.12 4" Workboard printer

connector was installed and on the other side there was a cable and a filter that ran to the vehicle's battery. These printers would also have a holder/cradle that the hand-held computer would dock into for communications and power to charge its batteries. Portable printing eliminates that capability, so today it is essential to have a cigarette lighter charger available when you get that low battery signal.

A DEX cable to perform DEX/UCS is essential in the United States and Australia. DEX is a standard, established in 1982, for the DSD personnel to exchange delivery data electronically with the retailer's receiving PC, using a set of pre-defined transactions to exchange the data over a two-wire serial interface. DEX ensures that only authorized items are delivered at the right price and in the right quantity. This process makes for faster deliveries, however if they have an error at this point, then the DSD personnel usually has to contact their management to get authorization to change the incorrect information and then has to go to the back of the receiving line and try again. The receiving personnel are not impacted, they simply move on to the next correct delivery (Fig. 15.13).

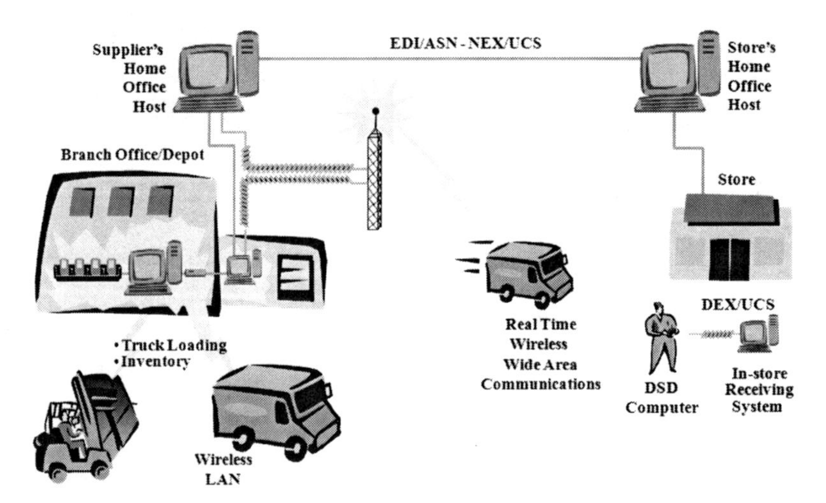

Fig. 15.13 Overall flow of NEX and DEX in DSD

DSD routes typically have a mix of accounts on a route that have either charge accounts (monthly billing) or cash accounts (pay in cash because they have a bad credit rating or are too small). Credit cards have a proven record in consumer sales that they generate at least a 10% uplift in sales on a per transaction basis. Business credit cards are becoming more popular, so by adding a snap-on credit card reader to those routes that have a lot of cash accounts you can generate more revenue and reduce the possibility for cash theft from your drivers or robbery. You also need authorization software that allows you to communicate over a wireless wide area network (WWAN; similar to cell phone text messaging) to verify the credit card and authorize the transaction (Fig. 15.14).

Fig. 15.14 Snap-on credit card reader

15.3.3 Communications

Communications is the third category of technology important to DSD. Historically, computers had two ways of communicating: multi-drop communications or modem. For those workers who did not return to the warehouse/distribution center/depot every night, they would use single docks with a modem either external or internal. As of 2007, the latest modem protocol is V.92 capable of 56 Kbps (bits per second). Within the depot, multi-docks were used and multi-drop RS485 communications were the initial implementation and later migrated to wired Ethernet. End of day communications involved only the transactions necessary for settlement of the route. Overnight communications would involve master file updates, route changes, route schedule, and other driver specific information, but it would also include software updates, which could take a considerable amount of time (Fig. 15.15).

Today, most computers come with an 802.11a/b/g (Institute of Electrical and Electronics Engineers standard number for wireless Ethernet in the 5 and 2.4 GHz frequency spectrum) radio that provides the user with wireless Ethernet capability. Going wireless saves the cost of the wired infrastructure which would include hubs, switches, and possibly routers for very large installs. All a customer has to do is connect an access point to their Ethernet LAN (local area network) to provide high speed access to multiple devices. Note that if you have more than 32 devices in a location, you could run into a bottleneck trying to download software in a small

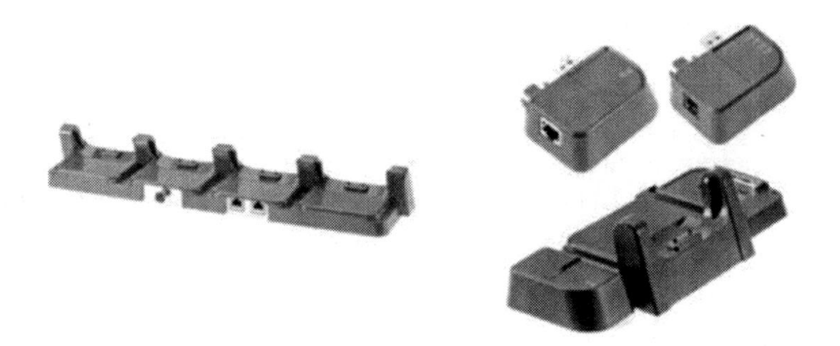

Fig. 15.15 Ethernet 4 position multi-dock. Single dock; modem and ethernet options

window of time, so more access points may be required. Many companies are already using a wireless LAN in their warehouse environment, which might make it easier for access depending on the LAN, routers, and host system locations.

Wireless networking opens up a much wider area to conduct your work and can save time/money, by taking inventory updates and performing settlement while the user is at their vehicle provided you have coverage in the yard. Wireless networks can be set up with no real security. Cisco constantly enhances security solutions to meet the industry's standards which may be implemented via CCX (Cisco Compatible Extensions) compliant radios.

Cable companies and phone companies are implementing digital phone systems in the home market. Essentially, those are Ethernet networks so you now have options for a single dock with Ethernet rather than a modem. Additionally wireless networks are appearing in the home too so expect users who go home after their routes to request these capabilities. If users are already paying for this capability it offers a "free" way of communicating. Some businesses are offering free hot spots but the challenge is navigating the sign-on process, accepting the terms and conditions, then launching a VPN (virtual private network) to secure the data.

Wireless wide area networking (WWAN) simplifies the remote communications challenges and offers almost real-time communication. WWAN radios are essentially cell phones in your hand-held computer. They offer both voice and data capabilities, allowing to eliminate a separate cell phone for the route person and to control the amount of voice activity they have on their route. The main solution globally is GSM/GPRS with CDMA as the second place contender, which varies by country and coverage area. None of these solutions are ubiquitous (capable of always being connected), so you always need to have "batch" or "stand-alone" capabilities are always needed. In the past, wireless data plans were expensive but prices dropped to the point that even companies that communicate a couple of times a day are considering WWAN. It is interesting to see that lesser developed countries even have better wireless coverage/performance than their wired phone systems, so WWAN becomes a primary mode of communication in those locales. GSM within Europe is almost a default on orders for hand-held equipment in DSD due to it being standard throughout Europe and the wireless network providers are very competitive.

WWAN opens up a lot of possibilities for dispatch, from accounts running out of inventory, to price updates prior to delivery, to early order communication that enables staging of product before the driver even returns to the depot. You can also coordinate deliveries with the pre-sales person so deliveries can be re-scheduled if the right personnel are not available.

A fundamental goal is to have people spend more time selling and merchandising than spending in the receiving room. You need to look at not only the route technology but also your host applications and picking solutions to provide the optimal environment. Using automated delivery technologies like EDI and the Internet to deliver advance shipment notices (ASN) and applying bar codes and/or RFID tags to "pallets" with serialized shipping container code (SSCC) labels your delivery personnel can move rapidly through the receiving area using honors check-in or exception checking. The receiving personnel will have received communications overnight that explain exactly what they will get on each "pallet" identified by the SSCC. Host systems will reconcile any item or pricing differences before the driver gets there. This combination of technology will free up more than double the merchandising/selling time currently experienced today!

Scan based trading (SBT) takes automated receiving one step further, by essentially creating a consignment inventory situation which may allow the DSD personnel to deliver anytime day or night that the store is open. The supplier is paid based on what is scanned at the PoS (point of sale) system. There are two main challenges to SBT: (1) Availability of PoS data, and (2) Agreement on how shrinkage ("missing product") will be shared.

Those that perform SBT today experience great benefit because they see an uplift of over 20% based on the delivery personnel controlling the merchandising space, timing, and product mix! However there are some locations that have had to stop due to irresolvable shrinkage problems.

15.4 Outlook

Each of the technologies displayed in the figure below (Fig. 15.16) will help to improve DSD in speed and decrease in power consumption over time, but you can capitalize on them today.

However you might ask where the next big improvement is going to be? It can be expected in optics and optical recognition (building off of 2D imaging) because there are a lot of innovations going on there today. Why is that important? Imagine to take a take a "snap shot" and automatically determine what products are on the shelves and how many are there, and even more importantly, what is missing (sold out), and if the promotional display is in compliance. Then have that information automatically loaded and the program calculating exactly what the user

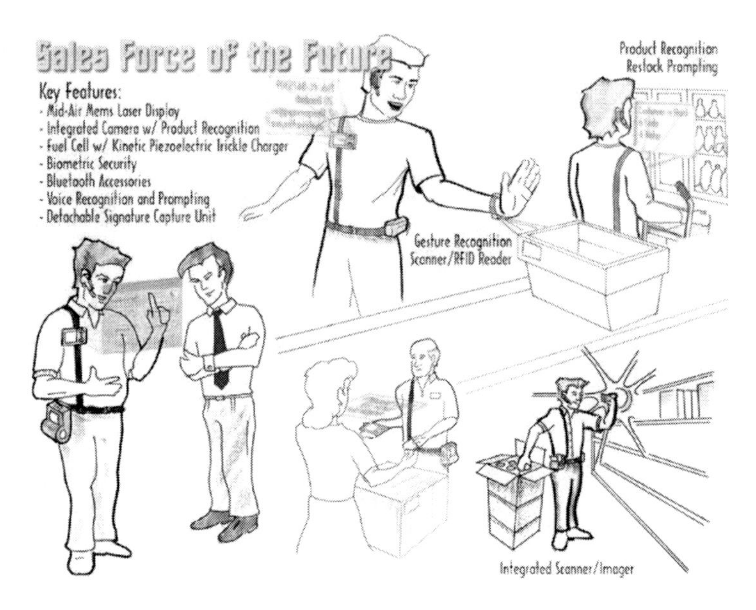

Fig. 15.16 Sales force of the future

needs to do. That would free the user up to spend increasing amounts of time on more sophisticated product mix and merchandising tasks, as well as, more time with store managers explaining how they can increase their revenues and profits. Now we are several years away from such a solution, but the technology people are hard at work today developing the next wave of DSD improvements.

Endnotes

[1] Key programming tips include:

- Load all DLLs (dynamic-link library) when initially loading the program because dynamic usage will consume scarce memory and processing cycles when they try to load and unload multiple times
- Regarding the bus speed for the display interface, having some standard formats and updating only the modified portions of the screen can also add speed to the application.

Chapter 16
Mobile Solutions for Direct Store Delivery

Wesley Mukai[1], Yuri Natchetoi[2], and Serhan Dagtas[3]

[1] SAP Research, 3475 Deer Creek Road, Palo Alto, CA 94304, USA,
tel.: +1 650-461-1891, e-mail: wesly.mukai@sap.com

[2] SAP Research, 111 Duke Street, Montreal, Quebec, H3C2M1, Canada,
tel.: +1 514 879 6739, e-mail: yuri.natchetoi@sap.com

[3] UALR, 2801 S. University Avenue, Little Rock AR 72204, USA,
tel.: +1 501-683-7267, e-mail: sxdagtas@ualr.edu

Abstract

Mobile phones are increasingly becoming a necessary platform for business applications. This "business mobilization" is driven by technology, IT policy, social trends, as well as business model evolution. DSD is a natural beneficiary of this increasing use of mobile phones as a business platform. This article provides a mobile perspective for future DSD applications and identifies the possible impact of current trends in this field. We show with several examples that multiple use cases for Mobile phone DSD exist today and complement/extend traditional use cases, especially for small to medium businesses. As mobile DSD continues to evolve and new areas such as social marketing and Mobile SOA technology advance, DSD has the potential to extend into new application areas. We foresee that increased home and office use of mobile platforms will complement traditional desktop models and play a major role in the future success of DSD applications.

16.1 Mobility for the Future DSD

Mobile phones are becoming a popular platform for business applications. There are almost 3.3 billion connected mobile devices in the world (IDC 2007) and the number of mobile users increases daily. In step with their massive popularity and flexibility, mobile phones are becoming equipped with powerful hardware and software technologies such as Java 2 Micro Edition (J2ME), Bluetooth, Global Positioning Systems (GPS), digital cameras, and more – all at a greatly reduced cost compared with fixed terminals. Logically, the wide use of mobile devices, low hardware costs and improved infrastructure make cell phones and other mobile devices a logical and convenient platform for business applications, such as Direct Store Delivery (DSD).

A. Otto et al., *Direct Store Delivery*,
DOI: 10.1007/978-3-540-77213-2_16, © Springer-Verlag Berlin Heidelberg 2009

A growing number of employees of CP Manufacturers and their customers (such as retail managers, small store owners) make business decisions using their mobile phones. The enhancement of mobile devices and software already enabled many functions typically performed by computer-based Point of Sale (PoS) with the help of specialized equipment: mobile touch-less payments using Near Field Communication (NFC) technology, scanning of bar-code labels and RFID tags, asynchronous connection to DSD back-end for automated replenishment, receipt printing, etc. As a result, mobile phones will play a critical role as devices used in the future of retail and logistics industries.

Another important trend that may eventually lead to a change in the paradigm of the marketing and retail industry is in the field of mobile peer-to-peer communications. Mobile applications on the consumers' cell phones can exchange data with the retailers' phones. When problems of standardization and data security are resolved, a significant part of the traditional retail and DSD business could be shifted to m-Business (Strategy 2006). This process has already started in the form of e-Business, involving desktop computers connected to Internet. However, so far e-Business has only gained a significant share in developed countries and among the younger generations.

There is a deep divide between developed countries and emerging economies. Developed countries have an older aging population, which can be more skeptical of e-Business. By contrast, in emerging economies the mobile phones play the role computers play in developed countries (IDC 2006) and the majority of the population is younger and much more mobile, flexible and favorable to the idea of using their phone for purposes other than voice calls. They are already using their phones as music players, cameras and terminals for internet access. Hence, they don't have a barrier against mobile payments and ordering goods using their phones. The young generation also intensively uses mobile social networks sites to communicate, share opinions and promote ideas which have direct consequences in the future of e-commerce, including DSD.

16.2 The Evolution of Mobility – Mobility in 2015

Mobility rises and dominates in both developed and emerging markets such as Asia, Eastern Europe, and Latin America. There, low-end mobile phones are a primary communication and information access device given the often underdeveloped traditional communication infrastructure. This multiplies the potential impact of mobility in both advanced and developing markets where the lack of advanced retail infrastructure adds to the need for alternative and effective distribution mechanisms.

Mobility will continue to see the technology and connectivity improvements we have observed throughout the IT industry, especially the desktop and laptop markets with increasing impact on e-commerce. Recent advances in the smart phone space is helping accelerate some technology trends, especially in the area of mobile web and usability. However, technology is not the only driver of the evolution of mobility, generational and social trends as well as business model evolutions will also play a major role on the future adoption and acceptance of mobile phones for enterprise applications, especially DSD applications.

16.2.1 It Won't be all About Technology

Discussions around the future of mobility usually begin and end with technology. More powerful CPUs, better screens, and longer battery life are often described as the keys to the future. While technology is important, there are also several other social and business related developments that will play a key role as to the future of mobile phones in the enterprise and more specifically in the DSD application arena.

There is no doubt that mobility in the enterprise is becoming mainstream. By 2011, the market intelligence firm IDC projects that there will be one billion mobile workers worldwide (IDC 2007). In addition, mobile employees on average spend over 40% of their time in the office away from their desks (Strategy 2006).

Consequently, mobile applications are appearing on more corporate IT initiatives than ever before. While some early adopters have experienced success with mobile solutions (e.g. tracking vehicles and packages), many others were discouraged by the costs associated with specialized devices, disparate and expensive networks, and customized software development.

However, over the last few years, the mobile landscape has experienced significant positive changes resulting in an enterprise environment poised for rapid mobile application growth. Several factors are contributing to this positive change:

- The rise of the mobile generation
- Industry consolidation and the rise of "full stack" software providers (i.e. large Enterprise Software vendors such as SAP, Oracle and Microsoft)
- The rapid proliferation of sophisticated cellular phones and smart phones in the consumer and enterprise space
- Dramatic increase in computational and visual capabilities in low-end cell phones
- Increased speed and ubiquity of mobile data networks.

While the evolution of mobility is not certain, these factors will play a key role to shape the future of mobility in the Enterprise and the DSD space.

16.2.2 The Rise of the Mobile Generation

Millennials are the Mobile Generation. Millennials, often referred to as Generation Y or the iGeneration, are described as those individuals in society born between 1980 and 2000. This is the generation that is comfortable in a Web 2.0 world. This is the generation who will be influencing work place and business processes over the next 7–8 years. With this generation, there is often a blurred line between work and play and little tolerance for lagging workplace IT. Mobility is a vital component of the everyday life of this generation.

The rise of this mobile generation also falls in line with the rise and dominance of mobility in emerging markets such as Asia, Eastern Europe, and Latin America. Here, lower end mobile phones are a primary communication and information access device given the often under-developed wired Internet and telephony infrastructure and the unwillingness of businesses to invest in expensive IT infrastructure and high end mobile devices.

The future of mobility lies with the social and cultural trends of this generation. One key area of impact will be the use of personal cell phones for business. A recent study from IDC (WCMDEA 2006), as shown in Fig. 16.1, identified a trend in IT and purchasing policies where individuals increasingly use their personal phones for work. This will have an impact on what types of devices need to be supported for enterprise applications and the high expectations for usability and performance that Generation Y individual will place on enterprises.

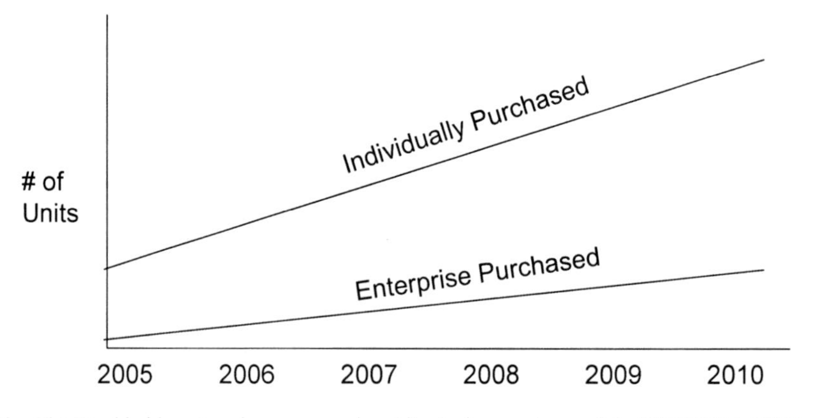

Fig. 16.1 Worldwide enterprise converged mobile device purchase origin (WCMDEA 2006)

This generation will also drive an unprecedented ubiquity of mobility in the workplace. Today, the picture of a business meeting is a room of multitasking individuals, each with an open laptop in front of him/her and a wireless LAN connection. Move ahead 5 years, and we will see a room full of individuals, each with a connected smart phone on the table or under the table, performing the same functions as they currently do on their laptop, but also texting friends and co-workers. Their device will also be aware of its surroundings and environment, gathering real-time information, acting in the background as a communications hub or perhaps harnessing local resources for mundane tasks such as printing or projecting. This is not only driven by technology (e.g. rising power and performance), but also by social norms. Likewise, one can expect this proliferation of mobile devices to move outside the conference room to the field, especially as retailers or manufacturers realize they won't necessarily want to equip all employees with sophisticated, customized devices, but rather adapt to what employees or customers already carry in their pocket.

This ubiquity of mobility in the workplace and the mixed business/personal use of individual mobile devices also provide a potential natural entry point for social networking and collaboration in the Enterprise. The mobile platform of the near future would be open, easy to deploy, context aware and collaboration-ready. One potential application could reflect the growing need in today's mobile workforce for situational access to specialized knowledge housed in people and systems. However, for many reasons, such specialized knowledge may be difficult to access (e.g. retiring "experts", personnel cutbacks, lack of system access.) Mobile intelligent solutions to enable knowledge sharing, selective and targeted information/ expertise provisioning for the right worker or worker profile at the right location and at the right time will become important.

16.2.3 Changing Industry Structure and Challenging Business Models

The mobile application and infrastructure industry has been a difficult one to make money. Specifically, in the mobile middleware space several start-up companies have found the road difficult and have been replaced by globally acting business software providers or big telecommunication companies. The rise of these "full-stack" software providers in the mobility space is creating an environment where better "end-to-end" and integrated mobile Enterprise applications will be possible. In the end, the potential for more comprehensive DSD solutions will rise with the consolidation in the industry.

Business models are also evolving that will make mobile enterprise applications more attractive. Traditional usage-based data plans have hindered the growth of mobile enterprise applications. Controlling cost was an issue when considering a wide-scale mobile enterprise application rollout. There has now been a shift in the market with regards to data plans. With the rollout of next generation mobile networks and increased competition for mobile subscribers in the mobile industry, the unlimited mobile data plan has taken off. In a future where mobile data is unlimited, the operational cost of mobile enterprise applications becomes predictable.

Lastly, it has been very difficult for mobile applications developers to make money in a world where there are too many mobile platforms to support. Development costs to support these platforms made for poor business models. Certifying applications for the multiple platforms and carriers is also a costly affair. However, a shift is underway that will pave the way for a new wave of profitable applications development.

16.2.4 The Rise of the Mobile Web

The introduction of the iPhone in January 2007 is significant because it has reinvigorated several technology trends that will impact the evolution of mobility over the next 5 years. Whether the iPhone itself becomes the dominant smart phone platform over time remains to be seen, but there is no doubt the iPhone's concepts, capabilities, and business model, along with those of Google Android and LiMO (Linux for Mobile Foundation), will be mirrored throughout the industry. The major impact areas of the iPhone are:

- The web browser as an application platform
- Usability and user interface
- Business model shift.

The richness of the web browsing experience on the iPhone has revitalized the momentum in the industry around mobile web applications. Despite technical drawbacks, there is a strong chance that mobile web applications, instead of native applications, will be the dominant type of mobile applications. The standards-based Safari browser on the iPhone makes for web-based applications that are rich and ubiquitous between PC and mobile. According to a recent study, "mobile Web browsing will be economically feasible and technically available to more than 80% of cellular subscribers in Europe by 2011. The equivalent for the U.S. will be 50% of subscribers" (Gartner 2007).

Developers can now confidently design a single application that will work both on PC and smart phone. Developer business models will improve dramatically as they no longer have to spend valuable resources on supporting multiple platforms. With the improved business model, one can expect new specialized and verticalized mobile applications that were once cost prohibitive. The iPhone browser is actually based on the WebKit engine, which is an open source application framework that provides a foundation for delivering web services. It features a small footprint and is fully standards-compliant. Besides the Safari browser on the iPhone, it also is used by Google Android, Nokia S60 and Opera.

Looking ahead, one can expect that other mobile device makers will eventually copy the iPhone's user interface design. In fact, just like the MacOS and Windows, there is a good chance that the industry will "copy" some, but not all aspects of the iPhone. Certainly, the new metaphors for input and output and richer displays are something to expect on high and low end mobile devices in the near future.

Lastly as discussed earlier, the iPhone reinforces business model trends (i.e. unlimited data plans) which will only improve the adoption of new mobile enterprise applications.

16.2.5 Technology and Connectivity Improvements Are a Given

From technology to social behavior back to supporting technology: along with the social and business-related developments over the next few years, one can expect the standard technology improvements to continue in the mobile space. Computational capabilities will continue to improve on the low-end and high-end devices. Greater integration of features on a single chip will allow for more features while maintaining or shrinking footprint. This will allow for more battery capacity and lower costs. Improvements in memory and storage costs will continue allowing for richer, multimedia applications and improved visual presentations. Connectivity will also improve as network bandwidth continues to increase and multi-radio capability provides better coverage options.

In general, the standard technology trends one has seen in desktop computing will continue in the mobile space, but the issues of resource conservation and simplicity will remain. While many will try to "converge" as much as possible onto a mobile device, the industry is now trending toward a mobile world where simplicity is key. There are a myriad of applications requiring only a single piece of-lookup data, or one-click actions. Mobile applications will be designed on-the-fly or easily mass-customized to change the daily life of each and every worker or consumer. Tools will allow each person or each micro-enterprise to make its simplest processes ubiquitous by pushing it out to a mobile device easily, personalizing them and making them aware of the user's context.

16.3 Enterprise Solutions for DSD: Mobile DSD Use Cases

DSD is a high-volume and very competitive business. It has never been easy or simple to track products, deliveries, sales volume, pricing, promotions and inventory. With IT business solutions for Direct Store Delivery, producers can control their complete DSD cycle from order entry to the sale and distribution of goods directly to a customer's store. Enterprise Resource Planning (ERP) solutions usually support multi-channel order entry, including order entry via telesales, as well as full integration of enterprise resource planning activities with back-office activities. Using ERP with Mobile access, field sales representatives and delivery personnel can for example handle new and revised orders from customers while reducing material losses, providing timely and accurate customer data and reducing paperwork.

Overall, adding the Service-Oriented Architecture (SOA) capability (see more below in section 16.4) and the mobile capabilities to ERP solutions for DSD can significantly lower operating and financial risk; optimize sequencing of routes; optimize capacity planning; provide pro-active exception management in the field; improve customer service and enhance planning based on historical data. Tracking high-volume real world information and relating that information and more into profitability has never been easy or simple. A Mobile DSD solution can automate mobile route accounting, sales and merchandising applications (Pohl et al. 2007). It can also automate a range of business processes including: sales history/planning; pricing and promotional data access; order and invoice creation/modification; vehicle load/unload cycles; distribution inventory management; goods tracking; inventory auditing; signature capture/proof of delivery and payment acceptance. The following is an example scenario that follows a delivery truck driver through a facilitated workday.

16.3.1 Consumer Goods Company Logistics (Truck Driver Scenario)

The working day of the delivery workers usually starts early in the morning when they load the truck with products and receive a list of work orders on their mobile phone. The routing software optimizes the delivery route for every truck in order to maximize truck load and minimize delivery time. The route is also downloaded to the mobile phone. If the truck driver's phone has embedded GPS, the delivery manager may monitor the location of every truck of his fleet. In combination with GPS, the phone provides driving directions to the worker. Traffic condition information such as traffic jams available from online services can cause re-routing. In this case, the new route is pushed from the server to the driver's phone.

When the truck arrives at the store, a delivery worker picks up the boxes, checks their RFID labels in order to prevent errors and sends billing documents to the Store Manager. If the receiver's signature on the delivery order is required, it can be captured by the phone camera and electronically attached to the delivery record. Otherwise, the receiver can send an electronically signed receipt using the Bluetooth protocol to the delivery worker.

In many cases the small retail stores do not have a line of credit from a producer and they have to pay upon receiving the delivery. In this case, the touch-less Near Field Communication (NFC) payment technology could be used. Some innovative cell phones already have a payment chip embedded and integrated with the phone. In the future, more phones will have NFC payment capability. If the receiver's phone does not have the NFC feature, he can use his credit or debit card with a speed pass chip which implements the NFC protocol.

Business-conscious truck drivers can use their phone not only for transaction processing tasks, but also for Business Intelligence (BI) analysis. Simple real-time data analysis can be performed on current data right on the cell phone. More complex analytics involving historical data can be performed by the backend ERP system of the logistics company. The results can be rendered by the back-end system into SVG charts with drill-down links and tables. Mobile dashboard applications render these charts and tables on the phone screen. When the user selects and clicks chart elements or Key Performance Indicators (KPI) numbers on the dashboard the drill-down information is requested from the BI server using a URL link attached to every KPI element.

16.4 Underlying Technologies for the Future Mobile DSD

When providing mobile access to existing DSD back-end applications, one must distinguish between the traditional understanding of full-fledged software applications and a specific functionality in a mobile enterprise software context. The core challenge is not to deploy the entire DSD business supporting system onto a mobile device. Rather, the challenge is to select only the relevant business information and software functionality required for a specific process, and in addition to simplify and optimize all steps of the application treatment.

16.4.1 An Example Framework with SOA

In an example Mobile Application Framework provided by SAP Research (Fig. 16.2), the business objects are serialized, compressed and transmitted between server and client sides in the form of a compressed message. The information is stored in the local Persistent Data Store in a compressed format, making it possibe

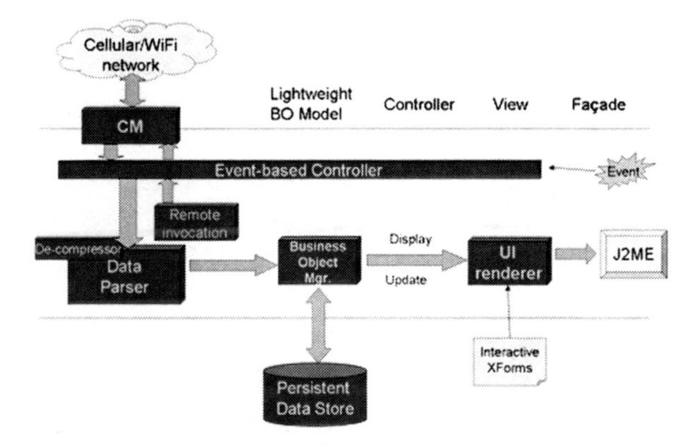

Fig. 16.2 Lightweight framework architecture for the mobile client (SAP Research 2008)

to store a significantly larger number of business objects than a traditional file system or relational database. The client application uses this local data to support off-line work. The framework also provides an asynchronous invocation of Web Services.

The important part of the Mobile lightweight architecture is an efficient connection to the back-end system. An asynchronous, message-based communication system is a better fit for a mobile environment in which the sender and receiver are loosely coupled. Mobile devices make use of many different network channels with different capabilities. Business data exchange is performed on demand, so that long offline phases are possible.

In this Mobile application framework, neither the business logic nor the user interface forms are hard-coded in the client application. Instead, the client application partially implements or uses open source interpreters of open industry standards like SOAP (Simple Object Access Protocol), RDF (Resource Description Framework), and XForms (XML format for the specification of a data processing model for XML data). The application logic and user interface can be easily modified or augmented at low cost, since they are using standard formats. In addition, a Business Process Execution Language (BPEL) interpreter on the mobile device enables the basic composition of workflow scenarios using local and remote services.

An SOA-based mobile architecture consists of Core Services and Composite Services. The Core Services provide a generic interface to business logic consisting of common building blocks. Composite Web Services account for more complex business processes and are implemented as a combination of core services. The core and composite Web Services are distributed across the client and an auxiliary proxy server and implement the business logic.

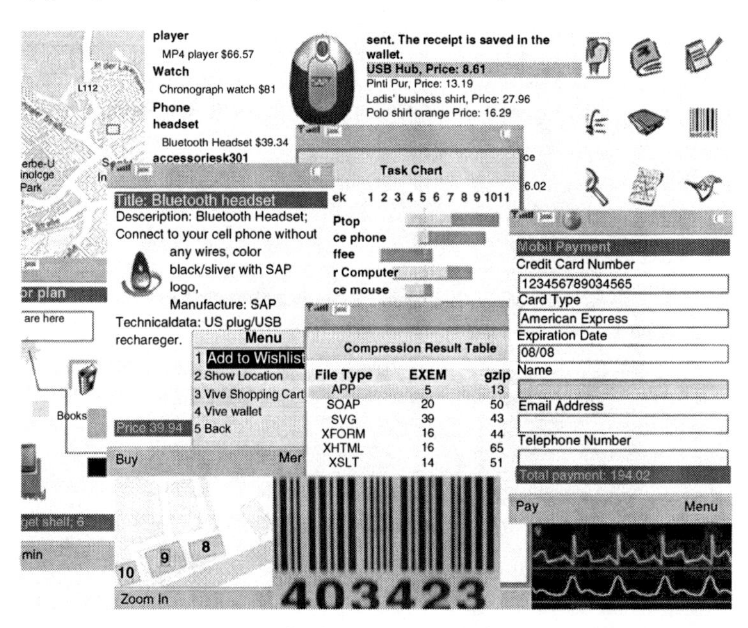

Fig. 16.3 Example M-business application that uses SAP framework (SAP Research 2008)

In the ERP area, the Enterprise Service-Oriented Architecture (ESOA) approach has been successfully used for years. The back-end Web Service is represented by a set of mobile application components based on the J2ME technology. These components provide user access to the Web Services implemented by ERP or Customer Relationship Management (CRM) back-ends. The client application provides customizable user-centric access to the service functionality. This approach enables the creation of widely distributed business processes that involve not only machine-based, but also user-performed operations. Thanks to the Open Service Gateway initiative-ready architecture of the mobile client (OSGi)[1], the new components can be easily created and integrated with Web Services and features available on the server side and on the mobile devices, such as the phone camera, Bluetooth, GPS, etc. A sample of screens for an m-business application is provided in Fig. 16.3.

The DSD is a complex interaction model, which requires an interaction between multiple clients and back-end ERP and CRM systems often produced by different software vendors. In this case the ESOA architecture and Web Service standardization become a crucial factor. Fortunately most large ERP providers already support Web Services and implement an SOA approach. However the Web Services provided by different vendors are incompatible. There is no DSD Web Service standard yet and even no standardization committee. In this situation the only possible solution is the mapping of Web Services from one system to another, based on an ontological knowledge of the DSD area.

In the Semantic SOA world the Web Service Definitions (WSDL) are enriched by the standard subject area Ontology, bound to the services. Using this Ontology and semantic query language (SPARQL) the application developers could find an appropriate Web Service in the UDDI registry with a relatively high probability of success (Yu 2007). The ontology-based mapping of the Web services could help in establishing interoperability between different client applications, available to Retailers and Producer's ERP Web Services, which enable JIT operations for DSD orders. However, even though this concept of Semantic Web services has existed for a while (Ankolekar et al. 2006), there are very few examples of really working semantic Web Services. The maturity of the products in this area is now increasing and one should expect the advent of Semantic SOA solutions in the near future.

16.4.2 Network Technology Trends Towards a Live DSD Supply Chain

The world is still working towards the holy grail of always-on, high bandwidth/speed and ubiquitous connectivity. Cellular networks and Wi-Fi are becoming ubiquitous and 3G/4G networks have started to emerge. Other types of networks could also emerge. E.g. the FCC bidding process for the "C Block" portion of the 747- to 792-MHz spectrum will certainly bring new opportunities for the Mobile Internet. The "C Block" frequencies are of high interest for mobile business because

---

[1] Open Services Gateway initiative: http://www.osgi.org

they offer a wider coverage, lower battery consumption and a better penetration of obstacles such as walls and buildings.

Mobile Rich Internet Applications (RIA) technologies are evolving at an unprecedented speed. One can mention WebKit-based browsers and widget engines, Flex Mobile, Silverlight mobile, JavaFX mobile, etc. The main characteristic of these technologies are:

- Simple development models (based on Web languages such as ECMA script)
- Simple distribution models (no or minimal installation and device dependency)
- Cover both occasionally connected and online modes
- Offer high quality multimedia and unified communication capabilities
- Offer integration mechanisms to device assets.

Having high speed always-on connectivity and mature mobile rich internet technologies will change how mobile applications such as DSD are built and utilized in most of the countries. It will also change how Enterprise systems architectures get designed. Enterprise systems will be more and more tailored towards service oriented and online models. The advances at the network level will also change how the firmware of future business devices is designed. According to the Yankee Group, business mobility is going from the opportunistic phase towards a strategic phase. Network, devices and firmware providers are a common architecture to address a large subset of the mobile workers (Yankee).

16.4.2.1 Client Side Architectural Shifts

The client side architecture will shift from a fully fledged fat offline client to an online client with caching mechanisms of web services in case of temporary disconnection. The client will also provide advanced messaging and collaboration features to support the delivery personnel in the field. This class of architecture requires little client side storage capabilities, low device management but much more networking capabilities in order to address the collaboration and unified communication requirements. The battery consumption should not be an issue for DSD business because the devices can be recharged in the delivery trucks.

16.4.2.2 Server Side Architectural Shifts

On the server side, the architecture will shift from purely data synchronization middleware to service/message based middleware. This shift will fully leverage current enterprise SOA efforts and potentially impose new performance and scalability challenges. Before the architecture reaches the fully service/message oriented stage it will certainly go through a temporarily transition phase combining both services and data synchronization approaches and for the near future, we will continue to witness a mix of server synchronization and service orientation.

The table below (Table 16.1) summarizes the key technology trends described in section 16.4 and their potential impact on main DSD processes, as listed in chapter 1.

Table 16.1 Key technology trends and DSD impact

	Technology trend					
DSD Process steps	Mobile Web 2.0	Location technologies (e.g. GPS)	Mobile processing/ Computing power	Mobile network bandwidth/ coverage	SOA Technologies	Mobile payment (NFC)
Order management	H	L	H	L	H	L
Route preparation	L	H	L	M	L	L
Check out	H	L	M	M	M	H
Physical dis-tribution	L	H	H	H	L	M
Check in	H	M	H	H	M	M
Route settlement	M	H	M	M	M	L

Degree of Impact: H = High, M = Medium, L = Low

16.5 Conclusion

The pairing of Mobile phones and DSD is inevitable with advances in technology, business models, and social norms. But the mobile phone should not be seen as just a replacement or extension of traditional DSD technologies. Mobile phones have the potential to introduce new modes, new processes, new ways of doing DSD given that: Mobile phones have the power to enhance ones own identity. The phone becomes the person and extends the capabilities of the person in both personal and business environment.

The architectural shifts and internet technologies advances will help provide an almost real-time end-to-end visibility to the supply chain. Mobile phones in particular are instrumental to the empowerment of business applications, driven by technology, IT policy, social trends, and business model evolution. In addition, as mobile DSD continues to evolve and new areas in social marketing advance, DSD has the potential to extend into the home, blurring the lines between personal lives and business. We believe that the increased home, personal and office use of mobile platforms will complement traditional desktop models and play a major role in the future success of DSD applications.

Acknowledgments

The authors acknowledge gratefully the contributions to this chapter of their colleagues from SAP Research. In particular, many thanks to Louenas Hamdi, Nolwen Mahe and Abdelghani Benharref.

References

Ankolekar, A.; Hitzler, P.; Lewen, H.; Oberle, D. and Studer, R. (2006): Integrating Semantic Web Services for Mobile Access, in: Wache, H.: Proceedings of the ESWC2006, Karlsruhe.

Gartner (2007): Mobile Web Trends 2007–2011, a market research report, June 18, 2007, Stamford.

IDC (2006): Worldwide Mobile Enterprise Applications 2006–2010 Forecast and Analysis.

IDC (2007): Worldwide Mobile Worker Population 2007–2011, Forecast, IDC, Dec. 2007.

Pohl, T.; Kothandaraman, R.; Seshasai, V.S. (2007): Developing Mobile Applications Using SAP NetWeaver Mobile, Bonn.

Signorini, E. (2007): Notebook Computers Go Truly Mobile at the Intersection of 3G and IT, Yankee Group Research, Inc., Boston.

Strategy (2006): Mobile Business Application Outlook 2006, Strategy Analytics, 2006.

WCMDEA (2006): Worldwide Converged Mobile Device Enterprise Adoption 2006–2010, Forcast, IDC, July, 2006.

Yu, L. (2007): Semantic Web and Semantic Web Services, Norwell.

Breinigsville, PA USA
12 May 2010
237841BV00003B/35/P

9 783540 772125